The Sunny Side
Diplomatic Life, 1875-1912

L. de Hegermann-Lindencrone

Alpha Editions

This edition published in 2024

ISBN : 9789364730907

Design and Setting By
Alpha Editions
www.alphaedis.com
Email - info@alphaedis.com

As per information held with us this book is in Public Domain. This book is a reproduction of an important historical work. Alpha Editions uses the best technology to reproduce historical work in the same manner it was first published to preserve its original nature. Any marks or number seen are left intentionally to preserve its true form.

Contents

NOTE ....- 1 -

THE ALPHABET OF A DIPLOMAT ....- 2 -

WASHINGTON, 1875-1880 ....- 4 -

ROME, 1880-1890 ....- 61 -

STOCKHOLM, 1890-1897 ....- 135 -

PARIS, 1897-1902 ....- 161 -

BERLIN, 1902-1912 ....- 188 -

NOTE

MADAME DE HEGERMANN-LINDENCRONE, the writer of these letters, is the wife of the recently retired Danish Minister to Germany. She was formerly Miss Lillie Greenough, of Cambridge, Massachusetts, where she lived with her grandfather, Judge Fay, in the fine old Fay mansion, now the property of Radcliffe College.

As a child Miss Greenough developed the remarkable voice which later was to make her well known, and when only fifteen years of age her mother took her to London to study under Garcia. Two years later Miss Greenough became the wife of Charles Moulton, the son of a well-known American banker, who had been a resident in Paris since the days of Louis Philippe. As Madame Charles Moulton the charming American became an appreciated guest at the court of Napoleon III. Upon the fall of the Empire Mrs. Moulton returned to America, where Mr. Moulton died, and a few years afterward she married M. de Hegermann-Lindencrone, at that time Danish Minister to the United States, and later periods his country's representative at Stockholm, Rome, Paris, Washington and Berlin.

THE ALPHABET OF A DIPLOMAT

lor	ıst a little below God.
	:st rung of the ladder.
	urd! Why, *never!*...
y	-yard where he is plucked.
	: of the walk.
	ɔn merely of time and place.
	ıe learns to make courtesies.
ıs	ı for all woes.
	st road to success.
ility	, whence no one returns.
corps)	s is there, but where is the *esprit?*
	Commandments.
	ɪ lane where two can walk abreast.
ıs	t pass in the night.
nanack)	ɛ of a Diplomat.
	make a deep courtesy.
	who does not agree with you.
	ıre side-light of truth.
	ıg beneath the dignity of a diplomat to notice.
(private)	ch every one already knows.

nts to let.

créance) impression.

rappel) llusion.

se) il to think of.

)eings with royal faults.

) be avoided like poison.

service.

ll to be seen with the naked eye.

t of service.

is) tic expression, meaning in French, *Une jambe en*

ly disguised thought as transparent as a soap-bu

: easily moved.

lways open for refuge.

paix) of dinners paid for by a lavish government.

ed and beribboned livery.

t important duty of a diplomat.

have, but easily dispensed with.

is iich seldom bears fruit.

iplomat does over his *rapports*.

ig a diplomat ought never to have too much of.

THE SUNNY SIDE OF DIPLOMATIC LIFE

WASHINGTON, 1875-1880

WASHINGTON, *November, 1875.*

Dear Mother,—After my hurriedly written letter of the 24th you will know that we have arrived here safely. My first introduction to my first post as diplomat's wife was made unwittingly by a gentleman walking with a friend just behind me. "Who is that gentleman?" said he, indicating Johan. "That? That is the Minister of Denmark." I, struggling with an armload of flowers culled from well-intentioned friends at different stations on the road, my maid and Johan's valet bringing up the rear with the overflow of small baggage, passed unnoticed. Now we are quite established here, and I have already commenced my diplomatic duties. There seems to be no end of card-leaving and card-receiving, and a list of rules on etiquette (the Ten Commandments of a Diplomat) as long as your arm. I never knew of anything so confusing. I try to remember the things that I must do and the things that I must not do. How many cold shower-baths of reproval have I already received; how many unruly things have I already done! We are invited to many dinners, luncheons, and entertainments of all kinds. I am knee-deep in engagements, actually wading in them. The engagement-book you gave me is already overfilled.

We were very much amused at the collection of newspaper cuttings you sent us. Johan thought the one describing him as "a massive blonde of magnificent proportions, whose pure heart and clean hands had won all hearts in Washington" [previous to winning mine], was much too personal. "The medals [his prized decorations] were not his fault, and should not be laid up against him; and as for the gold key which he wears on his back, it is considered a great honor, as few Danes have had it conferred on them, being, as it is, the key of the king's own bedchamber, and giving the wearer the privilege of entering there when he likes."

Another one which amused us says "the bride is to be congratulated on having annexed as fine a specimen of a viking as any one could desire, and, although she has not secured a golden crown for her marble brow, she has secured a name that ought to be good for a '*three-bagger*' on any diamond, and that just to see it written on a hotel register makes any hotel clerk faint." Johan asked me what a "three-bagger" was, but I could not tell him. Then the worst one! "Mr. de Hegermann is envoy extraordinary and parson to his Danish 'nibs.'" Johan was horrified at this *lèse majesté*. We looked the word "nibs" out in the dictionary, only to find that in cribbage "nibs" means the knave of trumps. This made matters worse; to call his sovereign a knave—even of trumps—seemed too disrespectful.

It was very nice of Norris, your Cambridge grocer, to placard the fruit in his shop window in our honor. "Lindencrone beauties" and "the Danish pair" show a certain amount of humor which ought to be applauded. Such a pun goes to my heart. I hope you encouraged him by buying them all and can tell me what a "Danish pair" looks like.

It would take more than one letter of mine written on foolscap paper to tell you of our colleagues and friends. I can do it in sections when I have time. But, oh, when can I get the time!

I have had my "audience" (Johan calls it an "audience"; I call it a "call on Mrs. President Grant at the White House"). There was nothing formal or formidable about it. Mrs. Grant and I sat on the sofa together and talked generalities. Johan could not tell me what to expect. He said *his* audience with the President had been a surprise, unprecedented by anything he had ever seen. As it was his first post as Minister, he had pictured to himself that it would be somewhat like the ceremonies abroad—very solemn and impressive. Of course he was in his red gala uniform, with all his decorations. A hired landau brought him to the steps of the White House, which he mounted with conscious dignity. His written speech, nicely folded, he carried in his hand. In Europe there would have been a crowd of gorgeous chamberlains to receive him, but here he found a negro, who, on seeing him, hurriedly donned a coat and, with an encouraging wave of the hand, said: "Come right along in, sir. I'll let them know you're here, sir." Johan was shown into a room and waited with patience until the President and Mr. Hamilton Fish came in. Mr. Grant was dressed in a gray walking-suit and wore a colored tie; and Mr. Hamilton Fish (Secretary of State) had evidently just come in from a walk, as his turned-up trousers signified.

Johan read his speech, and the President answered by reading, with some difficulty, a paper which Mr. Fish handed to him at the last moment. After this exchange of formalities Johan shook hands with the President, and without further ceremony he left the room, the door this time being opened by a white servant in black clothes. Mr. Fish at parting casually observed that the weather was fine.

I was officially presented on their reception days to the wives of all the Ministers, and made my visits to the members of the *Corps Diplomatique*. We were invited to dinner at the White House—a dinner given to the *Corps Diplomatique*. I was taken in by M. de Schlözer, the German Minister, and sat between him and Sir Edward Thornton (the English Minister), who sat on the right of Mrs. Grant. We were opposite to the President. I noticed that he turned his wine-glasses upside down, to indicate, I suppose, that he did not drink wine during dinner. Afterward we amused ourselves by walking in the long Blue Room. The President disappeared with some of the gentlemen to smoke and was lost to view. The company also faded gradually away. Mrs. Grant did not seem inclined to gaze on us any longer, and appeared to be relieved when we shook her outstretched hand and said "Good night."

A dinner to which we went, given by the Schiskines (the Russian Minister) in honor of the Grand-Duke Constantine of Russia, was most delightful. The Grand Duke is very charming, natural, with a sly twinkle in his mild blue eye. He has a very handsome face, is extremely musical, and plays the piano with great *finesse*, having a most sympathetic touch.

MRS. U.S. GRANT
From a photograph taken about 1876, when she was mistress of the White House.

SARAH BERNHARDT
From a photograph taken at the time of her visit to Boston.

After dinner we darned stockings. This sounds queer, but nevertheless it is true. The Schiskines had just bought a darning-machine. They paid eighty-six dollars for it; but to darn, one must have holes, and no holes could be found in a single decent stocking, so they had to cut holes, and then we darned. The Grand Duke was so enchanted with this darning that he is going to take a machine home to the Grand Duchess, his august mother.

The darning done, we had some music. M. de Schlözer improvised on the piano, and after the Grand Duke had played some Chopin I sang. M. de Schlözer went through his little antics as advance-courier of my singing: he screwed the piano-stool to the proper height (he thinks it must be just so high when I accompany myself); he removed all albums from sight for fear people might be tempted to glance in them; he almost snatched fans from the hands of unoffending ladies, fearing they might use them; no dogs were to be within patting distance, *and no smoking*; he turned all the chairs to face the piano so that no one should turn his back to it. These are all heinous crimes in his eyes. He would, if he could, have pulled down all the portières and curtains, as he does in his own house when I sing there. What must people think of him?

You ask me, "What kind of a cook have you?" Don't speak of it—it is a sore subject! We have the black cook from the White House (so her certificate says). She is not what our fancy painted her. Neither is the devil as black as he is painted (I don't know why I associate them in my mind). We had painted this cook white. I shudder to think how the White House must have lived in those years when she did the cooking. Our dinners are simply awful. Although she has *carte blanche* to provide anything and everything she wants, our dinners are failures. I look the fact in the face and blush. Our musical parties are better when I do the cooking and Johan does the serving—I mean when I sing and he fills the gaps. The diplomats groan. "Think," they say, "what a finished cook would do with all the delicious things they have here—all these wonderful birds and meats and vegetables, and only the one sauce!"

The charity concert, of which I was *dame patronesse*, went off with success. We made a great deal of money. M. de Schlözer paid twenty dollars for his ticket. My chorus covered itself with glory and was encored. As the concert finished at ten, we adjourned to the Zamaconas' (Minister of Mexico) first ball, and I hope, for them, their only one. It was one of those *soirées* where people appropriate the forks and spoons. It cost, they say, ten thousand dollars. The assemblage was promiscuous, to say the least. Every one who asked for an invitation got one, and went. The Minister had hired the house next the Legation, and cut doors into it so that there should be plenty of room, but even then there was not sufficient space to contain the crowd of miscellaneous guests. There were two orchestras, but no one wanted to dance. Every one wandered about through the rooms or lolled in the grottoes, which were lighted with different-colored lamps. In every corner were fountains of cologne, around which the gentler sex stood in crowds saturating their handkerchiefs—some of which had cross-stitch initials in red thread. Mirrors were placed at the end of each room to prolong the vista. "Mexico," in enormous letters formed by gas-jets, stood over the entrances. And as for the supper, it was in a room out of all proportion to the gathering! There was no question of getting into it; only prize-fighters and professional athletes could elbow their way through the crowd. The waiters had long since disappeared, frightened at their formidable task. The chairs intended for the guests were utilized as tables on which to put unfinished plates of food and half-empty glasses.

Everything that was not spilled on the floor was spilled on the table. Such things as bonbons, cakes, etc., that could be stowed away in pockets, vanished like magic. Gentlemen (?) broke the champagne-bottles by knocking them on the table, sending the contents flying across the room. The lady guests drew out the silver skewers which ornamented the *plats montées* and stuck them in their hair as mementoes of this memorable evening.

WASHINGTON, 1876.

Dear Aunt,—The best way I can spend this Ash-ful Wednesday is to write a penitent letter to you and beg you to forgive my long silence; but if you could imagine what a life we have been leading, I think that, being the being you are, you would make excuses for a niece who gets up with the sun and goes to bed with the morning star. When that morning star appears I am so tired I can think of nothing but bed and the bliss of laying my diplomatic body down to rest.

Dear old Mr. Corcoran (almost blind now) gave a unique banquet in honor of Johan and me. We went first to the theater to see "Rip Van Winkle" played by Jefferson. It was delightful, though I cried my eyes out. From the theater we went to Mr. Corcoran's house for a roasted-in-the-shell oyster supper. Johan, who had never before attended such a feast, thought he had got loose among a lot of milkmaids and firemen, each with his bucket and pail, and when he saw the enormous pile of oysters brought in on platters he wondered how many "r's" March had in her. However, like a lamb he sat next to his pail, and after having consumed about a bushel himself he became quite expert at opening the oysters and throwing the shells in his pail. It was a most amusing and original evening, and the amount of oyster-shells we left behind us would have paved the way to the Capitol.

Another original entertainment I must tell you about. We received a note from General Burnside (Senator from Rhode Island): "Will you come to my codfish dinner on Thursday next?" We of course accepted and went. General Burnside and Senator Anthony are great friends and live together. I never could understand, and never dared to ask, why such a little state as Rhode Island needed two Senators. However, that is neither here nor there. The other guests were Mr. Bayard, Mr. Blaine, Mrs. Blaine, Mrs. Lawrence, General Sherman. According to the rules of a codfish dinner, every one was provided with the same amount of boiled codfish, hard-boiled eggs, beets, carrots, and potatoes, and every English sauce ever made. Every one made his own mixture, which was passed about and "sampled." The lucky person who got the greatest number of votes received a beautiful silver bowl. The dining-room was arranged as if it were a camp. There were no ornaments of any kind, and we sat on little iron tent-chairs. You may imagine after we had finished with the codfish that our appetites were on the wane, and we felt that we had dined sumptuously, if monotonously, when, lo! our genial host surprised us with an enormous turkey (reared on his own estate), twenty-seven pounds in weight, with its usual accompaniments of cranberry sauce, sweet-potatoes, and so forth. Mr. Blaine and Mr. Bayard were fountains of wit.

Then another entertainment, a sort of *mardi-gras maigre* feast, was a champagne tea given for us at the Capitol by Mr. Blaine. He had invited a great many of the Senators and the Ministers, his wife, and some other ladies. These mighty people talked politics and had prodigious appetites. Sandwiches and cake disappeared in a hazy mist, and they drank oceans of champagne. They took cocktails before, during, and after! I amused myself—as I can't talk politics, and would not if I could—by noticing the ingenuity and variety of the spittoons placed about in convenient spots. The spittoons that tried to be pretty were the most hideous. I liked best the simplicity of the large, open, ready-to-receive ones filled with clean, dainty sand. There was no humbug about them, no trying to be something else; whereas the others, that pretended to be Etruscan vases or umbrella-stands or flower-pots, were failures in my eyes. Why are they ashamed of themselves? Why do they call themselves by the graceful name of "cuspidor"—suggestive of castanets and Andalusian wiles? Why such foolish masquerading? Spittoons will be spittoons—they risk not being recognized. I said as much as this to Mr. Blaine. "You are right," he said, "to fight their battles. Did you ever hear the story about the Western man who was not accustomed to such artistic objects, and said in one of his spitting moods, 'If you don't take that darned thing away I'll spit in it'?"

I forgot to tell you that the Emperor and Empress of Brazil are here "doing" Washington—doing it so thoroughly that they have almost overdone it. The Brazilian Minister is worn out. Every day he has a dinner and an entertainment of some kind. The Emperor wants to see everything and to know everybody. No institution is neglected, and all the industries are looked into thoroughly. He goes to the Senate very often and sits through the whole *séance*, wishing to understand everything. He always tries to get hold of the people who can give him the most information on any subject. Dom Pedro is most popular; one sees him everywhere. At the ball at the English Minister's for their Majesties, a gentleman presented to the Empress said, "*Je suis le Sénateur qui parle frangais.*" The Empress said to Johan, "I beg of you to keep near me and talk to me so that the '*Senateur qui parle français*' may be discouraged in his pursuit."

PHILADELPHIA, 1876.

My dear Aunt,—Is your heart melted with pity, or does it burst with national pride, and do you disregard such trifles as heat and exhaustion? I told you in my last letter that the diplomats were invited *en bloc* (at the country's expense) to be present at the opening of the Centennial Exposition. The country provided good rooms for us at this hotel, where we are invited to spend two days: one of those days was the day before yesterday, and I think that the other will be enough for me, for anything more awful than the heat at the present moment cannot well be conceived. It is as if Philadelphia had said to its friends, "You provide the exposition, and we'll provide the heat." There were carriages placed at our disposal for the opening, and we drove out to the grounds in great style. We were welcomed at the entrance by some officials and ushered to our seats on the red-hot platform draped with flags. President Grant then entered, accompanied by all his Ministers. After the opening speech by the President all the church-bells in the city began ringing, cannons were fired, the orchestra burst forth with national hymns—"Star-spangled Banner" and "Hail, Columbia." People waved handkerchiefs, and the display of patriotism was overpowering. In coming out, after the President had left the tribune, the crowd filled in after him, and we had to fight our way out as best we could.

DOM PEDRO
Emperor of Brazil.

The heat, which no thermometer could register—and there was no shade for the thermometer to register in—and the crowd were something fearful. People were almost crushed to death, and those who did the most crushing were the fat policemen, who stood in every one's way and on every one's toes and barred the whole procession. Johan looked like an enormous poppy in his red uniform; the sun blazing through the glass roof almost set him on fire (the diplomats were begged to come in uniform, and that meant coats padded and buttoned up to the chin). Johan tells fabulous stories of the number of stout old ladies he saved, who all threatened to faint away on his decorations. He says he carried them bodily through the crowd and deposited them on the grass outside and went back for more. I was miraculously saved. I clasped my arms around the fat body of a policeman and whispered endearing words with a foreign accent to the effect that a foreigner who had come there at the invitation of the country ought to be saved at any cost. He thought so too, and was very kind and sympathetic, but as I clung to his padded coat and felt his scorching buttons I wondered whether it were better to die crushed than to suffer suffocation. However, we were all saved; even Johan's chamberlain key clung to his back, and his decorations actually stayed in their places, which I think was wonderful, considering the stout ladies. My dress left a good deal of itself behind—only the front breadth held it onto my person; the back breadths were trampled on as far up as people could trample and were dirty beyond words.

A large dinner was prepared for us, where patriotic toasts were drunk galore.

We went out to the grounds the next day and rolled about in what they call "rolling-chairs," and had things explained to us by some nice gentlemen with gold-braided caps.

We will go once more to see what we left unseen, and then I turn my head toward Cambridge.

WASHINGTON, *March, 1877*.

The question of the annual *dîner diplomatique* was cleverly managed by Mr. Evarts. Mr. Hayes wanted to suppress wine and give tea and mineral water, but Mr. Evarts put his foot down. He said that the diplomats would not understand an official dinner without wine, and proposed, instead, a *soirée musicale*—in other words, a rout. The diplomats had a separate entrance (a novelty) from the garden side. There was an orchestra at the end of the Blue Room which drowned conversation when you were near it. I noticed that most of the young ladies found it too near, and sought other corners.

The supper *ne laissait rien à désirer*, and there was a sumptuous buffet open the whole evening; punch-bowls filled with lemonade were placed in the different *salons*. On the whole, it was a great success.

I think that the teetotality of the White House displeases as much our country-people as it does the foreigners. At one of our musical parties Mr. Blaine came rather late, and, clapping his hands on Johan's shoulder, said, "My kingdom for a glass of whisky; I have just dined at the White House." Others call the White House dinners "the life-saving station."

Mrs. Hayes was very nice to me. She sent me a magnificent basket of what she called "specimen flowers," which were superb orchids and begonias. On her card was written, "Thanking you again for the pleasure you gave me by your singing."

WASHINGTON, *March, 1877.*

My dear Mother,—We are now having a visit of the Queen of the Sandwich Islands. I suppose in Europe she would show to great advantage, but here her blackness is at a low premium. There was a large reception for her Royal Blackness at the White House, where all the diplomats were present. The queen talked with people with the aid of an interpreter. Her remarks necessarily being restricted, she said about the same thing to every one. She was bristling with jewelry, and the large white pearls on her broad, black bosom took on extra splendor. Robert (our colored valet), who was waiting in the corridor, caught sight of her as she walked by, and remarked, when he reached home, to my maid that he was "surprised that they should make such a fuss over a colored person"; and he attempted to turn his flat nose in the air; but, as it is not the kind that turns, it refused.

Robert wears a conspicuous decoration in his buttonhole whenever we have a dinner. The first time Johan noticed it he almost fainted away, as he knows every decoration under the sun, and, thinking it looked like the *Légion d'Honneur*, he proposed to question Robert about it; but Robert eluded the master's clutch as the door-bell was ringing. Johan was considerably disturbed until he learned the truth, which was that Robert belonged to a reading-club—a Browning and Tennyson club—and this was its badge. Our colleagues thought he was the Minister from Hayti!

WASHINGTON, *Spring, 1877.*

Dear Mother,—I must tell you the honor which has been conferred on me. I have been admitted into the enchanted circle of the Brain Club. I am an honorary member. Mrs. Dahlgren is the president, and I suppose all the set of intellectuals, "*Les élus des élus*" belong to it. I have only been twice to the meetings. I think I am a failure as far as brains go, but the members like my singing, and I am only called upon to take an active part when the members are falling off their chairs, trying with literary efforts to keep awake.

The first meeting was a ghastly affair. The subject to be discussed was the "Metamorphosis of Negative Matter." You may imagine that I was staggered. I had no more idea what negative matter was than the inhabitants of Mars. They took us alphabetically. When they got to "H," Mrs. Dahlgren (who, as president, sat in a comfortable chair with arms to it, while the others sat on hard dining-room, cane-bottomed chairs) turned to me and said, "Has Mrs. *Hegermann* anything to say concerning the Metamorphosis of Negative Matter?" I had on my blue velvet gown, and thought of it fast becoming chair-stamped, and I wondered if negative matter would comprise that. However, I wisely refrained from speech, and shook a sad smile from my closed lips.

"H" to "K" had a great deal to say. Every one looked wise and wore an appearance of interest. They slid down to "L." Then Mrs. Dahlgren said, "Has Mrs. *Lindencrone* anything to say on the Metamorphosis of Negative Matter?" I answered that I had not discovered anything since the last time they asked me. They were not accustomed to one lady having two names, each beginning with a capital letter.

The members had a beautiful time when they got to "R." Up rose a gaunt female who knew all about it and seemed positive about the "Negative" part. We were pulled suddenly up to time, and some one turned upon poor me and asked if I agreed. I answered hastily, "Certainly I do." Dear me! What had I said? Half the company rose with a bound. "Do you, really?" they asked in chorus. "That is more than we do. We cannot at all agree with a theory which is utterly false from the base." How I wished I knew what the false base had been. Was it the Negative, or the Metamorphosis, or the Matter? I murmured humbly, hiding behind a lame neutrality, that I had mistaken the cause for the effect. They all turned and looked at me with fierce eyes. I think they were staggered at this colossal utterance, for they gave up discussing, and "S" to "Z" never had a chance to say anything. Then they adjourned to the supper-room. After having eaten scalloped oysters and chicken salad, no more questions were discussed.

I was asked to sing. I am afraid that I am only looked upon as a bird on these mighty occasions. On the piano-stool I felt myself safe, and I sang. In the middle of my song some heavy person leaning against a shaky bookcase uprooted it, and it fell with a crash on the floor. I halted midway in my song. People rushing in from the supper-room asked, "What is the matter?" "Negative," answered Miss Loring, quick as thought, at which they all laughed. Mr. Brooks, to cover the confusion, said in a loud voice, "This is not the first time Madame Hegermann has brought down the house." There was more laughter, and I sat down again at the piano and sang "Tender and True," an exquisite song written by Mrs. Lincoln about a young soldier killed during the war, who wore to the last a knot of blue ribbon his sweetheart had given him.

M. de Schlözer is bubbling over with joy, for he has the famous pianist, von Bülow, staying with him at the German Legation. He says von Bülow is most amiable about playing, and plays whenever he is asked. His technique is wonderful and perfect. The ladies in Washington are wild over him, and figuratively throw themselves at his feet. He is giving two concerts here, and everybody has taken tickets. M. de Schlözer gave last evening one of his memorable dinners, followed by music. I know two people who enjoyed it—Schlözer and myself. Schlözer was going to ask Julian Sturgis, but Julian Sturgis had on some former occasion crossed his legs and looked distrait or had shown in some such trivial manner that he was bored, which so exasperated Schlözer that he barred him out, and invited Mr. Bayard instead, who perhaps loved music less, but showed no outward signs of boredom.

Von Bülow is not only a wonderful pianist, but a very clever man of the world. He sent me a book written by Wagner about music and wrote on the first page "*Voici un livre qui vous intéressera. De la part du mari de la femme de l'auteur.*" Clever, isn't it? You know that Madame Wagner is the daughter of Liszt. She ran away from von Bülow in order to marry Wagner.

Bülow dedicated a song to me, called "Adieu." It is pretty enough to sing when he plays the accompaniment, but otherwise I do not care for it. I sang it after dinner, and every one said it was charming, but I had the feeling that the ladies were more interested in my toilette than in Bülow's song. I don't blame them, for my dress *is* lovely (Worth called it "*un rêve*"), but I fancy I look like a Corot autumn sunset reflected in a stagnant lily-pond. It is of light salmon-colored satin, with a tulle overskirt and clusters of water-lilies here and there. I could have bought a real Corot with the same money.

Mr. Blaine, who is at present Speaker of the House, and Mr. Roscoe Conkling, one of the Senators from New York, are the two most prominent members of the Republican party, but are personally deadly enemies.

Mr. Blaine is an excellent talker, very popular with the ladies. In a drawing-room, he is generally found in a corner, quoting poetry (a specialty of his) to some handsome lady. He knows all the poetry in the world! They say that he is the best Speaker the House has ever known; it is quite wonderful to see the rapidity with which he counts the Ayes and Noes, pointing at each voter with the handle of his club. He grasps a situation in an instant, and gives a quick retort when he thinks it is deserved. Roscoe Conkling is quite a different type. He is very dignified and pompous—perhaps a little theatrical; not at all a society man, and, though he may be less vain than Mr. Blaine, he has the appearance of being more so.

The foreign Ministers have the "right of the floor," which means they have the right to enter the House of Representatives when they like. On one great occasion a member of the House offered M. de Schlözer his seat, which happened to be between two members who suddenly got up and began the most heated discussion over Schlözer's head. He found the situation dangerous and wished himself elsewhere. He said he felt like the Biblical baby when the two mothers were wrangling before the great Solomon. However, the storm spent itself in words, and fortunately the disputants did not come to blows.

Johan says he was very much struck the first time he went to Congress by seeing two opposing members, after bitterly attacking each other for hours, walk quietly away arm-in-arm, obviously the best of friends.

A little incident which occurred in the Senate amused Johan very much. Roscoe Conkling begged a colleague sitting next to him to read out loud something he wished to quote in his speech while he paused to draw a breath. The colleague read, and Conkling, without a word of thanks, took back the book; but when a colored man brought him a cup of tea (which he always takes during his speeches) he stood up and in a very loud voice, making a solemn bow, said, "I thank you, sir!"

I call that coquetting with the gallery, don't you?

We have been invited to take a trip to California by the railroad company. We can transport ourselves to Omaha; then all our expenses are to be defrayed by the lavish company. We have all accepted. Who could refuse such a tempting invitation?

CALIFORNIA, *Spring, 1877.*

Dear M.,—The rendezvous was to be at the third station before reaching Omaha, where we really did all meet. On arriving at the next one, some of the party asked the conductor how long the train would stop, and he answered, "Twenty minutes"; so off they started on foot to see the town.

We wise ones stayed in the train, which also started off, leaving our truants behind, but their bags remained with us.

When they returned to the station, before the twenty minutes had expired, they found the train gone! They hired a special train at great expense and delay, hoping to overtake us at Omaha. But before they reached Omaha an official appeared and said that he had received a telegram from headquarters at Chicago, acknowledging that the conductor had been at fault in starting a little earlier than he had said; therefore the company felt itself responsible and insisted on refunding the money the extra train had cost.

Where else but in America are mistakes so quickly and nicely remedied? Perhaps in this instance it could be explained by the fact that one of them was a prominent member of the Republican party, and the other no less than the Assistant Secretary of State. We were glad to receive our penitent wanderers, who promised to be more careful another time. We slept at Omaha, which is the jumping-off place, and to-morrow morning early we are going to "jump." We have already traveled seventeen hundred and fifty miles, and have not yet begun our real trip. Omaha has still wooden sidewalks and muddy roads; the post-office, school-house, and churches are all built on a grand scale, and the streets laid out in squares and broad avenues. Probably they have already designs for a grand-opera house. One can see FUTURE written all over it.

Mr. Cadwalader had bought in Philadelphia the best comestibles that it could provide, and had them stowed away in big hampers and put in the baggage-car. When the train stopped an hour for food, which it did three times a day, we preferred to spend that hour looking about us and (as Mr. Kasson said) stretching our legs rather than going into the overcrowded eating-rooms, which were reeking of food, loud talk, and ravenous passengers. The stations were always low wooden buildings with a piazza; sometimes no other houses were to be seen. On wooden boxes were enthroned the loafers, who must have ridden miles just to see passengers get in and out of the train. To show how kind these rough people must be when they are not engaged in killing people, chickens foraged about between their huge boots, and I saw a dog quietly asleep within an inch of a kick. As soon as the train started we went into the baggage-car and, seated about on the trunks, enjoyed our delicious feast.

We occupied almost one entire parlor-car. There were only two extra seats, and those were filled by two men surrounded by a mountain of newspapers and magazines of all kinds. I said, nodding toward one of these, "What a handsome man that is!"

"Do you know who it is?" asked Mr. Cadwalader.

"No. How should I?"

"That is the famous scout, Buffalo Bill."

"Really!" I exclaimed. "I had fancied him quite different from that. He looks like the pictures of Charles the First. His eyes are so soft, and he has such lovely brown curls and a could-not-hurt-a-fly look about him."

"Well," said Mr. Cadwalader, "he has killed more men than he can count on his fingers when he tries to go to sleep."

"I can't imagine it," I said, gazing with admiration at Buffalo Bill's fine and kind face and splendid figure. "His friend does not look so amiable."

"I should think *not*. That is the celebrated Mr. Holmes of Texas. He is a terror in this part of the world."

"He looks it," I said. "See all the pistols he has about him. I can see one in his coat pocket, and one in his vest pocket, and..."

"And many under his coat which you can't see."

Just at that moment the "terror" got up, and, lo! a pistol fell out of his clothing on to the floor. Fortunately, it did not go off, but it frightened us almost out of our senses (the ladies, of course). Buffalo Bill picked up the weapon and handed it back to Mr. Holmes, who put it quietly in his pocket, seeming rather abashed.

Buffalo Bill and his friend walked down the middle of the car, and we were somewhat agitated when he stopped in front of Johan and said in a soft, cooing voice, "Would you take a drink with me, sir?"

We gasped when we saw Johan shake his head and say politely with a smile, "No, thank you." We expected a volley of pistol-shots and the speedy wiping out of us all, but Buffalo Bill merely gave Johan an inquiring look and a tired but sarcastic smile.

Mr. Cadwalader said, hurriedly, to Johan, "Go, for Heaven's sake!"

Johan hastened to follow the good advice and Buffalo Bill, and said with diplomatic artifice, "On second thoughts, sir, I will not refuse your invitation, as I am a little thirsty." On which the three gentlemen went out together.

Johan came back refreshed and radiant. Never had he seen or talked to such a delightful person. Buffalo Bill had offered him some of his own favorite brand of whisky, which Johan found very good.

Johan asked B.B. later, being on more familiar terms, "Would you have been offended if I had refused to drink with you?"

B.B. answered, "If I had not seen that you were a foreigner I should not have liked it," meaning, I suppose, bloody murder and sudden death.

B.B. said the reason why he had chosen Johan out of the rest to drink with was that Johan looked so like the Grand-Duke Alexis, for whom he had been a guide on the prairies some years ago.

General Taylor, son of the former President, joined us at Cheyenne.

We have just passed thirty snow-sheds at Rock Creek, and have seen some wolves and some antelopes roaming about. We looked for buffaloes, but the only buffalo we saw was the mild Bill, who sat quietly reading a magazine, looking at us with his soft-brown eyes.

We were very high up in the Rocky Mountains. All around us was snow, and the view of the blue mountains, the tops of which were quite white, looked beautiful in the distance. There were some Indians on horseback drawn up in file as the train went by. They had all their war-paint on, were covered with picturesque blankets, and their feather head-dresses reached over their horses' backs; they had buckskin leggings covered with beads, which made them look very picturesque. They looked stolidly and indifferently at us while we stared at them admiringly from the car windows. The prairie-dogs looked like squirrels "sitting up so cute," as Miss C. said, "dodging in and out of their holes."

At one of the stations a whole band of Indians climbed into the train with guttural war-whoops and invaded the baggage-car. We thought we were being "held up," but they behaved themselves very well. The thought of Buffalo Bill, to say nothing of Mr. Holmes of Texas with his pistols, reassured us; and the only difference that the presence of the Indians made to us was that we avoided the baggage-car for our midday meal.

At another station a quantity of loafers, mostly Indians, smelling dreadfully of whisky, surrounded us and begged for money. Among them an old Indian woman who looked like the witch of Endor (they said she was over a hundred years old) stretched out a long, bony, orang-outang arm, and when we gave her a few cents the old thing actually grinned with joy. It was painful to see this creature with the accumulated look of greed on her withered old brown face.

Our baggage-master always kept his hat on, slouched at a tremendous angle. We wondered how it could keep on unless it was pinned to his ear. Mr. Kasson begged us to pretend not to notice it, because the man was very sensitive on the subject. He told us his story. The man had been fishing with some friends, near an Indian settlement, when the Indians attacked them and killed the others outright. The baggage-master saved his life by "playing 'possum" (as Mr. K. called pretending to be dead), and the Indians scalped him with a broken tin can. If he had made the slightest movement they would have despatched him. How horrible! We wondered if it could be true!

To-morrow "the distinguished party" mentioned in the paper are going to arrive at Salt Lake City. I will write from there unless I am snatched up by some craving widower, if there exists such a thing as a widower—or by some husband with too few wives.

A wild desire possessed us to sit on the cow-catcher in order to get a better view of the cañon. The engineer refused at first, but gave in at last. He said it was most dangerous.

"You might," he added, "scoop up a Chinaman, or some animal straying on the rails."

"How exciting!" we cried. "Who but a chosen few have the luck to scoop up a live Chinaman?"

Johan had the worst place, and therefore the least chance of getting the Chinaman. He sat up on a little iron seat attached to the boiler, holding on to the piston for dear life, and every time the whistle went off—and it went off very often—he nearly did the same. The fireman was obliged every other minute to whistle to frighten the cows away from the track. We others were more fortunate, having only to balance ourselves and clutch our neighbor. The least jar would have capsized us all. The Chinamen working on the railroad gazed at us in wonder; but we did not scoop any of them in, nor did we get any cows. The long tunnels were nasty and damp, and we were glad to breathe the fresh air again after having passed through them. After a ride of half an hour we got off our cow-catcher at the next station, feeling rather proud of the *bravoure* we had shown, but, all the same, thankful to be safe and sound.

Salt Lake City is such a pretty place, so beautifully situated. The great mountains capped with snow surround it and send the clearest mountain streams down through the streets. No town could be better drained than this one.

The lake is eighty miles away, and salted to exaggeration. Out of four quarts of water one can obtain one quart of salt. We thought of taking a bath in it and being sent home pickled and cured—of traveling.

We met on the train a Colonel Hooker, citizen of Utah. He introduced himself to us and gave us free passes on the railroad where the Mormon line branches off; so he must be some one of importance.

He telegraphed to announce our arrival at the hotel, and we flattered ourselves that all Mormondom would be agog. We did not, however, notice any great animation as we drove up to the hotel, and felt rather hurt that we did not create more of a sensation.

We had introductory letters to Brigham Young. The next day being Sunday, we went to the Tabernacle to attend their religious service. Happily, Brigham Young had returned the night before from St. Joseph, where he had sojourned with the "faithful." The Tabernacle is an enormous building which, we were told, can hold fourteen thousand people. It was filled to overflowing. The seating for the members was arranged in a semicircle of tiers, the minor elders sitting in the lowest seats. As the tiers mounted there were fewer seats and therefore fewer elders, and so on, until the highest point was reached, where the high priest—Brigham Young—sat alone in his glory. On the opposite side was the magnificent organ built in Boston. When they began building the Tabernacle, gigantic as they intended it to be, they did not know that the organ which had been ordered from Boston (probably wrong measurements had been sent) would be bigger than the Tabernacle. When it arrived they found that, instead of the organ having been made for the Tabernacle, the Tabernacle would have to be made for the organ.

To celebrate the Prophet's return they had the communion service. People all stayed in their pews, and the bread, cut in good healthy pieces, was handed about in bread-baskets; after which pitchers with ice-water were passed, and the water was poured in goblets, which were placed before the people. Brigham Young gave his flock a tremendous rating with lowering eyebrows and a thunder-cloud in each eye, and the flock trembled as one man. He said that during his absence they had not behaved themselves as they ought to have done. They had not only been found swearing and drunk, but they had mingled breath with the Gentiles. We feared he referred to Colonel Hooker, whose breath had mingled—the finger of wrath seemed to point that way. We felt very sorry for our companion and sat huddled together, a humiliated group of Gentiles, trembling to meet the glance of the wrathful Prophet.

After the service we were all received at Brigham Young's house, where he seemed to be expecting us. He looked like any old Vermont farmer, with his white fringe of beard under his fat, puffy cheeks, and his thick, jet-black eyebrows over his keen eyes. He talked to us about his mission in this world and told us about the hardships his people had borne when they came to St. Joseph, which was the first place they "struck" after their tramp over the desert, where most of the men died. It was there he received a mysterious message from on high telling him that bigamy would be pardonable under the circumstances. He told Johan that the Danes were some of his best subjects. Johan made his most diplomatic bow, as if he thought that this compliment to his nation ought to be acknowledged. We heard after that Brigham Young had said this because the Danes were known to take the most wives and ask no questions.

It seems that B.Y. is almost a widower now, poor man. He has only twenty-seven wives. Amelia reigns supreme just now; the others sit forlorn in rocking-chairs in their empty parlors, biting their nails and chewing the bitter gum of envy.

Johan thought we ought perhaps to demand an official "audience" of Amelia, but the others repulsed this inspiration. It was amusing to walk by Brigham Young's big house, a long rambling building with innumerable doors. Each wife has an establishment of her own, consisting of parlor, bedroom, and a front door, the key of which she keeps in her pocket.

We walked about after luncheon, and Colonel Hooker drove us through the streets and up the hill to show us the view, which was magnificent beyond words.

We left Salt Lake City next day with regret.

It was telegraphed to Reno that we were to arrive there, to be treated, escorted, and transported to Virginia City free of charge. They began the treating by giving us an excellent breakfast at the hotel. They asked us ladies if we wanted to go down the shaft with the gentlemen to see the famous silver-mine. We cried "Yes" with enthusiasm.

A dressing-room was put at our disposal, and the clothes we were to wear were neatly placed in piles. There were miners' jackets, miner's leather trousers, and felt hats. We chose the suits best fitting our different anatomies, and dressed. My choice fell on a boy's rather clean suit. We felt very rakish in the dressing-room, but very sheepish when we joined the gentlemen outside. In going down the shaft we had to stand on the platform of the cage, which had neither railing nor support of any kind. We went down thirteen hundred feet and stepped out into the alleys of the shining ore. After walking for what seemed miles, they showed us a hole and a shaft. We looked down a hundred feet deeper, where the men who were working were almost naked. The thermometer was fabulously high. There was a tank of cold water where the men who worked could plunge every two minutes out of the five. The air beginning to be rather oppressive, we requested to be taken up to our mother Earth. How glad we were to breathe the fresh air. A bath was awaiting us, and when we became ladies again we were taken all over the works, and saw the process of making silver bricks out of the walls we had been walking between, the beating of the metal, the sifting and weighing, and finally the silver bricks. They have 2,000 men working day and night. They are 1,400 feet below the surface now, and hope to go lower. The "pocket" is 175 feet long, but the poor stockholders' pockets are empty, for all that. (I am a stockholder and ought to know.)

Each lady was presented with a bag of silver ore-rocks they seemed to me. My bag had "500 dollars" written on it, in fun, I am sure. I left it at the hotel, as it was too heavy to carry.

We left Virginia City that evening for Carson City and slept there, glad to shake off the silver dust from our weary feet. The next day at 7 A.M. two carriages, one with four horses and the other with two, were before the door, and we drove up the mountain, took the little narrow-gage railroad which is there to carry the logs down to the lake. Sitting on the front logs, we rode down the mountain. The big beams of timber are brought to the mines in order to prop up the places where the ore has been taken out. These logs do a lot of traveling. They are cut on the other side of Lake Tahoe, dragged over the lake by a tug, sawed the right length by a sawing-mill, then carried up the mountain by this railroad and floated down by means of a wood trough, three feet wide, for twenty-two miles to another railroad, thence to Virginia City.

A steam-launch was waiting for us, and we cruised about this lovely lake, which is of the bluest water and the greenest shadows you ever saw. One sees a hundred feet down; the water is as clear as crystal. J. talked fishing with the pilot, who promised to take him out fishing with him. He caught a beautiful rainbow-trout (as they are called here) from the launch. When he gets home he will tell you how big the biggest fish was he lost.

We arrived at San Francisco at two o'clock. One of the men brought me some splendid cherries, big as plums, and Johan's consul met us on the ferryboat. This last was in a great hurry to get back to his home, as he did not know whether it was a boy or a girl.

We were driven to the Palace Hotel, which is very fine. Each of us had a complete apartment, *salon*, bed, and bathroom. Having been five days and nights in the train, you may imagine we were tired. I was not only tired, but dizzy and glad to go to bed.

Senator Sharon, who owns this hotel, sent us word begging us not to make any engagement for Saturday and Sunday next, as he intends inviting us to his country place. No bill is to be presented to us here. We are not expected to pay for anything. We are his guests, and, strange to say, not one of us knows him, excepting, of course, Mr. Kasson.

The drive out to the cliffs is enchanting. I had never seen a live sea-lion before, and here were thousands of them, barking, diving in the water and wriggling out of it, and basking in the sun on the rocks.

General McDowell took us out for an early tour the next day in his steam-launch. At five o'clock there was a dense fog covering everything, but suddenly it lifted as we approached. We made the circle of the Angel Island, then landed in a paradise of flowers. I don't think I ever saw such flowers as these. The heliotropes looked as big as cauliflowers, and I saw an ambitious and enormous tomato resembling a pumpkin, on the top of a veranda. The fuchsias were as large as dinner-bells, and when the sun rose over the bay no words can describe how beautiful it was—like one of Turner's pictures, only more exaggerated.

I think if I am going to be an angel, as I certainly am, instead of going to Paris when I die, I should prefer to go to this angelic island.

We ladies were invited by a well-known Chinese tea merchant to a Chinese feast. The table looked rather bare, having only a teacup and a plate before each person. The cups are double, the smaller one being placed on the other to keep in the tea-leaves. After drinking the pale water in which the leaves have soaked, we were served the viands. Each dish is brought in separately and put on the table. Every one of them is a *ragoût* of some kind. The Chinaman dives in with his chopsticks, and aims for the best piece he sees. Everything is eaten from the same plate—indeed, why should the plate be changed, since everything tastes and looks alike? I waited in vain for birds'-nest pudding, but I could probably not have distinguished it from the other *ragoûts* if it had been there.

The gentlemen went off on a purely masculine tour, with a policeman in tow. They wanted to see opium-dens and slums. They never told us a word of what they did see—the mean things! Philip V.R., accompanied by an American policeman, took us to a Chinese theater in the evening. I was so nervous I hardly dared to look about me.

The dusky mass of uncanny Chinamen with their shaved heads and their black pigtails sitting underneath us in the parquet was not pleasing, and the stage was merely a platform where some privileged of the audience sat unconcernedly. The scenery was—screens. How easy to shift. We had the policeman of course; but, though he kept a vigilant eye on us to prevent anything from happening in the way of an assault, as frequently happens here, the idea of fire frightened us to such a degree that our one wish was to get away. The upper gallery in which our box was situated was so low that you could touch the ceiling with your hand. The gas-jets had no globes, and the flickering flames suggested everything that was horrible. If there had been a fire no one could possibly have been saved. We felt no interest in the play. It had begun a month ago; the hero had not yet advanced further than his childhood. Perhaps next year when he grows up the play will be more interesting.

Nougats and other sweets, which looked as if they had circulated since the hero of the play was born, were passed about to the spectators. We were glad to reach the hotel in safety and bid our nice American policeman good night.

SAN FRANCISCO, *May, 1877.*

My dear Aunt,—The letters of introduction we brought to San Francisco have already procured us many invitations.

We were at a dinner last night, which Governor Stanford gave us. He has only twenty-five millions—hardly worth mentioning. Each of us ladies had a millionaire to take us in to dinner. Mine was most amiable. He passed all the other millionaires *en revue*; I wish I could remember all he said about them, but I only have a sort of vague recollection that every millionaire had come to San Francisco with only fifty cents in his pocket, and that all the millionaires' wives had gone, in former days, about in the streets of San Francisco selling milk or thread and needles. I was not spared the history of any of them. Mr. S. himself told me that he had made his fortune first in hosiery, and then he invested his money in stocks.

There were thirty people present, divided thus: distinguished party, ten; millionaires, twenty.

Every conceivable bird, alive or mechanical, was heard during this repast; besides, there were musical boxes at each end of the room, which made a tremendous confusion. I know to a cent how much this house cost—one million two hundred thousand dollars, my neighbor told me. It is a great, white, wooden, square house with a veranda around it, perched up on a sandy hill without any garden and without a view of any kind, and certainly without the least beauty.

The picture-gallery, which really has some fine pictures, cost four hundred thousand dollars.

They had had Italian workmen brought especially from Italy to put down the mosaic pavement in the hall, which was huge. We wandered through all the rooms, each one in a different style and epoch, and all in bad taste. I looked about in the so-called ballroom for a piano, and was surprised at not seeing one there; but I noticed several in the other rooms, decorated in the style of the room. They were in every color of wood and charged with brass ornaments. Evidently they were there *as ornaments, not to be used*. Some one must have said to Mr. S., "You must have a piano." And he must have answered: "Certainly. Of course we must. Let us have one in each room, by all means."

The servants all had mustaches and hair curled with tongs. I saw the eyebrows of my party go up at an angle when the servants offered them Johannesburg in gold cups, and still higher up when they saw the mustached waiters pouring white wine in glasses which were previously filled with red wine and alternated indiscriminately.

We were taken up-stairs to see Mrs. S.'s bedroom. It was worthy of an empress, having point-lace coverlids, satin down quilts trimmed with real Valenciennes.

What struck me the most in all this splendor was that so much money should have been expended in furnishing a perishable wooden palace which any tuppenny earthquake or fire could demolish in a moment. Another thing I noticed was that, though everything else was so handsome and costly, the glass and porcelain were of the most ordinary kind.

We enjoyed ourselves immensely and compared notes when we reached the hotel. Barring our individual millionaire, we hardly spoke to the others. We were simply insignificant meteors passing hastily in their midst.

Well, we went to the Senator's country place. A carriage with four horses was waiting for us at the station, and we drove up in fine style to the millionaire's mansion, where some Irish servants with baggy trousers, tumbled cravats, and no gloves opened wide the doors, ushering us into a large hall, where a gentleman whom we guessed was our host came forward to greet us.

We were glad that we were going at last to make his acquaintance. He is a millionaire and a Senator. That is all I can say about him at present, except that he is extremely hospitable. He did not know one of us from the other, except Kasson. He knew we were a "distinguished party" because the papers said so. When we were being dealt out to our rooms there was great confusion. Senator Sharon had an ancient *dame de compagnie*—the head priestess—who made it a particular point to dispose of Miss Clymer before any of the rest of us. She said, "Which of these gents is your husband?" At which Miss C. blushed and found no other answer than, "*None.*" J. and I finally secured the same room, because when Mr. S. in a moment of despair said, with an all-comprehensive wave of his hand, "Gentlemen, please take your wives," J. and I paired off. The Senator did not notice this little detail, for when dinner was announced he said to J.,

"Will you please take that young lady in to dinner?" pointing to me. Johan explained in which relation he stood to the young lady. The Senator was not in the least surprised, and merely answered: "Is that so? Well, then, take some one else."

A semi-millionaire took me in. He told me all his early life of poverty and threw in various reminiscences. I never knew the like of millionaires for telling you of their former miseries. They always do! When the ancient dame saw Mr. Kasson and me talking after dinner, she said to us with a kittenish smile, "Husbands and wives mustn't talk together." Hopeless! We did not even try to explain. The evening was forlorn. There were many dreary drawing-rooms, horribly furnished, but brilliantly lighted. A brawling musical box was supposed to enliven us. We talked in that desultory way that one does with people whom you meet for the first time and never want to meet again. Some of the millionaires hovered among us, but failed to impress us either with their past or present fortunes. Oh, joy! Bedtime came at last.

May 17th.

I have just had time to scribble these few words before the post comes for my letter.

We have been driving about, admiring landscapes, one another, every one else, millionaires! Everything that money can do to spoil Nature has been done here, but Nature will have her own way in the end; and in spite of the millionaires' millions and the incongruity of everything, we cannot but admire this beautiful and wonderful country.

Before our departure the Senator actually knew us one from the other. He said to me, struggling with my names, "Well, Mrs. *Lindermann Hegercrone*, I am very sorry you are going."

We started on visit No. 2—this time to Mr. Lathrop's beautiful place in Menlo Park. The grounds are perfectly laid out. Flowers of all kinds arranged in parterres, clusters of trees such as I had never seen before, roses as big as sunflowers, and the beautiful sparkling lake in front of the window and the blue mountains in the distance, made the place a perfect paradise. The stables were extra fine, the floor and ceiling being inlaid in two kinds of wood found only in California. The room where the bridles were kept had such beautiful polished panels that they shone like mirrors. There must have been harnesses for twelve horses hanging on the walls. Mr. L. gave me a box made of the thirty different kinds of wood found in California.

The following day we drove with four horses to Mr. Rathbone's, who also has a gorgeous place. His picture-gallery is worthy of a Rothschild.

We left San Francisco for Los Angeles; the directors of the road put everything at our disposition as usual. We had a *salon*, bed, and dressing-rooms in one car, and Miss Cadwalader and Miss Clymer had similar ones in another. There were kitchen, dining and reading rooms for the whole party, which had now grown to be sixteen in number, Senator Conover and his wife and some officers going with General Taylor to Fort Yuma having joined us.

We went to Santa Monica, which is the fashionable watering-place of these parts. Here we drove on the beach, which is thirty miles long. A gentleman of Los Angeles was attached to our party and showed us the sights. We saw all kinds of ranches—orange, grape, and bee ranches. Then we drove to a Mexican settlement, where they gave us a gorgeous dinner, really worthy of more time than we could give it, for we had to leave at five o'clock for Los Angeles, where we dined again.

The next day we started off on another tour. We drove through twenty-five miles of banana, pineapple, pomegranate groves and vineyards. We tasted all the wines and fruit-syrups, and drank native port and champagne. We had a special train and arrived at Merced the next morning, to start on our Yosemite Valley tour.

May 20th.

Just our luck! The first rain for four months pours down to-day. We drove, nevertheless, from 7 A.M. until 6 P.M. (only stopping for our meals), over barren, sandy, and desolate country. We saw whole flocks of sheep dead and dying by thousands from want of care and drought. We (seven and the driver) were packed away in an open three-seated wagon with four horses, and drove over the dreariest road one can imagine. We passed continually places where the ground was all upturned, evidently either worked-out or abandoned gold-diggings. It was very pathetic when one thought of the work, time, and hopes wasted there. At twelve o'clock we reached Hunter's (the name of the hotel), and then we drove over more dismal plains still to a hotel called Clark's. It must originally have been a lovely place, but now it is spoiled by the gold-diggings. Here we stayed all night in a very rough kind of tavern. During the night we heard the howls of wolves and jackals very near the hotel, which was not pleasant. We started at five o'clock the next morning in a big, open *char-à-bancs*, and went through the most beautiful forest. The trees are all from one hundred and fifty to two hundred feet high, and from six to seven feet in diameter; hardly any smaller trees among them. And such wonderful ferns! And the ice-plants! This has a brilliant red stalk and flowers coming from under the snow. We were so high up that there was snow on the ground all about us. The trees are perfectly beautiful. The mansanilla, the branches of which are like red coral, and the leaves the lightest of greens, the California laurel, and many others of which I do not know the names, were too beautiful. The white pine has cones one and a half feet long.

We drove up for four hours through the forest, until we reached the height of five thousand feet. Here was a magnificent view, as you may imagine. Then we began going down. That was something dreadful! The driver, with his six horses, drove at a diabolical rate, one foot on the brake, the other planted against the dashboard to keep his balance, holding a tremendously long whip in one hand and the six reins in the other. I shut my eyes and said my prayers. I cannot find words to describe my emotion when I saw the precipice on one side and the mountain on the other, especially when we came to a sharp corner and looked in front, when we actually seemed to be going into space.

We arrived exhausted at the Yosemite Valley, where the feeling of repose at being on flat ground and driving through those green pastures surrounded by the six-thousand-feet-high mountains was delicious. We found the hotel large, comfortable, with a good many other visitors. The *table d'hôte* dinner was well attended. Outside the hotel we spied an Indian lurking about. They told us that he was the last of the Yosemite tribe; he boasted that he had never spoken to a white man. I am sure no white man would ever care to speak to such an uncouth-looking tramp as he was, dressed in ragged clothes and wearing shabby boots, playing hide-and-seek in the most undignified manner, and utterly unworthy of the traditional Cooper Indian.

J. had time to put in a little fishing. The last of the Yosemites dodged behind the trees, watching him and probably envying him the lone minnow which was brought back in triumph.

The next morning we mounted horses and donkeys and rode up to Cloud's Rest to see the glorious view over the whole Yosemite range. Our horses picked their way most carefully over the stones and water puddles. J. had a donkey who pretended that he was weak in all his four legs. When he went up the mountain his fore legs stumbled at every moment, inviting J. to get off and lead him, and when he came down the mountain his back legs gave way and he sat down, so that J. could not help getting off. The result was that J. had to lead him both up and down and could have dispensed with his services entirely.

The Bride's Veil falls six thousand feet in a straight fall, becoming only a tiny spray and a fine mist before it reaches the rocks at the bottom.

Bright and early the next morning we drove to see Mirror Lake, which was really like a mirror. The air was deliciously fresh and fragrant with spring flowers. We bought some photographs and turned them upside down. The lake and mountains were so mirrored that you could not see which was top or bottom.

The next day being Sunday, we thought we would stay quietly in Yosemite Valley, enjoying the rest and beauty of our surroundings. The hotel was good, and the place was enticing. Here it was that the funniest thing happened we had yet encountered. A deputation of one knocked at our door at an early hour this morning. We had just finished a plain Sunday breakfast of hash, fried potatoes, corn cakes, griddle-cakes, and syrup fresh from the white-pine trees. But I am digressing, and the man is still knocking at our door. J. opened it and let him in. With many hums and haws he said that he had been sent to ask J. if he would read the prayers and preach a sermon in the drawing-room of the hotel, "its being Sunday and you being a minister."

J. was a little aghast, not exactly understanding, while I was shaking with laughter at the other end of the room, and would not have interfered for worlds for fear of losing a word of the dialogue.

"I read the gospel!" cried J.

"Yes, sir. You're a minister, ain't yer?"

"Well, yes, I am, but not the kind you mean."

The little man said, condescendingly: "We are not particular as to sect. Whether you're a *Baptist* or *Methodist*, it makes no difference as long as you will preach."

J. had difficulty in explaining in his best English that preaching was not a specialty of his. He did not add that all he did in that line was to administer occasionally a mild *savon* which he kept only for family use when we washed our linen at home.

The abashed ambassador left us, shaking his head, and evidently wondering why a minister, whether from Denmark or Lapland, couldn't preach, any more than a doctor who was a doctor couldn't practise.

You may be sure that this episode gave us plenty to laugh about to last all that beautiful day in the valley of Yosemite.

We stopped there altogether three days, and were lost in admiration and wonder at the beauty of everything. The greatest wonder the gentlemen met was the item on the bill for blacking boots, which was fifteen dollars. They paid without a murmur, because they wanted to tell their friends about it when they got home.

We took our leave of beautiful Yosemite Valley, throwing a disdainful look at the *boots*, and we saw the last of the Yosemites peeping at us from behind the shrubbery. We mounted the stage-coach which was to take us to Mariposa Grove. We drove up the mountain all right, but when the summit was reached the coachman began to whip up his six horses and started galloping them down and turning those corners in such a reckless manner that our hair stood on end; and in answer to our gentle words reminding him that there were human beings in the coach he said, coolly:

"Oh, I guess it'll be all right, but this is my first experience." On a sharp turn of the road we suddenly saw a great white pine about six feet in diameter lying right across our path. It had evidently fallen in the night. Fortunately, the driver saw it and managed to pull up his six horses in time to avoid a catastrophe.

How in the world should we ever get over this obstacle? All our projects would be disarranged if there came a single unexpected delay. A *conseil de guerre* was held, every one talking at once, and it was decided that the driver should unhitch the horses, and that each lady should hold two of them, while the men were to look about to find timber enough to improvise an inclined plane on both sides of this enormous tree-trunk, so that the coach could be hauled up on one side and dragged down on the other. The gentlemen managed to get the carriage over, then they led the horses over, and lastly we ladies were piloted across.

After a delay of an hour we were able to drive to Mariposa Hotel, where we found eight saddle-horses waiting for us. It was all most exciting, and we enjoyed every moment of the ride through the most beautiful forest in the world. The ordinary trees of this forest would be gigantic in any other part of the globe (six to seven feet in diameter), but when we "struck" the first big tree I almost fell off my horse with wonder. This tree was four hundred feet high and about thirty-three feet in diameter. I knew beforehand that they were monstrously big and high, but I did not know that they had such a beautiful color—a red cinnamon. The first branch was a hundred feet from the ground and six feet in diameter. In the Mariposa Grove there are three hundred of these giants. In one tree, which was partly hollowed out by fire, we seven people sat on horseback. That gives you an idea! We saw a carriage full of travelers drive through a hollow fallen tree as if through a tunnel. One must see these to imagine what they are like. The "Old Giant" was the most imposing and grandest of them all—thirty-seven feet in diameter, and high! One got dizzy trying to see the top, which is really not the top. The winds up there do not allow themselves to be encroached upon, and the young shoots are nipped off as soon as they appear.

We had to sleep at Mariposa Grove (Clark's Hotel) in the evening. We talked of nothing else but the wonderful trees until some one asked me if I was too tired to sing. I was willing enough. There was, in fact, a piano in the parlor—an old, yellow-keyed out-of-tune Chickering which had seen better days somewhere—and a spiral stool very rickety on its legs. There were wax flowers under dusty globes. Though no one of our party cared much for music, and the surroundings were anything but inspiring, still I longed to sing.

I sang a lot of things, and my tired audience no doubt thought I had done enough and ought to go to bed, which I did, after having received their thanks and seeing the heads of the servant-girls and various other heads and forms disappear from the veranda.

May 25th.

We left Clark's early in the morning without having made a second trip to the trees, as we wanted to, but the time was nearing when John Cadwalader was to leave us for his trip around the world. We were already too late as it was, and if anything should happen like another Gulliver across our downward path he would lose the steamer which starts from San Francisco in three days. I sat in the favorite seat next to the driver and waved a long farewell to the beautiful forest which I shall probably never see again.

Here another funny thing happened. Everything funny seems to happen at the end of our trip. The driver (a new one, not the one of yesterday) after a long silence, and having changed a piece of straw he was chewing from one side of his mouth to the other many times, made up his mind to speak. I did not speak first, though I longed to, as I am told it is not wise to speak to the man at the wheel, especially when the wheel happens to be a California coach and six horses.

"A beautiful day," the driver ventured.

"Yes," I said, "it is one of the most beautiful days I have ever seen."

He, after a long pause, said, "Was you in the hotel parlor last night?"

"Yes," I said, "I was."

"Did you hear that lady sing?"

"Yes, I did. Did you?"

"You bet I did. I was standing with the rest of the folks out on the piazza."

How curious it would be to hear a wild Western unvarnished, unprejudiced judgment of myself! "What did you think of her singing?" I asked my companion.

He replied by asking, "Have you ever heard a nightingale, ma'm?"

"Oh yes, many times," I answered, wondering what he would say next.

"Wal, I guess some of them nightingales will have to take a back seat when she sings."

I actually blushed with pride. I considered this was the greatest compliment I had ever had.

We arrived safely, without any adventure, at Sacramento, where John Cadwalader left us, and the rest of the party continued as far as Chicago together, where we bade each other good-by, each going his different way.

CAMBRIDGE, *June, 1877.*

My dear Sister,—Sarah Bernhardt is playing in Boston now, much to Boston's delight. I went to see her at the Tremont House, where she is staying. She looked enchanting, and was dressed in her most characteristic manner, in a white dress with a border of fur. Fancy, in this heat! She talked about Paris, her latest successes, asked after Nina, and finally—what I wanted most to know—her impressions of America.

This is her first visit. I found that she seemed to be cautious about expressing her opinions. She said she was surprised to see how many people in America understood French. "Really?" I answered. "It did not strike me so the other evening when I heard you in 'La Dame aux Camelias.'" "I don't mean the public," she replied. "It apparently understands very little, and the turning of the leaves of the librettos distracts me so much that I sometimes forget my rôle. At any rate, I wait till the leaves have finished rustling. But in society," she added, "I find that almost every one who is presented to me talks very good French." "Well," I answered, "if Boston didn't speak French I should be ashamed of it." She laughed. "Sometimes," she said, "they do make curious mistakes. I am making note of all I can remember. They will be amusing in the book I am writing. A lady said to me, 'What I admire the most in you, madame, *c'est votre température.*'" She meant "temperament." "What did you answer to that?" I asked. "I said, '*Oui, madame, il fait très chaud,*' which fell unappreciated."

She is bored with reporters, who besiege her from morning till night. One—a woman—who sat with note-book in hand for ages ("*une éternité*" she said) reporting, the next day sent her the newspaper in which a column was filled with the manner she treated her nails. Not one word about "*mon art*"! "Some of my *admirateurs*" she said, "pay their fabulous compliments through an interpreter." She thought this was ridiculous. When I got up to leave she said, "*Chère* madame, you know Mr. Longfellow?" "Yes," I replied, "very well." "Could you not arrange that I might make his bust? You can tell him that you know my work, and that I can do it if he will let me."

I told her that I would try. She was profuse in her thanks in anticipation, but, alas! Mr. Longfellow, when I spoke to him, turned a cold shoulder on the idea. He begged me to assure Sarah Bernhardt nothing would have given him more pleasure, but, with a playful wink, "I am leaving for Portland in a few days, and I am afraid she will have left Boston when I come back"—thus cutting the Gordian (k)*not* with a snap. But, evidently regretting his curtness, he said, "Tell her if she is at liberty to-morrow I will offer her a cup of tea." Then he added: "You must come and chaperon me. It would not do to leave me alone with such a dangerous and captivating visitor." He invited Mr. Howells and Oliver Wendell Holmes to meet her. I wrote to Sarah Bernhardt what the result of my interview was and gave the invitation. She sent back a short "I will come." The next afternoon I met her at Mr. Longfellow's. When we were drinking our tea she said, "*Cher* M. Longfellow, I would like so much to have made your bust, but I am so occupied that I really have not the time." And he answered her in the most suave manner, "I would have been delighted to sit for you, but, unfortunately, I am leaving for the country to-morrow." How clever people are!

Mr. Longfellow speaks French like a native. He said: "I saw you the other evening in 'Phèdre.' I saw Rachel in it fifty years ago, but you surpass her. You are magnificent, for you are *plus vivante*. I wish I could make my praises vocal—*chanter vos louanges*."

"I wish that you could make *me* vocal," she said. "How much finer my Phèdre would be if I could sing, and not be obliged to depend upon some horrible soprano behind the scenes!"

"You don't need any extra attraction," Mr. Longfellow said. "I wish I could make you feel what I felt."

"You can," she said, "and you do—by your poetry."

"Can you read my poetry?"

"Yes. I read your 'He-a-vatere.'"

"My—Oh yes—'Hiawatha.' But you surely do not understand that?"

"Yes, yes, indeed I do," she said. "*Chaque mot.*"

HENRY W. LONGFELLOW

JAMES G. BLAINE
When Speaker of the House of Representatives.

"You are wonderful," he said, and fearing that she might be tempted to recite "*chaque mot*" of his "Hiawatha," hastened to present Mr. Holmes, who was all attention.

At last the tea-party came to an end. We all accompanied her to her carriage, and as she was about to get in she turned with a sudden impulse, threw her arms round Mr. Longfellow's neck, and said, "*Vous êtes adorable*," and kissed him on his cheek. He did not, seem displeased, but as she drove away he turned to me and said, "You see I did need a chaperon."

Johan has just come home from Boston, bringing incredible stories about having talked in a machine called telephone. It was nothing but a wire, one end in Boston and the other end in Cambridge. He said he could hear quite plainly what the person in Cambridge said. Mr. Graham Bell, our neighbor, has invented this. How wonderful it must be! He has put up wires about Boston, but not farther than Cambridge—yet. He was ambitious enough to suggest Providence. "What!" cried the members of the committee. "You think you can talk along a wire in the air over that distance?" "Let me just try it," said Bell. "I will bear half the expense of putting up the wire if you will bear the other half."

He was ultra-convinced of his success when, on talking to his brother in Cambridge from Boston in order to invite him to dinner, adding, "Bring your mother-in-law," he heard, distinctly but feebly, the old lady's voice: "Good gracious! Again! What a bore!"

There is also another invention, called phonograph, where the human voice is reproduced, and can go on for ever being reproduced. I sang in one through a horn, and they transposed this on a platina roll and wound it off. Then they put it on another disk, and I heard my voice—for the first time in my life. If that is my voice, I don't want to hear it again! I could not believe that it could be so awful! A high, squeaky, nasal sound; I was ashamed of it. And the faster the man turned the crank the higher and squeakier the voice became. The intonation—the pronunciation—I could recognize as my own, but the *voice*!... Dear me!

[*Johan, desiring me to know his family, suggested that we spend the Christmas holidays in Denmark, and we arrived safely after a slow and very stormy voyage.*]

"BJÖRNEMOSE," *December 20, 1877.*

Dear Mother,—Denmark looks very friendly under its mantle of snow, glistening with its varnish of ice. It is lovely weather. The sun shines brightly, but it is as cold as Greenland. They tell me it is a very mild winter. Compared with Alaska, it may be! The house, which is heated only by large porcelain stoves, is particularly cold. These stoves are filled with wood in the early morning, and when the wood is burned out they shut the door and the porcelain tiles retain the heat—still, the ladies all wear shawls over their shoulders and shiver. I go and lean my back up against the huge white monument, but this is not considered good form.

The Baltic Sea, which is at the foot of the snow-covered lawn, is filled with floating ice. It must be lovely here in the summer, when one can see the opposite shores of Thuro across the blue water.

My new family, taken singly and collectively, is delightful. I shall tell you later about the dear, genial General—my father-in-law—the kind mother, and the three devoted sisters. *Now* I shall only write—as I promised you—my *first* impressions.

We live in a manner which is, I fancy, called "patriarchal," and which reminds me continually of Frederika Bremer's book called *Home*. A great many things in the way of food are new to me. For instance, there is a soup made of beer, brown bread, and cream, and another made of the insides of a goose, with its long neck and thin legs, boiled with prunes, apples, and vinegar. Then rice porridge is served as soup and mixed with hot beer, cinnamon, butter, and cream. These all seem very queer, but they taste very good, I asked for oatmeal porridge, but I was told that oatmeal was used only for cataplasms. Corn is known only as ornamental shrubbery, and tomatoes, alas! are totally unknown.

Every one I have met so far has been most kind and hospitable. We have been invited out to dinner several times. I will describe the first one, which was unique as a *début*.

The distances are enormous between country houses in this land; and, as the hour named for dinner was six o'clock, we had to begin dressing in the afternoon at the early hour of three. At four we were packed in the family landau, with a mountain of rugs and different things to keep our feet warm. We jogged along the hard, slippery highroad at a monotonous pace; and, as it is dark at four o'clock, nothing could have been more conducive to slumber and peaceful dreams. Finally we arrived. Every one was standing up when we entered the *salon*. There seemed to be a great number of people. I was presented to all the ladies, and the gentlemen were brought up one by one and named to me. They bowed, shook my hand, and retired. I noticed that all the ladies wore long trailing skirts—lilac or gray—and had real flowers in their hair and on their bosoms. Dinner was announced. Then there came a pause. The host and the hostess were looking about for some one to undertake *me*—some one who could *tale Engelsk* (talk English). Finally they decided upon a lank, spectacled gentleman, who offered me his arm and took me in.

My father-in-law, who was the person highest in rank, sat on the left of the hostess. I thought this peculiar, but such is the custom here. From the moment we sat down until we rose from the table my English-speaking friend never stopped talking. He told me he had learned my language when a boy, but had forgotten a great deal; if he had said he had forgotten it entirely he would have been nearer the truth.

He wanted to tell me the family history of a gentleman opposite us, and began by saying: "Do you see that gentleman? He has been washing you all the time."

"Washing me?" I exclaimed. "What do you mean?"

"Yes, the one with the gray hairs and the bird."

I looked about for a canary perched on some one's nose.

"It is a pity," he went on to say, "that he has no shield."

"How is that?" I asked. "I thought every one had a shield of some sort?" To make it clearer to me, he said, uIn Danish we call a shield a *barn*."

"Is he a farmer?" said I, much puzzled.

"Oh dear, no! He is a lawyer like me."

"Then what does he want with a barn?"

"Every couple [pronounced copol] wants *burn*," he replied.

"What is it they want?" I asked. "What do you call *burn*?"

"Burn," he explained, "is *pluriel* for barn. *Eight* barn, two *burn*."

"What?" I cried, "eight barns to burn! Why do they want to burn eight barns? They must be crazy!"

All this will sound to you as idiotic as it did to me, but you will get the explanation at the end of the chapter, as I did—on the drive home—the two hours of which were entirely taken up in laughing at the mistakes of the good lawyer, who did his best.

Our conversation languished after this. My brain could not bear such a strain. Suddenly he got up from his chair. I thought that he was going to take himself and his English away, but after he had quaffed a whole glass of wine, at one swallow, bowed over it, and pointed his empty glass at Johan, he resumed his seat, and conversation flowed again.

It seems that Johan had honored him with a friendly nod and an uplifted glass, which obliged him to arise and acknowledge the compliment.

In Denmark there is a great deal of *skaal*-drinking (*skaal*, in Danish, means drinking a toast). I think there must be an eleventh commandment—"Thou shalt not omit to *skaal*." The host drinks with every one, and every one drinks with every one else. It seems to me to be rather a cheap way of being amiable, but it looks very friendly and sociable. When a person of high rank drinks with one of lower the latter stands while emptying his glass.

When we left the table I did not feel that my Danish had gained much, and certainly my partner's English had not improved. However, we seemed to have conversed in a very spirited manner, which must have impressed the lookers-on with a sense of my partner's talent for languages.

On our return to the *salon* we found more petroleum-lamps, and the candelabra lighted to exaggeration with wax candles. The lamp-shades, which I thought were quite ingenious, were of paper, and contained dried ferns and even flattened-out butterflies between two sheets of shiny tissue-paper. The *salon* had dark walls on which hung a collection of family portraits. Ladies with puckered mouths and wasp-like waists had necks adorned with gorgeous pearls, which had apparently gone to an early grave with their wearers. I saw no similar ones on the necks of the present generation. After the coffee was served and a certain time allowed for breathing, the daughter of the house sat down, without being begged, at an upright piano, and attacked the "Moonlight Sonata." This seemed to be the signal for the ladies to bring out their work-bags.

The knitting made a pleasing accompaniment to the moonlight of the sonata, as if pelicans were gnashing their teeth in the dimness. The sterner sex made a dash for the various albums and literature on the round table in the center of the room, and turned the leaves with a gentle flutter. The sonata was finished in dead silence. As it was performed by one of the family, no applause was necessary. I was asked to sing; and, though I do not like to sing after dinner, I consented, not to be disobliging. Before taking my seat on the revolving piano-stool I looked with a severe eye at the knitting-needles. The ladies certainly did try to make less noise, but they went on knitting, all the same.

The flushed-with-success lawyer, wishing to show his appreciation of my singing, leaned gracefully across the piano, and said, "*Kammerherrinde* [that is my title], you sing as if you had a beard in your throat."

"A what?" I gasped. "A beard?"

"Yes! a beautiful beard," and added, with a conscious smile, "I sing myself."

Good heavens! I thought, and asked, "Do you know what a beard is?"

"In Danish we call a beard a *fugle*" (pronounced *fool*.)

"Then," I said, pretending to be offended, "I sing like a fool?"

"Exactly," he said with enthusiasm, his eyes beaming with joy through his spectacles.

This was hopeless. I moved gently away from the man who "talked English."

The candles had burned down almost to their *bobèches*, and we were beginning to forget that we had eaten a dinner of fifteen courses, when in came a procession of servants with piles of plates in their arms and trays of *smördröd* (sandwiches), tea, beer (in bottles), and cakes, which are called here *kicks*. Everything seemed very tempting except the things handed about by the stable-boy, who was dressed for the occasion in a livery, much too large, and was preceded and followed by a mixed odor of stable and almond soap.

What struck me as unusual was that the host named the hour for his guests to go home. Therefore all the carriages were before the door at the same time.

Johan explained the mistakes on the way home.

"The man with the gray hairs and the *beard*" (pronounced like *heard*) had been *watching* me. *Shield* meant *child! A child* in Danish is *et barn*, which sounds the same as *eight barn*. *Two children* (in Danish) are *to börn*, pronounced *toe burn*. *Bird* he pronounced like *beard*, because it was written so. A bird in Danish is *fugle* (fool).

Do you wonder that I was somewhat bewildered?

January, 1878.

Dear Mother,—After Christmas Johan and I went to Copenhagen, where I was presented to the King and the Queen. I was first received by the *Grande Maîtresse*, Madame de Raben, and three *dames d'honneur*, who were all pleasant but ceremonious. When the Queen entered the room and I was presented to her she was most gracious and affable. She motioned me to sit down beside her on the sofa. She said that she had heard much about me. She spoke of my father-in-law, whom she *loved*, and Johan, whom she *liked* so much. She was most interested to hear about you and the children. She had heard that Nina promised to be a beauty.

"If children would only grow up to their promises!" I said.

"Mine have," said the Queen; "they are all beautiful."

She showed me the photographs of the Princess of Wales and the Grand-Duchess Dagmar of Russia. If they resemble their pictures they must indeed be beautiful.

The *salon* in which we sat was filled with drawings, pastels, and photographs, and was so crowded with furniture that one could hardly move about.

"I've been told," the Queen said, "that you have a splendid voice and sing wonderfully. You must come some day and sing for me; I love music." Then we talked music, the most delightful of subjects. The King came in. He was also perfectly charming, and as kind as possible. He is about sixty years old, but looks younger, having a wonderfully youthful figure and a very handsome face. The King preferred to speak French, but the Queen liked better to talk English, which she does to perfection.

"Have you learned Danish yet?" the King asked me.

"Alas! your Majesty," I answered, "though I try very hard to learn, I have not mastered it yet, and only dare to inflict it on my family."

"You will not find it difficult," he said. "You will learn it in time."

"I hope so, your Majesty—Time is a good teacher."

He told me an anecdote about Queen Desiree, of Sweden, wife of Bernadotte, who on her arrival in Stockholm did not know one word of Swedish.

She was taught certain phrases to use at her first reception when ladies were presented to her. She was to say, "Are you married, madame?" and then, "Have you any children?" Of course, she did not understand the answers. "She was very unlucky," the King laughed, "and got things mixed up, and once began her conversation with a lady by asking, 'Have you any children?'"

The lady hastened to answer, "Yes, your Majesty, I have seven?"

"Are you married?" asked the Queen, very graciously.

"You must not do anything like *that*," said the King, smilingly.

I promised that I would try not to.

The *Grande Maîtresse* came in, and I thought it was the signal for me to go—which apparently it was. There was a little pause; then the Queen held out her hand and said, "I hope to see you again very soon." The King shook hands kindly with me, and I reached the antechamber, escorted by the ladies.

My next audience was with the Crown Princess. She is the daughter of the late King of Sweden (Carl XV.) and niece of the present King Oscar, whom I used to know in Paris. This audience was not so ceremonious as the one I had had with the Queen. There was only one lady-in-waiting, who received me in the *salon* adjoining that of the Princess. She accompanied me to the door, presented me, and withdrew, leaving us together. In the beginning the conversation palled somewhat. I had been warned that it was not etiquette for me to start any subject of conversation, though I might enlarge on it once it had been broached. The Crown Princess was so kind as to speak of something which she thought would interest me, and the conventional half-hour passed pleasantly and quickly.

I had other audiences. The Queen Dowager, the widow of King Christian VIII., lives in one of the four palaces in the square of Amalienborg. She is very stately, and received me with great etiquette. She was dressed in a stiff black brocade dress, with a white lace head-dress over her bandeaux; she wore short, white, tight kid gloves. She spoke French, and was most kind, telling me a great deal about Denmark and its history, which interested me very much.

As Mademoiselle de Rosen, her first *dame d'honneur*, re-entered the room I made my courtesy, kissed the Queen's hand, and the audience was over.

Johan accompanied me to the fourth audience, which for me was the most difficult one. It was with the Princess Caroline, widow of Prince Ferdinand, brother of King Christian VIII., who died when he was heir-apparent to the throne. She spoke only Danish to us, so I sat and gazed about, not understanding a word she said to Johan.

She wore flaxen braids wound above her ears, through which the cotton showed like the petal of a flower. She had a lace cap on her head with long lace ends, and these caught in everything she wore—her eye-glasses, her neck-chain, her rings and bracelets, and she seemed to do nothing but try to extricate herself while talking. This she did steadily, in order (I suppose) to prevent any one else from talking. She is so deaf that she cannot hear a word. She had once been burned, and the effects of that, with the mark of former smallpox, makes her face look far from handsome. But all these things have not prevented her from reaching the ripe old age of eighty.

Johan supplied what little there was of conversation on our side. She asked him, "How did you come to Denmark?" He, enchanted to be asked something he could answer, replied that he had come on one of the big German boats, and, to accentuate the fact that it was something *big* he came in, he made a wide circular movement with his arms and became quite eloquent, flattering himself that he was very interesting. The Princess fixed a pair of earnest eyes on him, and said, in hushed tones, "And what became of the child?"

We took our leave. In stooping to kiss her Royal Highness's hand her cap caught in an ornament I had on my bonnet, and there we stood tied together. Johan tried in vain to undo us, but was obliged to call in the lady-in-waiting, who finally disentangled us.

DENMARK, *January, 1878.*

Dear Mother,—The Queen of Denmark is an adorable and lovely queen. I am happy to call her *my* Queen.

A few days after my audience we were invited to a dinner at Amalienborg. We met in the *salon*, before their Majesties came in. When they had made a little *cercle* and said a word to every one, dinner was announced. The King gave one arm to the Queen and the other to the Princess Anne of Hesse—the Queen's sister-in-law. The King and the Queen sat next to each other. There were about forty people at table. Admiral Bille took me in; he talked English perfectly, and was—like all naval officers!—very charming.

The Queen said to me: "I should so like to hear you sing. Will you come to-morrow? I will send my carriage for you, and please don't forget to bring some music."

As if I should forget! I was only too delighted.

The next morning the Queen sent her own coupé for me at eleven o'clock. I felt very grand; all the people in the street bowed and courtesied, thinking I was one of the royal family. I let down the glasses on both sides of the coupé so that every one could have a chance to bow.

I was at once ushered into the Queen's *salon* by an old red-liveried majordomo who had many decorations on his breast. The Queen was alone with the *Grande Maîtresse*, and after having talked a little she said, "Now we'll have some music," and led the way into the ballroom, where there were two pianos. The Queen sat on the sofa, wearing an expression that was half pre-indulgent and half expectant. The *Grande Maîtresse*, who was there, *not* in her official character, but as a musician, accompanied me when I sang "*Voi che sapete.*" When I came to the phrase, "*Non trovo pace notte ne di,*" the Queen raised her hand to her eyes, which were filled with tears, and after I had finished, said, "Please sing another."

I spread out the music of "Biondina" in front of the eye-glasses of the *Grande Maîtresse*, but the first bars convinced me that if I were to sing *that* song, *she* was not to play it, and, against all etiquette, I placed my hands over hers and gently pushed her off the seat, saying, "May I?"

I confess I deserved the daggers she looked at me, but the Queen only laughed and said, "You are quite right; you must play *that* for yourself."

The Queen seemed to be delighted, and after some more music I returned to the hotel in the same regal manner I had come.

COPENHAGEN, *February, 1878.*

Dear Mother,—Some days have passed between this and my last letter, but I have been very busy. I have tried to do some sight-seeing—there are many interesting and enchanting things to see here. Then I have had a great many visits to pay, and I go often to sing with the Queen.

Yesterday I lunched at the palace. The Queen had said to me before: "When you come to me, come straight to my room. Don't bother about going first to the *dames d'honneur.* The servant has orders."

So yesterday, when I arrived, the old decorated servant who sits in the antechamber simply opened the door of the Queen's private apartments, where I found her and the Princess Thyra alone.

The Queen said, "You will stay to luncheon, will you not?" I hesitated, as we had invited some friends to lunch with us, but that was evidently no obstacle. She said: "Never mind that. I will send word to your husband that I have kept you." Of course I stayed. We had a great deal of music. I sang "Beware" for the first time. The Queen said, "Oh, the King must hear that," and rang the bell, sending the servant to beg Prince Valdemar to come in.

On his appearing, the Queen said, "Valdemar, you must tell papa that he must come." Prince Valdemar soon returned, saying, "Papa has lumbago, and says he cannot come." The Queen shook her head, evidently not believing in the lumbago, and said, "Lumbago or not, papa *must* come, even if we have to *bring* him."

The King came without being "brought," and I sang "Beware" for him, and then "*Ma mère était bohémienne,*" the Queen accompanying me in both.

"Now," said the Queen, "please sing that song which you play for yourself—the one with such a dash." She meant "Biondina."

"Please, madame," said the King, when I had finished, "sing 'Beware' again."

Then we went down a little side-staircase for luncheon. The dining-room is quite small and looks out upon the square. The table could not have seated more than twelve people. Besides the King and Queen, there were Prince Hans and Prince Wilhelm (brothers of the King), Prince Valdemar,

Princess Thyra, and myself. There were no ladies or gentlemen in waiting, except the King's adjutant.

On a side-table were the warm meats, vegetables, and several cold dishes. No servants were allowed in the room. It is the only meal when the family are quite alone together; the serving was all done by the royalties themselves. I felt quite shy when the King proposed to shell my shrimps for me! "Oh, your Majesty," I said, "I can do that myself!"

"No," said he, "I am sure you cannot. At any rate, not as it ought to be done."

He was quite right. I never could have done it so dexterously as he did. He took the shells off and put the shrimps on some bread—they looked like little pink worms. I did not dare to get up and serve myself at the side-table, and rather than be waited on by royalty I preferred eating little and going away hungry.

The King was very gay. He asked me how I was getting on with my Danish. I told him some of my mistakes, at which they all laughed.

COPENHAGEN, *February, 1878*.

Dear Mother,—After our music and luncheon the other day at the palace the Queen asked me if I would like to drive with her to see Bernstorff Castle, where they spend their summers. I accepted the invitation with delight. To drive with her was bliss indeed.

Bernstorff is about an hour's drive from Copenhagen. When the open landau appeared in the *porte-cochère* the Queen got in; I sat on her left and the lady of honor sat opposite. The Danish royal livery is a bright red covered with braid. The coachman's coat has many red capes, one on top of the other, looking like huge pen-wipers. J. had told me it was not etiquette for any one driving with the Queen to bow. We happened to pass J. walking with a friend of his, and it seemed odd that I was obliged to cut him dead.

When people see the Queen's carriage coming they stop their own, and the ladies get out on the sidewalk and make deep courtesies. Gentlemen bow very low and stand holding their hats in their hands until the royal carriage has passed.

The castle of Bernstorff is neither large nor imposing, but looks home-like and comfortable. The Queen showed me all over it—her private rooms, and even upstairs where her *atelier* is; she paints charmingly—as well as she plays the piano.

She pointed out on the window-panes of a room over the principal *salon* different things that her daughters had written with their diamond rings on the glass: "Farewell, my beautiful clouds!—Alexandra." "Till the next time.—Dagmar." "*A bientôt*—Willie" (the young King of Greece).[1]

She told me that Bernstorff was the first home she and the King had lived in after their marriage, when he was Prince, and they love it so much that they prefer it to the larger castles. They go to Fredensborg in the autumn. The Grand-Duchess Dagmar and the Princess of Wales, when they come to Bernstorff in the summer, sleep in the room which they shared as children.

I cannot tell you how nice the royal family are to me.

We were present at a state ball at Christiansborg. On arriving we passed up a magnificent staircase and went through many large *salons*, the walls of which were covered with fine tapestries and old Spanish leather, and a long gallery of beautiful pictures, before we reached the *salon* where I belonged according to my rank (every one is placed according to the rules of the protocol).

Their Majesties entered. The Queen looked dazzlingly brilliant. She wore all the crown jewels and had some splendid pearls on her neck. The King looked superb in his uniform. They were followed by the Princess Thyra (the young and sympathetic Princess with eyes like a gazelle), and the youngest son, Prince Valdemar.

The Crown Prince and Princess were already there. She also had some wonderful jewels, inherited, they said, from her mother, who was of the royal family of Holland.

Their Majesties were very gracious to me. The King even did me the honor to waltz with me. He dances like a young man of twenty. He went from one lady to another and gave them each a turn. I was taken to supper by a person whose duty it was to attend to me—I forget his name. The King danced the cotillon. You will hardly see that anywhere else—a gentleman of sixty dancing a cotillon.

The principal street in Copenhagen is Ostergade, where all the best shops are. It is very narrow. People sometimes stop and hold conversations across the street, and perambulating nurses, lingering at the shop windows, hold up the traffic.

There is a very pretty square called Amagertorv, where all the peasant women assemble, looking very picturesque in their national dresses, with their little velvet caps embroidered in gold, and their Quaker-like bonnets with a fichu tied over them. They quite fill up the square with flowers, fruits, and vegetables, and stand in the open air by their wares in spite of wind, rain, and weather.

Around the corner, in front of Christiansborg Castle, by the canal, your nose will inform you that this is the fish-market, where the fish are brought every morning, wriggling and gasping in the nets in which they have been caught overnight. It is a very interesting sight to see all the hundreds of boats in the canal, which runs through the center of the town.

The other evening there was a large musical *soirée* given at Amalienborg. I won't tell you the names of those who were present, as you would not know them, but they are the most prominent names here.

Their Majesties sat in two gilded arm-chairs, in front of which was a rug. There was a barytone from the Royal Theater who sang some Danish songs; then the Princess Thyra and an English lady and I sang the trio from "Elijah," and a quartette with the barytone. I sang several times alone. There was an English lady, whose name I do not remember, who played a solo on the *cornet à piston*. Her face was hidden by her music, which was on a stand in front of her. After I had sung the "*Caro Nome*" from "Rigoletto," and the English lady had played her solo, the deaf Princess Caroline—who, with her ears filled with cotton and encompassed by her flaxen braids, sat in front—said, in a loud and penetrating voice, "I like *that* lady's singing better than the other one's"—meaning me. Every one laughed. I had never had a *cornet à piston* as a rival before.

March 1, 1878.

Dear Mother,—Our last day here. I lunched at Amalienborg, and was the only stranger present. The King, who sat next to me, said, "I feel quite hurt that you have never asked me for my photograph."

"But I have one," I answered, "which I bought. I dare not ask your Majesty to sign it."

"One must always dare," he answered, smilingly. "May I 'dare' to ask you to accept one from me?" He got up from the table and left the room, being absent for a few minutes. When the door opened again we saw the King standing outside, trying to carry a large picture. His Majesty had gone up to the room in which the picture hung, and the servant who had taken it from the wall brought it to the door of the dining-room, whence the King carried it in himself. The mark of the dusty cord still showed on his shoulder. It was a life-size portrait of himself painted in oil.

He said, "Will you accept this?"

I could not believe my ears. This for me! I hesitated.

The Queen said, "My dear, you must take it, since the King desires it."

"But," I replied, "how can I?"

Her Majesty answered, "Your husband would not like you to refuse. Take it!—*you must!*" and added, "The ribbon [the blue Order of the Elephant] is beautifully painted"—as if the rest were not!

The Princess Thyra said, "Papa has only had six portraits painted of himself. This one is painted by Mr. Shytte. I don't think that it is half handsome enough for papa. Do you?"

"Well," said the King, "I shall have it sent to your hotel." I could not thank his Majesty enough, and I am sure I looked as embarrassed as I felt.

As we were going away the next day, this was my last visit to the Queen. On bidding me good-by she pressed something into my hand and said, "You leave me so many *souvenirs*! I have only one for you, and here it is."

It was a lovely locket of turquoises. On opening it I found the Queen's portrait on one side and the Princess Thyra's on the other.

She kissed me, and I kissed her hand, with tears in my eyes.

We return to Björnemose to bid our parents good-by; then farewell to Denmark.

We leave in four days for New York.

WASHINGTON, *February, 1879.*

Dear Mother,—Monsieur de Schlözer is one of the colleagues whom we like best. I wish you knew him! I do not know anything more delightful than to see him and Carl Schurz together. They are not unlike in character; they are both witty, refined, always seeing the beautiful in everything, almost boyish in their enthusiasm, and clever, *cela va sans dire*, to their finger-tips. They bring each other out, and they both appear at their best, which is saying a great deal. We consider that we are fortunate to number them among our *intimes*.

Would it interest you to know how these *intimes* amuse themselves? Life is so simple in Washington, and there are so few distractions outside of society, that we only have our social pleasures to take the place of theaters and public entertainments. It is unlike Paris and other capitals in this respect.

We have organized a club which we call "The National Rational International Dining Club," to which belong Mrs. Bigelow Lawrence, her sister Miss Chapman, Mr. de Schlözer, Carl Schurz, Aristarchi Bey (the Turkish Minister), Count Dönhoff (Secretary to the German Legation), and ourselves. So when we are free, and not invited elsewhere, we dine together at one another's houses. I am the president, Mrs. Lawrence the vice-president, Schurz the treasurer, Schlözer the sergeant-at-arms, and Johan has the most difficult—and (as Mr. Schurz calls it) the "onerous"—duty of recognizing and calling attention to the jokes, which in his conscientious attempts to seize he often loses entirely.

The "rational" part is the menu. We are allowed a soup, one roast, one vegetable and dessert, and *two* wines, one of which, according to the regulations, *must be good*. We do not even need so much, for there is more laughing than eating. A stuffed goose from the Smithsonian Institution serves as a *milieu de table*, and is sent, on the day of the dinner, to the person who gives it.

We always have music. Schurz and Schlözer play the piano alternately, and I do the singing. I must say that a more appreciative audience than our co-diners cannot be imagined.

We have laws and by-laws written on large foolscap paper, bearing a huge seal which looks very official. Mr. Schurz carries it in his inside pocket, and sometimes at large dinners he pulls it out and begins reading it with the greatest attention, and every one at the table believes that there is something very important going on in politics. But we, the initiated, know that the document is the law of the N.R.I. Dining Club. Then, when all eyes are fastened on him, he puts the paper deliberately back in his pocket, with a sly wink at the members.

Mr. Schurz is now Secretary of the Interior, and a great personage. When one thinks that he hardly knew a word of our language when he came to this country (a young man of twenty), and that now he is one of our first orators, one cannot help but admire him. Because he has entirely identified himself with the politics of our country he has risen to the high position which he now holds. You said, when you heard him deliver that oration at Harvard College, that you were astonished that any foreigner could have such complete command of the language. He is integrity itself, with a great mind free from all guile, and is filled with the enthusiasm and vivacity of youth. During the revolutionary movement in Germany in 1848 he helped a political friend escape from the Schandau prison, and on account of that was himself condemned to death. However, he managed to evade pursuit and took refuge in America, where he has lived ever since.

Le Chevalier, as we call Senator Bayard, because he is so entirely *sans reproche*, sent his photograph to Mrs. T. and wrote on the back of it, "*Avec les regards de T. Bayard*." She showed it to her friends with the scathing remark, "People should not write French if they don't understand the language." Others, who understood the language, thought it very clever.

Schlözer has let it be known in the Foreign Office in Berlin that a secretary who has money to spend is more desirable in America than one who has not. He thinks that it is more advantageous for a young man to travel through the country and learn things than to sit copying despatches in the *chancellerie* in Washington.

In this respect Count Dönhoff, his new secretary, ought to satisfy him, for never was a person so determined to see everything, know everybody, and do all that is doing. He begged Mr. Schurz to give him permission to accompany General Adam, who, because he knew the Indians and their little ways and how to deal with them, was sent out to Montana to rescue the family of one of the commissioners who had been captured.

These two gentlemen (Adam and Dönhoff) went to the place where the women and children were concealed, and remained there a week, trying to induce the Indians to give them up. They were finally successful, but it was known afterward that the Indians during the time they were there were holding council every night to decide whether or not they would hang the two "pale-faces" to the first tree in the morning.

Both Schurz and Schlözer were relieved to see Count Dönhoff when he returned safe and sound. They reproached themselves for allowing him to start on such an expedition, as it was a very reckless adventure, and a great risk for him.

WASHINGTON, *March, 1879.*

My dear Mother,—We have taken the Fant House for this winter. People say it is haunted. As yet we have not seen any ghosts nor found any skeletons in the closets. The possible ghosts have no terrors for me. On the contrary, I should love to meet one face to face! But the rats are plentiful and have probably played ghosts' parts and given the house its reputation. Those we have here are so bold and assertive that I have become quite accustomed to them. I meet them on the staircase, and they politely wait for me to pass. One old fellow—I call him Alcibiades, because he is so audacious—actually gnaws at our door, as if begging to be allowed to come in and join us. We put poison in every attractive way we can think of all about, but they seem to like it and thrive upon it. Johan, having had a Danish sailor recommended to him, allows him to live in a room up-stairs and to help a little in the house while waiting for a boat. He is very masterful in his movements, and handles the crockery as if it were buckets of water, and draws back the portieres as if he were hauling at the main-sheet.

Mr. Robeson (Secretary of the Navy), who ought to know *le dernier cri* on the subject of the habits of rats, told us that the only way to get rid of them was to catch one and dress him up in a jacket and trousers—red preferable—tie a bell round his neck, and let him loose. "Then," he said, "the rat would run about among his companions and indicate the pressure brought upon rats, and soon there would not be one left in the house."

This was an idyl for our sailor. He spent most of his days making a jacket with which to clothe the rat, and actually did catch one (I hoped he was not my friend of the staircase) and proceeded to put him into this sailor-made costume, which was not an easy thing to do, and had he not been accustomed to bracing up stays and other nautical work he never could have accomplished the thing. However, he *did* accomplish it; he tied the bell on the rat's neck and let him loose.

The remedy (though uttered from an official mouth for which we have great respect) was worse than the evil. The rat refused to run about to warn his friends. On the contrary, he would not move, but looked imploringly into the eyes of his tormentor, as if begging to be allowed to die in his normal skin. Then, I believe, he went and sulked in a corner and committed suicide—he was so mortified. We said one rat in a corner was worse than twelve on the staircase.

The Outreys (the French Minister) had their diplomatic reception, and sent cards to every one they knew and many they did not know. The ladies who went expected Madame Outrey to be dressed in the latest fashion; being the wife of the French Minister, it was her duty to let society into the secrets of Parisian "modes," but she was dressed in a simple, might-have-been-made-at-home black gown. This exasperated the ladies (who had gone with an eye to copying) to such a degree that many went home with pent-up and wounded feelings, as if they had been defrauded of their rights and without supper—which, had they stayed, they would have found to be the latest thing in suppers.

WASHINGTON.

The grass on our small plot has reached the last limit of endurance and greenness, and is sprouting weeds at a great rate; also our one bush, though still full of chirpiness, is beginning to show signs of depression.

We were invited to a spiritualistic *séance* at the L____'s *salon*. The Empress Josephine has consented to materialize in America after having visited the Continent. We saw her, and a more unempress-looking empress I cannot imagine. To convince a skeptic she displayed her leg to show how well it had succeeded in taking on flesh. I have no patience with people who believe such nonsense. The famous spiritualist Poster is also here in

Washington. He is clever in a way, and has made many converts simply by putting two and two together. We went, of course, to see him, and came away astounded, but not convinced. He produced a slate on which were written some wonderful things about a ring which had a history in J.'s family. J. could not imagine how any one could have known it. Foster said to me: "I had a premonition that you were coming to-day. See!" and he pulled up his sleeve and there stood "Lillie," written in what appeared to be my handwriting in gore, I suppose—it was red. I urged Baron Bildt to go and see him, knowing that he liked that sort of thing. The moment he appeared, Foster, smelling a diplo-rat, said, "Madame Hegermann sent you to me," upon which Baron Bildt succumbed instantly.

Teresa Carreno, the *Wunderkind*, now a *Wunder-mädchen*, having arrived at the age when she wisely puts up her hair and lets down her dresses, is on a concert tour with Wilhelmj (the famous violinist). He is not as good as Wieniawski, and can't be named in the same breath with Ole Bull. They came here to lunch, together with Schlözer, who brought the violin. I invited a good many people to come in the afternoon—among others, Aristarchi, who looks very absorbed when music is going on, but with him it means absolutely nothing, because he is a little deaf, but looks eager in order to seize other people's impressions.

Wilhelmj played, and Teresa Carreno played, and I sang a song of Wilhelmj's from the manuscript. He said, "You sing it as if you had dreamed it." I thought if I had dreamed it I should have dreamed of a patchwork quilt, there were so many flats and sharps. My eyes and brain ached.

After a good deal of music Wilhelmj sank in a chair and said, "I can no more!" and fell to talking about his wines. He is not only a violinist, but is a wine merchant. Schlözer and J. naturally gave him some large orders.

Washington is very gay, humming like a top. Everything is going on at once.

The daily receptions I find the most tiresome things, they are so monotonous. Women crowd in the *salons*, shake hands, leave a pile of cards on the tray in the hall, and flit to other spheres.

At a dinner at Senator Chandler's Mr. Blaine took me in, and Eugene Hale, a Congressman, sat on the other side. They call him "Blaine's little boy." He was very amusing on the subject of Alexander Agassiz (the pioneer of my youthful studies, under whose ironical eye I used to read Schiller), who is just now being lionized, and is lecturing on the National History of the Peruvians. Agassiz has become a millionaire, not from the proceeds of his brain, but from copper-mines (Calumet and Hecla). How his dear old father would have liked to possess some of his millions.

Sam Ward is the diner-out *par excellence* here, and is the king of the lobby *par préférence*. When you want anything pushed through Congress you have only to apply to Sam Ward, and it is done. I don't know whether he accomplishes what he undertakes by money or persuasion; it must be the latter, for I think he is far from being a rich man. His lobbying is mostly done at the dinner-table. He is a most delightful talker and full of anecdotes.

Mrs. Robeson's "Sunday evenings" are very popular. She has given up singing and does not—thank Heaven!—have any music. She thinks it prevents people from talking (sometimes it does, and sometimes it has the contrary effect). She prefers the talking, in which she takes the most active part. Mr. Robeson is the most amiable of hosts, beams and laughs a great deal.

The *enfant terrible* is quoted incessantly. She must be overwhelmingly amusing. She said to her mother when she saw her in evening dress; "Mama, pull up your collar. You must not show your stomach-ache!" Everything in anatomy lower than the throat she calls "stomach-ache"—the fountain of all her woes, I suppose.

Mr. Blaine and Mr. Robeson, supplemented by General Schenck, are great poker-players. They are continually talking about the game, when they ought to be talking politics for the benefit of foreigners. You hear this sort of thing, "Well, you couldn't beat my full house," at which the diplomats prick up their ears, thinking that there will be something wonderful in Congress the next day, and decide to go there.

Mr. Brooks, of Cambridge, made his Fourth-of-July oration at our *soirée* on Thursday. This is the funniest thing I have ever heard. Mr. Evarts almost rolled off his seat. It is supposed to be a speech made at a Paris *fête* on the Fourth of July, where every speaker got more patriotic as the evening went on. The last speech was the climax:

"I propose the toast, '*The United States!*—bordered on the north by the aurora borealis; on the east by the rising sun; on the west by the procession of equinoxes; and on the south by eternal chaos!"

WASHINGTON, *April, 1879.*

Mr. Schurz, as Secretary of the Interior, was to receive a conclave of Indians, and could not refuse Mrs. Lawrence, Miss Chapman, and myself when we begged to be present at the interview. They came to make some contracts. The interpreter, or agent, or whatever he was, who had them in charge proposed to dress them suitably for the occasion, but when he heard there were to be ladies present he added colored and striped shirts, which, the Indians insisted upon wearing over their embroidered buckskin trousers. They caused a sensation as they came out of the clothes-shop. They had feather head-dresses and braids of hair hanging down by the sides of their brown cheeks. They wore bracelets on their bare arms and blankets over their shoulders. They sat in a semicircle around Mr. Schurz. After Mr. Schurz had heard what the interpreter had to say he and the other members of the committee (they call them "undershirts") talked together for a while, and Mr. Schurz said, "I cannot accept," which was translated to the chief, who looked more sullen and treacherous than before. Then there was a burst of wild Indian, and the chief held forth in a deep bass voice, I fancy giving pieces of his mind to Mr. Schurz, which were translated in a milder form. Mrs. Lawrence, who looks at everything in a rosy, sentimental light, thought they looked high-spirited and noble. I, who am prosaic to my finger-tips, thought they looked conceited, brutal, and obstinate. They all sat with their tomahawks laid by the side of their chairs. The chief was not insensible to the beauty of Miss Chapman, and sat behind his outspread fingers, gazing at her and her jewelry. We were glad to get away from the barbarous-looking people. All the same, the interview was very interesting.

General and Mrs. Albert Meyer gave a dinner in honor of the President and Mrs. Hayes, to which some diplomats were invited. You know Mr. Meyer is the man called "Old Prob," because he tells one beforehand what weather one can expect for the next picnic.

This was the first dinner that the Presidential couple had gone to, and we were a little curious to see how it would be managed. As neither Mr. nor Mrs. Hayes drinks wine, they were served all the different known brands of mineral waters, milk, and tea. But the others got wine. Mr. Meyer was very funny when he took up his glass, looked at it critically, and said, "I recommend this vintage." The President did not seem to mind these *plaisanteries*. We were curious to see what they would do when *punch à la Romaine*, which stood on the menu in a little paragraph by itself, would be served. It was a rather strong punch (too strong for any of the diplomats) and the glasses were deep, but they seemed to enjoy this glimpse into the depths of perdition and did not leave a mouthful. Taking it, you see, with a spoon made a difference.

The Lesseps were among the guests. There are thirteen little Lesseps somewhere; only one daughter is with them. Monsieur Lesseps is twenty-five years older than Madame, if not more. When the three came in the *salon*, young Miss Bayard said, "The girl is taking her mother and grandfather into society."

A weird menu was at the side of each plate; it was in French—on account, I suppose, of the Lesseps. One of the items was *L'estomac de dinde à l'ambassadrice, pommes sautees*. Mr. John Hay, who sat next to me, remarked, ironically, "Why do they not write their menu in plain English?"

"I think," I answered, "that it is better in French. How would 'turkey to an ambassadress's stomach' or 'jumped potatoes' sound?"

He could find no answer to this.

Madame Lesseps confided to me in our coffee-cups that she and her husband were in "Vasheengton *en touristes, mais aussi, ils avaient des affaires*." The *affaires* are no less than the Panama Canal.

CAMBRIDGE, *Summer, 1879.*

Ole Bull (the great violinist) has taken James Russell Lowell's house in Cambridge. He is remarried, and lives here with his wife and daughter. He has a magnificent head, and that broad, expansive smile which seems to belong to geniuses. Liszt had one like it.

He and Mrs. Bull come here often on Sunday evenings, and sometimes he brings his violin. Mrs. B. accompanies him, and he plays divinely. There is no violinist on earth that can compare with him. There may be many who have as brilliant a technique, but none who has his *feu sacrè* and the tremendous magnetism which creates such enthusiasm that you are carried away. The sterner sex pretend that they can resist him, but certainly no woman can.

He is very proud of showing the diamond in his bow which was given to him by the King of Sweden.

He loves to tell the story of King Frederick VII. of Denmark, who said to him: "Where did you learn to play the violin? Who was your teacher?"

Ole Bull answered, "Your Majesty, the pine forests of Norway and the beautiful *fjords* taught me!"

The King, who had no feeling for such high-flown sentiments, turned to one of his *aides-de-camp* and said, "*Sikken vrövl*'"—the Danish for "What rubbish!"

Mr. John Owen (Mr. Longfellow's shadow) swoops down on us occasionally on the wings of poesy. I don't always comprehend the poesy, and sometimes would like to cut the wings, but Owen can't be stopped. Every event is translated into verse; even my going to Newport by the ten-o'clock train, which sounds prosy enough, inspires him, and the next morning he comes in with a poem. Then we see it in the *Boston Advertiser*, evening edition.

OLE BULL
From a photograph taken in New York in 1880.

CAMBRIDGE.

A Dane, a friend of Johan's, who had come to America to write a book on American institutions, asked the consul to find him a quiet boarding-house in a quiet street. The consul knew of exactly such a retreat, and directed the Professor to the place. It was not far from the Revere House. He arrived there in the evening, unpacked his treasures, congratulating himself on his cozy quarters and his nice landlady, who asked such a modest price that he jumped at it.

The next morning, at four o'clock, he was awakened by a strange noise, the like of which he had never heard outside a zoological garden. At first he thought he was still dreaming, and turned over to sleep again, but the noise repeated itself. This time it seemed to come from under his bed, and sounded like a lion's roar. Probably a circus had passed and a lion had got loose and was prowling about, seeking what he could devour! He thought of ringing up the house, but demurred, reflecting that whoever answered the bell would probably be the first victim. Again the roar! Fear overcame his humane impulses; he rang, hoping that if the lion's appetite was appeased by the first victim, he might be spared.

The landlady appeared in the flesh, calmly and quietly. "Did you ring, sir?" she asked, placidly.

"I did indeed," he answered. "Will you kindly tell me whether I am awake or asleep? It seems to me that I heard the roar of a lion. Did no one else hear it?"

The landlady hesitated, embarrassed, and answered, "I did, sir—you and I are the only persons in the house."

"Then the lion is waiting for us?" he said, quaking in his slippers.

"I beg your pardon, sir," the woman answered. "I had hoped that you had not noticed anything—"

"Good gracious!" he said, "do you think I can be in the house with a roaring lion and not notice anything?"

"He happens to be hungry this morning, and nothing will keep him quiet," said the kind lady, as if she were talking of her kitten.

"Madam," screamed the infuriated Dane, "one of us is certainly going mad! When I tell you that there is a lion roaming over your house you stand there quietly and tell me that he is hungry?"

"If you will wait a moment, sir, I will explain."

"No explanation is needed, madam. If I can get out of this house alive I will meet you in some other un-lion-visited part of Boston and pay you." And he added, with great sarcasm, "He is probably a pet of yours, and your ex-boarders have furnished his meals."

Instead of being shocked at this, the gentle landlady's eyes beamed with content. "That's just it—he is a pet of mine, and he lives in the back parlor."

"The lion is here in your back parlor, and you have the face to keep boarders?" shrieked the Dane.

"My other boarders have left me."

"I should think so, and this one is going to do like-wise, and without delay"—beginning to put his things in his bag.

She said she was sorry he thought of going, but she could understand he was nervous.

Nervous! If he could have given his feelings words he would have said that never in all his life had he been so scared.

The meek lady before him watched him while he was making up his packages and his mind. What he made up was his reluctance to flee from danger and leave the lion-hearted little woman alone.

"I will not go," he said, in the voice of an early Christian martyr.

"You see, sir, this is how it happened," began the woman. "A very nice sailor came to board here, but could not pay his bill, so to settle with me he offered me his pet dog. I thought it a puppy, and as I had taken a fancy to the little thing—he used to drink milk with the cat out of the same saucer—I consented to keep it."

"And he turned out to be a lion? How did you first notice it?"

"Well, sir, I soon saw he attracted attention in the street. He wanted to fight all the other animals, and attacked everything from a horse to a milk-pan. It was when I was giving him a bath that I noticed that his tail was beginning to bunch out at the end and his under-jaw was growing pointed. Then the awful thought came to me—it was not a dog, but a lion! This was a dreadful moment, for I loved him, and he was fond of me, and I could not part with him. He grew and grew—his body lengthened out and his paws became enormous, and his shaggy hair covered his head. But it was when he tried to get up in my lap, and became angry because my lap was not big enough to hold him, that he growled so that I became afraid. Then I had bars put up before the door of my back parlor, which was my former dining-room, and I keep him there."

"Do you feed him yourself?"

"Yes, sir, but it takes a fortune to keep him in meat."

"How old do you think he is?" the Dane asked, beginning now to feel a respectful admiration for the lone woman who preferred to give up boarders rather than give up her companion.

"That I do not know," she replied, "but from his size and voice I should say he was full-grown."

"I can vouch for his voice. Will you show him to me?" He had never seen a lion boarding in a back parlor, and rather fancied the novelty. He told the consul afterward that he had never seen a finer specimen of the Bengal lion. To his mistress he was obedient and meek as a lamb. She could do anything she liked with him; she passed her hand lovingly over his great head, caressing his tawny locks, while the lion looked at her with soft and tender eyes, and stuck out his enormous tongue to lick her hand.

The Dane stayed on, like the good man he was. He had not the heart to deprive the little woman of the few dollars he paid for his room, which would go toward buying food for her pet. He himself became very fond of "Leo," and would surreptitiously spend all his spare money at the butcher's, who must have wondered, when he sent the quarters of beef, how such a small family could consume so much—and the Dane would pass hours feeding the lion with tidbits held on the end of his umbrella.

We were told afterward that the police discovered that the noises coming from the house were not the usual Boston east winds, and, having found out from what they proceeded, suggested that the Zoological Gardens should buy the animal, for which they paid an enormous price. So the sailor did pay his debt, after all!

CAMBRIDGE, *March, 1880.*

Dear L.,—I love to write to you; my thoughts run away with me, my pen flies like a bird over the paper. You need not remind me of the fact that my handwriting is execrable. I know it, therefore don't waft it across America. Spare me this mortification. Tear the letters up after reading them, or *before*, if you like. When I see the stacks of never-looked-through letters being dragged from one place to the other, tied up in their old faded ribbons, I feel that I do not wish mine to have the same fate.

I read the other day H.'s lively letters full of dash, written in her happy girlhood, and think of her as she is now, the tired mother of six children, without a sparkle of humor left in her, and nothing more spicy in her epistles than a lengthy account of the coal bill or the children's measles. All the life taken out of her for ever! Just deadly dull!

I feel in the above pathetic mood whenever I look out of my window and see the veteran Washington elm facing wind and weather, bravely waiting the end. With what care they bolster up its weary limbs, saw off its withered branches, and deluge its old roots! They spend days belting and tarring its waist, trying to destroy the perverse caterpillars; but with all this they can never give it back its fresh and green youth. It goes on patiently year after year putting forth its leaves in spring and coquetting in its summer garb with its younger rivals. In autumn the pretty colored leaves fly away, and it remains bare and grim under its coating of snow and ice. Some day it will blow down, and nothing but the monumental stone will be left on which future generations will read, "Under this tree George Washington first took command of the American Army, July 3, 1775."

If I stay in Cambridge long enough I shall become a beacon of wisdom. Every one is so learned. If I happen to meet a lady in the street she will begin to talk of the "old masters" as if it were as natural a subject of conversation as the weather.

Washington, *March 23, 1880.*

Johan has this moment received the news that he is transferred to Rome. We feel dreadfully sad to leave Washington and all our dear friends. Our good Schlözer would say "*Que faire? La diplomatie a des exigences qu'il ne faut pas négliger.*"

The Queen of Denmark writes, "I hope that you are sure that I never omit to name your husband when a change is coming on in diplomacy, and I hope soon to see something advance to fulfil my wish. Alas, no great benefit to me personally, as you will not live in Copenhagen, but you would come here in an easier way, and you would be in Europe. Farewell, dear Lilly, farewell, and think of me as I of you. Yours.... Louise. The King's best compliments."

From this I fancy it was the gracious Queen whose finger pointed to the post Rome. This will be the last letter you will get from me from this side of the Atlantic, as I am going to be very busy—as busy as the bee I only hope that people will let the busy B.

ROME, 1880-1890

ROME, PALAZZO ROSPIGLIOSI, *December, 1880.*

Dear Mother,—We are now almost settled in the Eternal City, after a process which has seemed to me as eternal as the city itself, and I am so far established as to be able to take up the threads of my new life. The first of these will be this letter to you.

We found an apartment in this palace which is large and comfortable. It looks onto the Piazza Quirinal on one side, and on the other into the courtyard, where we see the procession of tourists with red Baedekers under their arms, filing into the Palazetto to admire the famous "Aurora."

Johan had been received by King Umberto before I arrived. The ceremony seems to have been full of splendor and surrounded with etiquette. A magnificent gala coach drawn by two splendid horses brought Signor Peruzzi (master of ceremonies), accompanied by an escort of carabineers, to the Hôtel Bristol, where Johan was stopping, attracting a large crowd in the Piazza Barberini—less than this is sufficient to collect gazers-on in Italy, where the natives pass most of their time in gazing at nothing at all.

As the carriage entered the *grande cour* of the palace, the guards presented arms and the military band played. A second master of ceremonies met Johan at the foot of the principal staircase, while the Grand Master of Ceremonies waited for him at the head of it. Accompanied by these gentlemen, Johan passed through the long gallery, which was lined on both sides by the civil and military members of the household. At the extreme end of the gallery stood the prefect of the palace, Signor Visone, who preceded Johan to the King's apartment and retired after having announced him to his Majesty. This seems complicated, but you see it takes all these functionaries to present a Minister to a King.

Johan had prepared his obligatory speech about *les bonnes relations* which had always existed between Italy and Denmark, and so forth, but the King did not give him the opportunity to make any speech at all. He held out his hand and said in a most friendly and cordial manner, "*Je suis bien content de vous voir, et j'èspère que vous vous plairez parmi nous.*" His Majesty then asked Johan about King Christian, and spoke about the visit he had made to Denmark some years ago. Before the end of the audience Johan succeeded in making the King accept his *lettres de créance*, and presented the greetings of King Christian; but the speech remained unspoken.

The contrast seemed very striking between the ceremonious manner in which he was conducted to the King, and the simple and unconventional manner in which he was received by his Majesty.

Yesterday I asked for an audience with the Queen. The Marquise Villamarina (the *Grande Maîtresse*) wrote that the Queen, though desiring to see me, thought it better to defer the audience until after the reception of the *Corps Diplomatique*, which was to take place in a few days. I am rather glad of the few days of rest before the first of January, as I am completely tired out.

January, 1881.

Dear Mother,—The great event of the season has just taken place! The *Corps Diplomatique* has been received by their Majesties at the Quirinal, and I have made my first official appearance and worn my first court train. This splendid ceremony took place at two o'clock in the afternoon, a rather trying time to be *décolletée* and look your best. In my letter from Paris I told you about my dress made by Worth. It really is quite lovely—white brocade, with the tulle front—all embroidered with iridescent beads and pearls. The *manteau de cour* is of white satin, trimmed with Valenciennes lace and ruches of chiffon. I wore my diamond tiara, my pearls on my neck, and everything I owned in the way of jewelry pinned on me somewhere.

Johan was in full gala uniform—the red one—on the back of which was the chamberlain's key on the blue ribbon.

On arriving at the Quirinal we drove through the *porte-cochère* and stopped at the grand staircase, which was lined all the way up by the tall and handsome guards, dressed in their brilliant uniforms.

We were received in the *salon* adjoining the throne-room by the Marquise Villamarina and the *Préfet du Palais*. In crossing this *salon* one lets one's train drag on the floor and proceeds, peacock-like, toward the ballroom. It seems that this is the proper thing to do, as it is expected of you to allow all beholders to admire your train and to verify its length. It must be four and a half yards long. I was told that the train of one of the diplomatic ladies last year was not long enough, and she was officially reproached. She excused herself by saying that she thought it would go "*that once*," but she found that it didn't go, and it was considered very disrespectful of her to disregard the court's regulations.

On entering the ballroom you pick up your train and go to your place—for every lady has her place according to her *ancienneté*. I, being the wife of the newest Minister, was naturally at the very end, and next to me was the newest Minister himself. While waiting for their Majesties you let your train fall, and it lies in a heap at your left side.

Behind each lady was a red-velvet *fauteuil*, in which she could rest for a moment, if her colleagues would screen her from public view by "closing up," according to military language. We did not, fortunately, have long to wait. The doors were opened and their Majesties entered. The ladies courtesied low, and the gentlemen bowed reverentially.

I was quite overcome by the Queen's dazzling beauty and regal presence. She wore a beautiful dress of very pale salmon-colored satin, embroidered in the same color. A red-velvet *manteau de cour* covered with heavy embossed silver embroidery hung from her shoulders. Her jewels were handsomer than anything I had ever seen before, even more magnificent than those of the Empress Eugénie. The King and Queen separated. The King turned to the *doyen* of the *Corps Diplomatique*, talked a long time with him, and then passed on, having a word for each gentleman, not overlooking even the youngest secretary.

The Queen went directly toward the Countess Wimphen, the *doyenne*, and, holding out her hand, leaned forward as if to kiss her cheek. The Ambassadress sank almost to the ground. Then the Queen talked with all the Ambassadresses and to the Ministers' wives. Madame Westenberg, the wife of the Minister from Holland, being the *plus ancienne* of these, stood, full of importance at the head of her flock. The Queen's ready mind found something of interest to say to every one, and she seemed brimming over with conversation. There were continual glances between their Majesties, as if they were mutually comparing notes, which I fancy were something like this, "You'd better hurry, or I shall finish before you do."

Every time the Queen turned, Marquis Guiccioli (the Queen's chamberlain) bent down to the ground and arranged her train, spreading it out flat on the floor. When the Queen caught sight of me a smile of recognition passed over her face, and when she gave me her hand she said: "I am so glad to see you again, and so happy to know that we are going to have you in Rome. I've never forgotten your singing. Your voice is still ringing in my ears."

I answered, "I have never forgotten your Majesty's kindness to me when I was here before."

"I remember so well," she said, "how beautifully you and the Marquise Villamarina sang that duet from 'La Pavorita.' We shall have some music later, I hope," and she added, "The King was delighted with Monsieur de Hegermann."

I said that Monsieur de Hegermann was very much flattered by the King's gracious manner when the King received him.

On leaving me the Queen crossed the room, directing her steps toward the *doyen* Ambassador. In the mean while the King came toward the ladies, passing rapidly from one to the other. He made quick work of us, as he did most of the talking himself, hardly ever waiting for an answer.

He said to me, "The Queen tells me that you have been here before."

"I have, your Majesty," I answered; "I was here five years ago and had the honor to be presented to you."

"Really?" said the King. "I don't remember."

"But I've known you longer even than that," I said.

"How so?" asked the King, abruptly.

"When your Majesty was in Paris in 1867."

"That makes us very old friends," he said, smilingly.

Finally, when their Majesties had finished the circle, they met at the end of the ball-room; every one made a *grande reverence*, and they bowed graciously in response and withdrew.

We ladies, in walking out, allowed our *manteaux* to trail behind us. We entered the room where refreshments were served, and crowded around the buffet, which groaned under the weight of all sorts of good things. We drank one another's health and Happy New Year in champagne.

January, 1881.

Dear Mother,—You would never believe that my official duties weigh as heavily on me as they do. I received a letter from the Marquise Villamarina, saying that "her Gracious Sovereign would be pleased to receive me on the seventh at three o'clock." Therefore, dressed in my best, I drove to the Quirinal. It is so near our palace that I had hardly entered the carriage before I had to get out of it. The gorgeously dressed and long-bearded *concierge* who stood pompously at the entrance of the palace waved the carriage to the other end of the courtyard, and pounded his mace on the pavement in an authoritative manner.

I mounted the broad, winding staircase, went through the long gallery lined with lackeys, and reached the *salon*, where the Marquise Villamarina was waiting to receive me. After the usual greetings she said, "*Sa Majesté vous attend*," and led me through many *salons* to the one where the Queen was. I noticed, as we walked along, that the Marquise removed her right-hand glove, I took this as a hint that I should do the same. The Queen was standing when I entered the room. I made a deep courtesy before going in. She came forward and gave me her ungloved hand, over which I bowed deeply. The Marquise retired, leaving me alone with the Queen, who motioned me to sit beside her on the sofa. She spoke French, and so rapidly that I could hardly follow her. She was kindness itself, as affable and charming as one could possibly be, and put me at my ease immediately.

She had a little diamond ball hanging on a chain in the folds of her dress, the prettiest little watch I ever saw. After a half-hour, which passed like a flash, the Marquise reappeared in the doorway. This was a signal for me to take my leave. The Queen rose, gave me her hand, and said, "Good-by, Madame de Hegermann; I'm so glad to have you here in Rome."

I should have liked to kiss her hand, but I was told that the wife of a foreign minister never kisses the hand of any queen save her own.

I feel now that I am really launched. Let us hope that my barque will ride the waves successfully! In Europe visits are not as with us in America. Here the residents wait until the stranger makes the first visit; in America it is just the contrary. I must say I like the European way best. It would be very awkward for *me* to receive visitors now, especially when my household is in its present chaotic state. I hope it will be only a question of cards for some time yet.

January 20, 1881.

Dear Mother,—Last night the Princess Palavicini gave what she intended to be the finest ball of the season, for which no expense was spared. They had sent to Paris for the cotillon favors, to Nice for flowers to decorate the magnificent *salons* of the Palazzo Rospigliosi, and to Naples for the famous Neapolitan orchestra.

The Princess Palavicini is one of the Queen's ladies of honor, belongs to one of the most aristocratic families in Italy, and claims to have the most select society in Rome. The King and the Queen had consented to grace the ball with their presence. That the King had promised to go was a great exception, as he has never been willing to go to any function outside of the Quirinal since the much-talked-of ball at the Duke di Fiano's. I believe that it is only his keen sense of duty that makes him attend his own entertainments.

All the guests were assembled and awaiting the arrival of their Majesties, but they did not come. The reason given was that the present members of the Ministry took exception to the fact that neither they nor their wives had been invited. The Ministers sent word to the King that if their Majesties attended the ball they would give in their resignations *en bloc.* The result was that the ball was a complete failure. All the spirit had gone out of the guests, who moved about aimlessly, talking in groups, and then quietly disappeared. The dancers of the cotillon waited for the supper, which they said was magnificent and sufficient for a hungry army.

ROME, *February 1881*.

Dear ____,—The two sons of the King of Sweden (Prince Oscar and Prince Carl) are here for a fortnight's visit, and are seeing Rome thoroughly in the company of two chamberlains, two cicerones, and some friends. The young princes gave a dinner at the Hôtel Quirinal, to which we were invited. They had engaged the Neapolitan singers from Naples, who sang the most delightful and lively songs. We felt like dancing a *saltarello*, and perhaps might have done so if we had been in less princely presences. The Scandinavian Club gave a feast—the finest and greatest in the annals of the club—in honor of the two princes, to welcome the Swedish and Norwegian Minister's bride, and also to welcome us—a great combination—and to celebrate the carnival by a fancy ball.

People were begged to come in costume, which, to be amiable, every one was delighted to do. The costumes were not original. Roman peasants were abundant. This costume needs only a towel folded square and put on the head, and a Roman apron, easily obtained at the Campo di Fiore for a song. Flower-girls with hats turned up on the side and baskets of flowers were also popular. The handsome Prince Carl, who is six feet six, needed only a helmet to personify to perfection a youthful god Mars. Prince Oscar merely wore his naval mess-jacket. Herr Ross (the Norwegian artist) was the head and spirit of the ball and directed everything. He was dressed appropriately as a *pierrot*, with a wand in his hand, and pirouetted about to his heart's content.

All was done on the most economical basis, as the club is entirely composed of artists, who, consequently, are poor. The lines were drawn apparently at the food, but in *skaals* (toasts)—the thing dearest the Scandinavian heart—they were extremely liberal and reckless. All six of us were toasted to a crisp brown, and at each separate toast we stood up and listened to the tale of our virtues.

The celebrated Ibsen honored this feast with his presence, and especially honored the Chianti and Genzano wines, which were served copiously, in *fiascos*. When you see Ibsen, with his lion face and tangle of hair, for the first time, you are fascinated by him, knowing what a genius he is, but when you talk with him, and feel his piercing, critical eyes looking at you from under his bushy brows, and see his cruel, satirical smile, you are a little prejudiced against him. We meet him often at our friend Ross's studio at afternoon teas, where there is always a little music. Ibsen sits sullen, silent, and indifferent. He does not like music, and does not disguise his dislike. This is not, as you may imagine, inspiring to the performers. In fact, just to look at him takes all the life out of you. He is a veritable wet blanket. I have read all his works in the original. I think they lose a great deal in being translated. The Norwegian language is very curt and concise, each word conveying almost the meaning of two in English, which enables the author to paint a whole situation in a few words. I can see the difference, in reading the English translations, and where they fail to convey his real meaning. Strangers who wish to see Ibsen must go to the cheap Italian restaurant, "Falcone," where he sits before a small iron table, eating deviled devil-fish. No wonder that he is morbid and his plays weird!

February, 1881.

Dear Mother,—I know you would like to hear about the first ball at the Quirinal. It was very splendid. Since the last and famous ball at the Tuileries I had seen nothing like it. When we had mounted the guard-lined staircase and passed through innumerable *salons* we were received by the *Grande Maîtresse*, surrounded by numerous *dames de palais*, all so beautiful that I wondered if they had been chosen for their beauty alone. I never saw so many handsome women grouped together. Numerous chamberlains preceded us into the ballroom and showed us the benches where the *Corps Diplomatique* have their places. The benches looked inviting enough, with their red-velvet coverings and their gilded legs, but I did not feel as if I should care to sit on them for hours.

Madame Minghetti sat on one of the *taborets* on one side of the throne, and Madame Cairoli (wife of the Minister of Foreign Affairs) occupied the *taboret* on the other side. These two ladies are the only ones who have the right to sit on the little square stools that are called *taborets*.

We waited in our places until we heard the orchestra start the national hymn, then every one stood up as the King and the Queen entered arm in arm, followed by splendidly dressed and bejeweled *dames d'honneur* and the numerous suite. Their Majesties went to the throne, stood there a moment, then stepped down and spoke to the two ladies on the *taborets*. The *quadrille d'honneur* commenced almost immediately. Count Wimphen approached the Queen, making the deepest of bows, offered her his hand, and led her to her place on the floor. M. de Keudell and the Countess Wimphen took their places opposite the Queen. There were only two other couples. Every one stood while this quadrille was being danced.

The Queen looked exquisite, and seemed to be in the best of spirits. She was the *point de mire* of all eyes. She wore a superb gown of light-blue brocade, the front entirely trimmed with old Venetian lace. Her necklace and tiara were of enormous pearls and diamonds. She was truly a vision of beauty and queenly grace.

After the *quadrille d'honneur* the dancing became general. The Queen first talked to the Ambassadresses, then to the wives of the Ministers, sitting down on the bench beside the lady she desired to converse with, the one on the other side moving on discreetly to make more room for the Queen.

The King never came anywhere near the ladies, but talked only with the gentlemen, frequently keeping one by his side and addressing him while he talked with another.

The dancing continued until the Queen had returned from a tour of the other *salons*, where she had been talking with those assembled there. Re-entering the ballroom, preceded as always by her chamberlains and followed by her ladies, she joined the King, and both, bowing graciously as if to say good night, retired.

QUEEN MARGHERITA
Mother of the present King of Italy as she appeared in 1886. The tiara was a present from the King on the preceding Christmas. In the necklace are some of the crown jewels, pearls and six remarkable emeralds.

ROME, *February, 1881.*

Dear ____,—Mrs. Elliot brought Ouida to see me on my reception-day. Ouida is, I am afraid, a little bit of a *poseuse*, but geniuses have privileges which cannot be endured in ordinary people. She was dressed with a lofty disregard of Roman climate and its possibilities, and in utter defiance of common sense. She wore a dress open at the throat, with short sleeves, and the thinnest of shoes and stockings, which she managed to show more than was quite necessary. She spoke in an affected voice, and looked about her continually as if people were watching her and taking notes.

Among the ladies of the Queen here are three Americans who have married Italians and have entered the charmed circle of the court. Their services are only required upon certain gala occasions. One is the daughter of Hickson Fields (whom we used to know so well in Paris), who has married Prince Brancaccio. Another American lady, the wife of Prince Cenci, who is of the same family as the lady with the turban. Both the Prince and the Princess are at court, he as chamberlain and she as *dame de palais*. He is called the "*Boeuf à la mode*," not because he in any way looks like a *boeuf*, but because he is fine-looking, masterful, and *à la mode*.

Count Gianotti, first master of ceremonies, has also an American wife. She was a Miss Kinney, a daughter of Mrs. Kinney whom we knew in Washington. She is tall and striking-looking. Her Friday receptions are well attended, especially when she lets it be known that there will be *particularly* fine music. While the artist at the piano thinks he is making a heavy and great success and is wrestling with his *arpeggios* on a small piano, the guests come and go and rattle their teacups, regardless of the noise, while the music goes on. This is often the case in Roman *salons*.

The Marquis de Noailles is the French Ambassador. You recollect him and the Marquise, who were in Washington the first year we were there. He, as you know, is of the bluest blood of France. She is of Polish extraction and lived in Paris, where she had a *succès de beauté* in the Napoleonic days. After her first husband's death (Count Schwieskoska) she married de Noailles. They have an offspring, an *enfant terrible*, if there ever was one, who is about nine years old, and a worse torment never existed. Nobody on earth has the slightest control over him—neither father, mother, nor tutor. The Marquis makes excuses for his bringing-up by saying that, having had a very severe, rod-using father himself, he was determined that if he ever had a child he would spare the rod. He can flatter himself that he has thoroughly succeeded in spoiling the child.

When we were at a very large and official dinner at the Farnese Palace (the French Embassy), where the beautifully decorated tables filled the whole length of the Carracci Gallery, the guests were amazed as seeing Doudou (the name of the infant) come in on a velocipede and ride round and round the table, all the servants dodging about to avoid collision, holding their platters high in the air, for fear of being tripped up and spilling the food. The astonished guests expected every moment to have their chairs knocked from under them. This made this should-be-magnificent dinner into a sort of circus. No persuasion or threats could induce this terrible child to go away, and he continued during the dinner to do his velocipede exercises. He must be a very trying boy. His mother told me herself that he forces both her and his father to take castor or any other oil when the doctor prescribes it for him. People tell horrible stories about him. I am sure you will say what every one else says—"Why don't his parents give him a good spanking?"

At a small dinner at the English Embassy I met the celebrated tenor, Mario. I had not seen him since in Paris in 1868, when he was singing with Alboni and Patti in "Rigoletto." Alboni once invited the Duke and the Duchess of Newcastle, Mr. Tom Hohler, and ourselves to dinner to meet Mario in her cozy apartment in the Avenue Kleber. I was perfectly fascinated by Mario and thought him the beau ideal of a Lothario. His voice was melodious and *caressante*, as the French say, and altogether his manners were those of a charmer. It was a most interesting dinner, and I was all ears, not wanting to lose a word of what Alboni and he said. What they talked about most was their many reminiscences, and almost each of their phrases commenced, "*Vous rappelez vous?*" and then came the reminiscence. After fourteen years I meet him here, a grandpapa, traveling with his daughter. He is now the Marquis di Candia (having resumed his title), *et l'homme du monde parfait*; he is seventy years old and has a gray and rather scanty beard instead of the smooth, carefully trimmed brown one of *autrefois*. Why do captivating and fascinating creatures, such as he was, ever grow old? But, as Auber used to say, "the only way to become old is to live a long time."

At the Embassy dinner he did not sit next to me, alas! but afterward we sat on the sofa and talked of Alboni, Paris, and music. I told him that the first time I had heard him sing was in America, when he sang with Grisi.

"So long ago?" he said. "Why, you couldn't have been born!"

"Oh yes," I answered; "I was born, and old enough to appreciate your singing. I have never forgotten it, nor your voice. One will never hear anything like it again. Have you quite given up singing?" I asked.

"Why, I am a grandfather! You would not have a grandfather sing, would you?"

"I would," I answered, "if the grandfather was Mario."

ROME, *1881*.

Dear ____,—The opening of the Parliament is a great occasion in Rome (where one would like to be both inside and outside at the same time). The children's governess had a friend who offered them seats in her window, and this is what they saw outside:

The streets lined with soldiers from the Quirinal to the House of Parliament, the large places in the Square swept clean and sanded (an unusual sight in Rome), thousands of citizens hanging out of the windows, flags and pennants waving in the air; brilliant cavalcades followed one another, accompanied by military bands playing inspiring music, and then came the Bersagliere, in their double-quick step, sounding their bugles as they marched along, their hats cocked very much on one side, with long rooster feathers streaming out in the wind. This is the most unique regiment (I was going to say cockiest) one can imagine. Their uniforms are very dark green, their hats are black patent leather, and they wear black gloves and leggings. I am told that these soldiers do not live long—that they hardly ever reach the age of forty. The strain on the heart, caused by their quick pace, which is something between a run and a trot, is too great, especially for the buglers, who blow their bugles while running. At last came the splendid gala coaches of the King and the Queen, followed by many others, and then the military suite, making a splendid procession.

KING VICTOR EMMANUEL
From a photograph given to Madame de Hegermann-Lindencrone in 1893.

Inside, the large building was crowded to its limit. The state Ministers were in their seats in front, the members of Parliament behind them. The balconies were filled with people, and every available place was occupied. When the Queen entered the royal *loge* with her ladies and chamberlains, there was a great deal of clapping of hands, which is the way an Italian shows his enthusiasm and loyalty. Every one arose and remained standing while the Queen came forward to the front of her *loge*, bowed and smiled, and bowed and bowed again until the clapping ceased; then she took her seat, and every one sat down.

The *loge* reserved for the Diplomatic Corps is directly opposite the Queen's. After a few moments' pause the platform supporting the throne was noiselessly invaded by numerous officers in their glittering and brilliant uniforms, and members of the court in their court dress covered with decorations, who took their places on each side of the throne. The King came in quietly without any pomp, and was greeted by the most enthusiastic and prolonged demonstration. He acknowledged the ovation, but evidently chafed under the slight delay, as if impatient to commence his speech. Before doing so he turned toward the Queen's *loge* with a respectful inclination of the head, as if to acknowledge her presence, then, bowing to the Diplomatic *loge* and turning to the audience, read his proclamation.

It was most difficult to hear what the King said, perched as we were high above him; but we understood by the frequent interruptions and the enthusiastic *benes* and *bravos* and the clapping of hands that what he said pleased his subjects. The speech over, the King, accompanied by his suite, left as quietly as he had entered, amid the vociferous applause that followed. The Queen then arose, smiled and bowed to the assembly, and withdrew.

The streets were thronged with soldiers and people, and it was as much as his life was worth for the coachman to draw up in front of the door.

Mr. and Mrs. Field have almost completed their enormous palace out by Santa Maria Maggiore, but they have not, as they hoped, succeeded in making that part of Rome fashionable. They have bought land as far as the Colosseum; Nero's gold house, which stands in a *finocchi* patch, is theirs too. The tenement-houses near them continue to festoon the façades with the week's wash in every state of unrepair. There is no privacy about the Italians washing their dirty linen, though they do wash at home.

I seem to be introducing you to all Rome.

Mr. and Mme. Minghetti are old friends—that is, I have known her from 1866. Then she was Princess Camporeale, very handsome and captivating.

She is just as attractive now and holds Rome in her hand. Her *salon* is the *salon* where all fashionable Rome flocks. She has arranged it in the most artistic manner. It is crowded with furniture, with cozy corners and flirtatious nooks between *armoires* and palm-trees. Valuable old pictures and tapestries decorate the walls. The *salon* is two stories high and has an ornamental little winding staircase on which an enormous stuffed peacock stands with outspread tail, as if guarding things below. On her Sunday afternoons one is sure to hear some good music. No one refuses, as it gives a person a certain prestige to be heard there.

Mr. Minghetti, possessing the order of the Annunciata (the highest decoration of Italy), is called "*Le cousin du Roi.*" He is a great personage. He has been Prime Minister and still plays a very conspicuous part in politics. He has written many books on constitutional law. He is tall, handsome, and altogether delightful.

The Storys still live in the third heaven of the Barberini Palace, where on Fridays there is a steady procession of tea-thirsty English and Americans who toil upward.

The two sons are what Mr. Story calls "promising." Waldo (the elder) promises to rival his father as a sculptor. Julian promises to be a great painter. His picture of Cardinal Howard, all in red against a red background, is a fine study in color besides being an excellent likeness.

The Haseltines are flourishing like green bay-trees. Their beautiful apartment in the Altieri Palace, where his *atelier* is, is filled with his exquisite water-colors and paintings. Her brother, Mr. Marshall, is staying with them. He is very amusing. Last evening he held the table in a roar when he told of a recent experience.

At the Duchess Fiano's costume ball he had worn a costume of a Mignon-Henri-II. He described it to us. A light-blue satin jacket, and trunk-hose, slashed to exaggeration, with white satin puffs, a jaunty velvet cap with a long feather, and white satin shoes turned up at the ends.

Worth had made it and put a price on it almost equal to Marshall's income, and just because it had cost so much and he had received a good many compliments he thought it was his duty to have it and himself photographed as a memento of his reckless extravagance before the costume was consigned to oblivion. On the day of his appointment with the artist he was dressed and ready in his costume. As it was a rainy day, he provided himself with an umbrella and a pair of india-rubbers big enough to go over the gondola-like shoes. He also carried a stuffed falcon in his hand so that there should be no doubt as to what he was.

Unluckily, the horse fell down on the slippery *Corso*, and the coachman insisted upon Marshall's getting out.

"You may imagine my feelings," he said, "at being obliged to show myself in broad daylight in this get-up. A crowd of gaping idiots gathered about me and made particularly sarcastic remarks. One said, '*E il Re!* ('It is the King'). Another screamed, '*Quante e bello i piccolo!*' There was I stranded in the middle of the *Corso*, holding an umbrella over my head in one hand and that ridiculous falcon in the other, my feather dripping down my back; and when I looked down at blue legs fast turning another color and my huge india-rubbers I realized what a spectacle I was making of myself...."

We laughed till the tears rolled down our cheeks. He showed us the photograph, and I must say that a less Mignon-Henri-II-like Mignon and a more typical American face and figure could not be imagined. If Henri II had caught sight of him with his thin legs, side-whiskers, and eye-glasses he would have turned in his grave.

Dr. Nevin, our pastoral shepherd, has really done a great deal for the American church here and ought to have a vote of thanks. He has collected so much money that he has not only built the pretty church, but has decorated it with Burne-Jones's tall angels and copies of the mosaics from Ravenna. He has also built a comfortable rectory, which he has filled with rare *bric-à-brac*. They say that no one is a better match for the wily dealers in antiquities than the reverend gentleman, and the pert little cabmen don't dare to try any of their tricks on him.

He shows another side of his character when in the pulpit.

The mere sound of his own voice in reading the Scriptures affects him to tears. Last Sunday he almost broke down completely when he was reading about Elijah and the bears (a tale which does not seem in the least pathetic to me). He is a great sportsman and plays all games with enthusiasm, and is a fervent but bad whist-player, and when he revokes (which he often does) we suppose he is thinking out his next Sunday's sermon. In the summer vacation he goes to the Rocky Mountains and kills bears.

A few Sundays ago it was, if ever, the occasion to say, "Don't kill the organist; he is doing his best." Signor Rotoli (the organist), who does not know one word of English, was dozing through Dr. Nevin's usual sermon, and, having the music open before him of the solo that Mr. Grant (the tenor) was going to sing, heard the first words of the prayer, "O Lord, grant—" thought that it was the signal for the anthem, and crashed down the opening chords.

Dr. Nevin looked daggers at him, as if he could have killed him on the spot, and had there been anything at hand heavier than his sermon he certainly would have thrown it at him.

March, 1881.

Dear ____,—The carnival is over. As it is the first carnival I have ever seen, I must describe it to you. It lasts almost a week. It commenced last Wednesday and finished yesterday. Mr. Saumares, of the English Embassy, had taken a balcony just opposite the Palazzo Fiano, where the Queen always goes. He invited us for the whole week, and when we were not in the fray ourselves, we went there at five o'clock to take tea and to see the *corso di barbeir* (the race of the wild horses). The first day of the carnival we were full of energy and eagerness. We were all in our shabbiest clothes, as this is the customary thing. The coachman and the valet also had their worst clothes on, which is saying a good deal, and the horses were even worse than usual, which is saying a good deal more. The carriages were filled to overflowing with flowers, bonbons, and confetti by the bushel. Our servant, Giuseppe, had been since early morning bargaining for the things, and after tucking us in the carriage he contemplated us with pride as we drove off.

We started from the Piazzo del Popolo at three o'clock, and pelted every one, exhausting our ammunition recklessly. Dirty little beggar-boys would jump on the step of the carriage and snatch what flowers they could, even out of our hands, and would then sell them back to us, scrambling for the soldi which we threw at them; and, what was worse, they picked the same bouquets up, which by this time had become mere stems without flowers and covered with mud, and threw them at us. They wanted their fun, too.

At five o'clock we stood on the balcony to watch the race of the wild horses. These are brought straight in from the country, quite wild and untamed. They are covered with all sorts of dangling pointed tin things and fire-crackers, which not only frighten them dreadfully, but hurt them. They started at the Piazza del Popolo and were hooted and goaded on by the excited screams of the populace all the way down the narrow *Corso*, which is a mile long. It is a wonder that the poor creatures in their fright did not dart into the howling crowd, but they did not. They kept straight on their way, stung to desperation by the fireworks on their backs. At the Piazza di Venezia the street narrows into a very small passage, which divides the palazzo from its neighbor opposite. Here sheets (or, rather, sails) were hung across this narrow place, into which the horses, blinded with terror, puzzled and confused, ran headlong, and were easily caught. The one who gets there first gets the prize, and is led back through the streets, tired and meek, wearing his number on a card around his neck. It is a cruel sport, but the Italians enjoy it, believing, as they do, that animals have no souls, and therefore can support any amount of torture.

Nothing is done on Friday. The following Tuesday—Mardi-gras—was the last day. Then folly reigned supreme. After the horses had run their race and twilight had descended on the scene, the *moccoletti* began. This is such a childish sport that it really seems impossible that grown-up men and women could find any amusement in taking part in it. Lighting your own small tallow candle and trying to put out your neighbor's—that is what it amounts to. Does it not sound silly? Yet all this vast crowd is as intent on it as if their lives and welfare were at stake. At eight o'clock, however, this came to an end, the last flickering light was put out, and we went home—one would think to play with our dolls.

ROME, *1881.*

Dear ____,—Since we are bereft of balls and *soirées* we devote our time to improving our Italian. Johan and I take lessons of a monsignore who appears precisely at ten every morning. We struggle through some verbs, and then he dives into Dante, the most difficult thing to comprehend in the Italian language. Then he tries to explain it in Italian to us, which is more difficult still. He makes us read aloud to him, during which he folds his hands over his fat stomach and audibly goes to sleep. He will awake with a start and excuse himself, saying that he gets up at five o'clock in the morning for *matines*, and that naturally at eleven he is sleepy; but I think he only pretends to sleep and takes refuge behind his eyelids, in order to ponder over the Italian language as "she is spoke."

Sgambati, the very best composer and pianist in Rome, gives lessons to Nina, who he says has "*molto talento.*" Sgambati has a wonderful and sympathetic touch, which is at once velvety and masterful. His gavotte is a *chef-d'oeuvre.* He calls it a gavotte, but I tell him he ought to call it "The Procession of the Cavaliers," because it has such a martial ring to it. It does not in the least resemble a Gavotte Louis XV. I seem to see in my mind's eye Henry V. trying to rally his comrades about him and incite them to combat. Sgambati looks like a *preux chevalier* himself, with his soft, mild blue eyes and long hair and serene brow. He brought a song that he composed, he said, "*per la distinta Eccellenza Hegermann* expressly by her devoted and admiring Sgambati." Although the song was beautiful as a piano piece and as *he* played it, I could not sing it. I said:

"My dear Sgambati, I can never sing 'Mio' on a si-bemol. Can I not change it for an 'A'?"

"No!" answered Sgambati. "The-whole meaning would be lost; but you can broaden it out and sing 'Miaa.'"

Another shining light is Tosti, who comes to us very often. He is by far the best beloved of popular composers. He understands the voice thoroughly and composes songs which are melodious and easy to sing. Therefore every one sings them. He has not much of a voice, but when he sings his compositions he makes them so charming that they sell like wildfire. He is the most amiable of geniuses, and never refuses to sing when he is asked.

Yesterday I sang something I had composed as a *vocalize*. He liked it so much that he asked why I did not sing it as a song.

I said, "I cannot write either it or the accompaniment."

"That is easy enough," he replied. "I will write it for you," and scribbled it off then and there.

He dedicated a piece to me called "Forever," which I sing on every occasion.

I have a great friend in Madame Helbig, the wife of Herr Helbig, the German archæologist in Rome. She is born a Russian princess, and is certainly one of the best amateur musicians, if not the best, I have ever met. She is of immense proportions, being very tall and very stout. One might easily mistake her for a priest, as she is always dressed in a long black garment which is a sort of water-proof; and as her hair is short and she never wears a hat, you may well imagine that she is very well known in Rome. When she hails a cab to take her up the very steep Caffarelli Hill, where they live, the cabbies, who are humorists in their way, look at her, then at their poor, half-fed horses and the weak springs of their dilapidated *bottes* (cabs), shake their heads, and, holding up two dirty fingers, say, "*In due volte*" (which means "in two trips"). Mr. Ross, the Norwegian painter, whose English is not quite up to the mark, said she was the "hell-biggest" woman he ever saw; and when she undertook a journey to Russia, said, "Dear me, how can she ever travel with that corpse of hers?"

ROME, HOLY WEEK, *1881*.

My dear Aunt,—The churches are open all day. St. Peter's, Laterano, Santa Maria Maggiore each has one of the famous sopranos. The music is—well, simply divine! I can't say more. You must hear it to appreciate it. (Some day I hope you will.) Good Friday is the great day at St. Peter's. The church is so crowded that one can hardly get a place to stand. There are not chairs enough in any of the churches during Holy Week for the numerous strangers that pervade Rome. My servant generally carries a camp-stool and rug, and I sit entranced, listening in the deepening twilight to the heavenly strains of Palestrina, Pergolese, and Marcello. Sometimes the soloists sing Gounod's "Ava Maria" and Rossini's "Stabat Mater," and, fortunately, drown the squeaky tones of the old organ. A choir of men and boys accompanies them in "The Inflammatus," where the high notes of M.'s tearful voice are almost supernatural. People swarm to the Laterano on Saturday to hear the Vespers, which are especially fine. After the solo is finished, the priests begin their monotonous Gregorian chants, and at the end of those they *slap-bang* their prayer-books on the wooden benches on which they are sitting, making a noise to wake the dead. I thought they were furious with one another and were refusing to sing any more. It seemed very out of place for such an exhibition of temper. A knowing friend told me that it was an old Jewish custom which had been repeated for ages on this particular day and at this hour. It closes the Lenten season.

On Easter Sunday I sang in the American church. Dr. Nevin urged me so much that I did not like to refuse. I chose Mendelssohn's beautiful anthem, "Come unto Me."

ROME, *1883.*

Dear ____,—We have moved from the Palazzo Rospigliosi to the Palazzo Tittoni, in Via Rasella, which leads from the Palazzo Barberini down to the Fontana di Trevi. I never would have chosen this palace, beautiful as it is, if I could have foreseen the misery I suffer when I hear the wicked drivers goading and beating their poor beasts up this steep hill. The poor things strain every muscle under their incredible burdens, but are beaten, all the same. I am really happy when I hear the crow—I mean the bray—of a donkey. It has a jubiliant ring in it, as if he were somehow enjoying himself, and my heart sympathizes with him. But it may be only his way of expressing the deepest depths of woe.

Mrs. Charles Bristed, of New York, a recent convert to the Church of Rome, receives on Saturday evenings. She has accomplished what hitherto has been considered impossible—that is, the bringing together of the "blacks" (the ultra-Catholic party, belonging to the Vatican) and the "whites," the party adhering to the Quirinal. These two parties meet in her *salon* as if they were of the same color. The Pope's singers are the great attraction. She must either have a tremendously long purse or great persuasive powers to get them, for her *salon* is the only place outside the churches where one can hear them. Therefore this *salon* is the only platform in Rome where the two antagonistic parties meet and glare at each other.

We went there last Saturday. The chairs were arranged in rows, superb in their symmetry at first, but after the first petticoats had swept by everything was in a hopeless confusion. Two ladies sitting on one chair, one lady appropriating two chairs instead of one, and another sitting sideways on three. The consequence was that there was a conglomeration of empty chairs in the middle of the room, while crowds of weary guests stood in and near the doorway, with the thermometer sky-high! When one sees the Pope's singers in evening dress and white cravats the prestige and effect are altogether lost. This particular evening was unusually brilliant, for the monsignores and cardinals were extra-abundant. There were printed programs handed to us with the list of the numerous songs that we were going to hear.

The famous Moresca, who sings at the Laterano, is a full-faced soprano of forty winters. He has a tear in each note and a sigh in each breath. He sang the jewel song in "Faust," which seemed horribly out of place. Especially when he asks (in the hand-glass) if he is really Marguerita, one feels tempted to answer, "*Macché*," for him. Then they sang a chorus of Palestrina, all screaming at the top of their lungs, evidently thinking they were in St. Peter's. It never occurred to them to temper their voices to the poor shorn lambs wedged up against the walls.

Afterward followed the duet, "*Quis est homo*," of Rossini's "Stabat Mater," sung by two gray-haired sopranos. This was extremely beautiful, but the best of all was the solo sung by a fat, yellow-mustached barytone. I never heard anything to compare to his exquisite voice. We shall never hear anything like it in this world, and I doubt in the next. Maroni is the man who always directs the Pope's singers. He makes more noise beating time with his roll of music on the piano than all the cab-drivers below in the Piazza del Popolo.

The supper-room was a sight to behold—the enormous table fairly creaking under the weight of every variety of food filled half the room, leaving very little space for the guests. The sopranos got in first, ahead even of the amiable hostess, who stopped the whole procession, trying to go abreast through the door with a portly cardinal and a white diplomat, leaving us, the hungry black and white sheep, still wrestling with the chairs.

You must have heard of Hamilton Aidé, the author of *The Poet and the Prince* and other works. He comes frequently to see us, and always brings either a new book or a new song—for he is not only a distinguished author, but a composer as well. He sings willingly when asked. He is very fond of one of his songs, called "The Danube River." If he had not brought the music and I had not seen the title as I laid it on the piano, I should never have known that it was anything so lively as a river he was singing about. Though I could occasionally hear the word "river," I hoped that as the river and singer went on they would have a little more "go" in them; but they continued babbling along regardless of obstacles and time.

I was extremely mortified to see that several of my guests had dozed off. The river and the singer had had a too-lullaby effect on them.

ROME, *1883.*

Dear ____,—Next to the Palazzo Tittoni lives a delightful family—the Count and Countess Gigliucci, with a son and two daughters. The Countess is the celebrated Clara Novello of oratorio fame. The three ladies are perfectly charming. I love to go to see them, and often drop in about tea-hour, when I get an excellent cup of English tea and delicious muffins, and enjoy them in this cozy family circle.

Though they live In a palace and have a showy *portier*, they do not disdain to do their shopping out of the window by means of a basket, which the servant-girl lets down on a string for the daily marketing. Even cards and letters are received in this way, as the porter refuses to carry anything up to their third story. "*Sortita!*" screamed down in a shrill voice is the answer to the visitor waiting below in the courtyard.

When the three ladies are sitting at the tea-table dispensing tea, one of them will suddenly commence the trio from "Elijah"—"Lift thine eyes"—the other two joining in (singing without an accompaniment, of course) in the most delicious manner. Their voices are so alike in *timbre* and quality that it is almost impossible to distinguish one from the other. After the trio they go on pouring out tea as if nothing had happened, whereas for me it is an event. It is such perfection!

Countess Gigliucci comes sometimes and sings with me. Her voice is still beautiful and clear as a bell. What must it have been in its prime? In her letters to me she calls me "my delicious blackbird."

ROME, *March, 1883.*

The King of Sweden came to Rome on an official visit to their Majesties. I suppose it is called official because he is staying as a guest at the Quirinal, therefore he is hardly seen in private. You remember that I saw a good deal of him when he was in Paris in 1867. He was then hereditary Prince to the throne of Sweden, and was called Prince Oscar. He only stayed three days at Rome. There was a gala dinner to which all the diplomats were invited. He greeted me very cordially, shook hands in his genial manner, and talked about the past (sixteen years ago) as if it were yesterday. He said, smilingly:

"You see, since I have become King I have cut my hair."

I had no idea what he meant and looked puzzled.

"Don't you remember," he said, "you called me 'the *Hair* Apparent' on account of my long locks?"

"Oh, your Majesty," I said, "how could I have been so rude?"

"It was not rudeness," he said, kindly. "You said what you liked in those days. You were not then a diplomat's wife."

The day of his departure from Rome we went to the station. The King was very gracious, and said to Johan, "I hope you and your wife will come some day to Sweden," and gave my hand an extra-hearty squeeze. A hearty squeeze from his hand was something to remember!

The Queen has asked me to sing with her, and I go regularly twice a week to the Quirinal at two o'clock. We sing all kinds of duets, classical and the ultra-modern. The Queen's singing-master, Signor Vera, and sometimes the composer, Signor Marchetti, accompany us—they bring new music which has appeared, which we *déchiffrons* under their critical eyes. It is the greatest delight I have to be able to be with her Majesty in such an informal way. She is so enchanting, so natural, so gay, and so fascinating. No one can resist her. Am I not a greatly privileged person? I presented Nina to her last week—her Majesty told me to bring her with me on one of our singing-lesson days at half past one—so we had a half-hour of conversation before the singing-master came. The Queen said, after Nina had gone: "What a beauty she is! She will set the world on fire."

May, 1883.

The visit of the newly married couple, Prince Tomaso, brother of the Queen, and Princess Isabella of Bavaria, has been the occasion of many festivities.

Yesterday there was a garden party in the Quirinal gardens. It was a perfect day, and the beautiful toilets of the ladies made the lawn look like a *parterre* of living flowers. The grounds are so large that there were several entertainments going on at the same time without interfering with one another.

A band of gipsies in their brilliant dresses were singing in one place, and in a *bosquet* a troupe of Neapolitans were dancing the tarantella in their white-stockinged feet. There were booths where you could have your photograph taken and your fortune told. Everywhere you were given souvenirs of some kind. One played at the *tombola* and always got a prize. Buffets, of course, at every turn. We went from one surprise to another. The Prince of Naples was omnipresent and seemed to enjoy himself immensely. Whoever arranged this *fête* ought to have received a decoration. Twilight and the obligation of having to dress for the evening concert put a stop to this delightful afternoon. In the evening there was a gala concert which was very entertaining. It commenced by a piece written by the Baron Renzie and very well performed by amateurs, and some mandolinists, who played several things more or less acceptably, and then came a long and tedious symphony which was too classical for the majority of the audience. The Queen and the Duchess of Genoa seemed to enjoy it. I did, too, but the King looked bored to death, and the bridegroom went fast to sleep. The Queen, who was sitting next to him, gave him a vigorous pinch to wake him up. The pinch had the intended effect, but the groan he gave was almost too audible. In the interlude when ices were passed the Princess talked with the wives of the diplomats who were brought up to her. The Queen, still laughing at her brother's discomfiture, passed about among the other guests.

December, 1883.

We returned to Rome a week ago. It was said that their Majesties had expressed the desire that as many diplomats as possible should be present when the Crown Prince of Germany came for his visit to the Quirinal.

During the stay of the Crown-Prince Frederic the crowds waited patiently outside the Quirinal, hoping to catch a glimpse of him. He is very popular, and whenever he shows himself he is cheered to *outrance*. Sometimes he came out on the balcony, and once he took the Prince of Naples up in his strong arms and cried "*Evviva l'Italia*" The people clapped their hands till they were worn out.

There were fireworks from the Castel St. Angelo in his honor which were wonderfully fine.

To reach the balconies reserved for the *Corps Diplomatique* we were obliged to leave our carriages in a little side-street and go through a long carpeted passage, the walls of which were hung with fine old tapestries taken from the Quirinal in order to hide the unsightly objects concealed behind them. The balconies were erected on the outside of the dilapidated houses which overlook the Tiber and facing the Castel St. Angelo. How they ever managed to make this passage is a mystery! In the daytime one could not see the possibility of cutting through the labyrinth of these forlorn tumble-down houses. We sat trembling for fear that the shaky planks would suddenly give way and plunge us into the whirling Tiber under our feet. The fireworks were the most gorgeous display of pyrotechnics I ever saw. And the bouquet as the *finale* was a magnificent tornado of fire which left a huge "F" blazing, which lighted up the December night. We were thankful when we reached home alive.

The next and last evening of the festivities was a gala opera, where there was a great deal of clapping and enthusiasm which accompanied a rather poor performance of "Aida." They said that Verdi was in the audience, but he did not appear, nor was there any demonstration made for him.

ROME, *January, 1884*.

My dear ____,—There are a few changes in the Embassies. Sir Saville Lumley has succeeded Sir August Paget at the English Embassy. Sir Saville's own paintings now cover Lady Paget's chocolate cherubs—only those above the door and their bulrushes are left to tell the tale. Monsieur Decrais, the new French Ambassador and his wife, who replace the De Noailles in the Farnese Palace, are already established. The iciness of Siberia continues to pervade the palace in spite of all efforts to warm those vast *salons*, enormous in their proportions—I do not know how many *mètres* they are to the ceiling. The Carracci gallery separates the bedrooms from the *salons*. Madame Decrais says that they are obliged to dress like Eskimos when they cross it, as they do twenty times a day.

How the Roman climate must have changed since the time when the Romans went about in togas and sandals and lay on slabs of marble after their bath!

We are delighted to have our dear friend M. de Schlözer here. He is Minister to the Vatican, and is (or ought to be) as black as ink, while we Quirinalers are as white as the driven snow; but he has no prejudice as to color, nor have we, so we see one another very often and dine together whenever we can. As soon as his silver was unpacked we were invited straightway to dinner. His rooms in the Palazzo Capranica (belonging to the family of Madame Ristori's husband) are as bare as those he occupied in Washington—barer, even, for here there are no *portières*. In the *salon* he had his beloved Steinway grand, one stiff sofa, four enormous *fauteuils*, destined for his cardinals, a few small gilt *chaises volantes* (as he calls little chairs that are easy to move about), one table on which reposes the last piece of marble picked up while strolling in the Forum, and, as a supreme banality, his niece's Christmas present, a *lamp-mat*, on which stands the lamp in solitary glory.

Schlözer's dinners are of the best, and are most amusing. He superintends everything himself and gives himself no end of trouble. Each course as it is served receives an introductory speech: "*Ce paté, mon cher, est la gloire de ma cuisinière*" etc.

He says that all *volaille* ought to be carved at the table, therefore he carves the birds and the chickens himself, brandishing the knife with gusto while sharpening it.

And as for the wines! Dear me! After filling his glass he holds it against the light, tastes the wine, smacks his lips, and says: "*Ce vin de Bordeaux est du '64. Il faut le boire avec recueillement. Je l'ai débouché moi-même.*"

He has a great liking for Lenbach (the famous painter), although they are utterly different in character and ways. Lenbach is not musical, and is rather rough and gruff in his manners. Even his best friends acknowledge that he does not possess the thing called manners. He is clever and witty in his way, but his way is sarcastic and peevish. Sometimes when he is talking to you he beams and scowls alternately behind his spectacles. You think that he is listening to you, but not at all! He is only thinking out his own thoughts, in which he seems always to be wrapped.

Lenbach occupies the same apartment in the Palazzo Borghese that Pauline Bonaparte lived in. Probably the very couch is still there on which she reclined for her famous statue. You remember what a modest lady friend said to her, "*Cela m'étonne que vous ayez pu poser comme cela!*"—meaning, without clothes; to which the Princess replied: "But why do you wonder? Canova had a fire in the room."

Lenbach asked permission to paint Nina. We did not refuse, and expected great things. He photographed her twenty times in different poses, turning her head (physically, not morally) every which way, and painted thirteen pictures of her, but there was only one (a very pretty profile in crayon with a pink ear and a little dash of yellow on the hair) which he thought good enough to give us.

Do not ask me what we have done or whom we have seen. We are out morning, noon, and night. Every day there is a regular "precession of the equinoxes"—luncheons, dinners, and *soirées* galore.

I sing twice a week with the Queen—red-letter days for me. I look forward with joy to passing that hour with her. I never knew any one so full of interest, humor, and intelligence. It is delightful to see her when she is amused. She can laugh so heartily, and no one, when there is occasion for sympathy, is more ready to give it. Her kind eyes can fill with tears as quickly as they can see the fun in a situation.

Nina and I go out every morning from ten to twelve. Johan is then busy with his despatches and shut up in the chancellery. It is the fashion during those hours to drive in a cab in the *Corso*. It is not considered *chic* to go out in one's own carriage until the afternoon. I am glad of the excuse of buying even a paper of pins in order to be out in the sunshine.

Another queer fashion is that on Sundays gentlemen (the highest of the high) who have their own fine equipages, of which on week-days they are so proud, drive to the fashionable places, like Villa Borghese and Villa

Doria, in *cabs*. Sometimes you will see the beaux most in vogue squeezed (three or four of them) in a little *botte* (the Italian name for cab), looking very uncomfortable. But as it is the thing to do, they are proud and happy to do it. But on other days!—horrible! Nevertheless, it is on Sundays (*especially* on Sundays) that Principe Massimo causes people to stop and stare because he drives abroad on that day in his high-seated phaeton, his long side-whiskers floating in the wind, his servants in their conspicuous dark-red liveries covered with armorial braid, pale-blue cuffs and collars, sitting behind him. Then it is that the Romans say to themselves, Our aristocracy is not yet dead.

Our colleagues, the de W.'s, had a *loge* in the Argentina Theater and invited us the other evening to go with them to see the great Salvini in "Hamlet." The theater was filled to the uppermost galleries; you could not have wedged in another person. The people in the audience, when not applauding, were as silent as so many mice; this is unlike the usual theater-going Italian, who reads and rustles his evening paper all through the performance, looking up occasionally to hiss.

Salvini surpassed himself, perhaps on account of the presence of her Majesty, whose eyes never wandered from the stage, except in the *entr'actes*, when she responded to the ovation the public always makes wherever she appears. She rose and bowed with her sweet smile, the smile which wins all hearts.

There was only one hitch during the performance, and that was when Hamlet and Polonius fought the duel; the latter, unfortunately, missed his aim and speared Hamlet's wig with his sword, on which it stuck in spite of the most desperate efforts to shake it off. Salvini, all unconscious, continued fencing until he caught sight of his wig dangling in the air and, realizing his un-Hamlet-like bald head, backed out into the side-wing, leaving Polonius to get off the stage as best he could.

In the *entr'acte* Monsieur de W. and I talked over the play, and, unfortunately, I said, "Did Hamlet ever exist?" A bomb exploding under our noses could not have been more disastrous! He burst out in indignant tones, and we almost came to literary blows in our violent discussion. M. de W. insists upon it that Shakespeare knew all about Hamlet and where he lived, the medieval clothes he wore, and that he was the sepulchral Prince with whom we are so familiar; that Ophelia was a very misused and unhappy young lady, who drowned herself in a water-lily pond; and that Hamlet's papa used to come nights and scare the life out of the courtiers.

"Wait a little," I said. "I flatter myself that I know the story of Hamlet thoroughly. I spent all last summer studying the old Danish chronicle, which was written in Latin in 1200 by a monk called Saxo Grammaticus, then translated into old-fashioned Danish, which I translated, to amuse myself, into English. If what Saxo says is true Hamlet lived about two or three hundred years before Christ."

"Impossible!" almost screamed my friend.

I went on, regardless of M. de W.'s dangerous attitude: "Denmark at that time was divided into several kingdoms, and Hamlet's father was king in a part of Jutland, which, let us say, was as small as Rhode Island—"

"What nonsense!" interrupted M. de W., indignantly.

"He probably went about in fur-covered legs and a sheepskin over his shoulders, as was then the fashion. He was called Amleth; Shakespeare simply transposed the h. He was a naughty little boy, vicious and revengeful. He despised his mother and hated his uncle, who was his stepfather."

TWO YOUNG QUEENS
From a photograph, taken in 1878, of the two daughters of the King of Denmark. They were then the Princess of Wales and the Grand Duchess Dagmar. They are now the widows of two European sovereigns, Dowager Queen Alexandra of England and the Dowager Empress of Russia. They spend their summers together in a small cottage near Copenhagen. Alexandra is on the right of the picture.

"Why?" asked, in a milder tone, M. de W.

"Because his mother and the uncle, wishing to marry and mount the throne, killed Hamlet's father. Hamlet passed his youth haunted by thoughts of revenge and how he could punish the two sinners."

"It was clever of Shakespeare to let the father do the haunting and leave to Hamlet the *rôle* of a guileless and sentimental youth; the authorities do not agree as to whether Hamlet was really a fool or only pretended to be one."

"Fool he certainly was not," I replied. "He was clever enough to play the part of one, and he played it so well that no one, even at that time, could make out what he really was."

"Then," declared M. de W., "Shakespeare got that part of it right—perhaps you will concede that much. How about Hamlet's grave? Surely there is no humbug about that? I have seen it myself. Has it been there since two hundred years B.C.?"

"Hamlet's grave at Helsingör is an interesting bit of imagination. A unique instance of inaccuracy on the part of the Danes! Hamlet lived to be king in his little land and was buried where he died—if he ever lived—as an Irishman would say."

"How confusing you are," said my opponent. "You destroy my dearest illusions—I, who adore Shakespeare's Hamlet."

"I adore Shakespeare's Hamlet, too, but I do not adore Saxo's. Hamlet's love for his father was the only redeeming point about him. Did you know that he married the daughter of the King of England?"

"Shakespeare only mentions Ophelia, and we are led to believe that Hamlet died unmarried."

"Well," I answered, "if Saxo is right, he was married, had lots of children, and continued the dynasty till *dato*."

"Go on! You interest me."

"He made himself very disagreeable at home with his silly talk and his hatred of the King and the Queen. In a conversation he had with his mother he flung away all disguise and also hurled some unpleasant and extremely unvarnished truths full in the maternal face."

"That does not speak well for him," said Mr. de W.

"To get rid of him," I continued, warming to my subject, "the Danish court sent him to the English court with a nice letter of introduction, and at the same time sent a letter to the King of England, begging him to have Hamlet killed somehow or other, but clever Hamlet stole and read the letter and killed the messenger himself."

"That shows he was no fool," acknowledged M. de W.

"The King of England gave him a fine dinner, and I think the English court must have opened its eyes when Hamlet pushed away the food, saying it was '*too bad to eat*.' He told them that the bread tasted of dead men's bones and the wine of blood, and, worst of all, that the Queen was not a born lady. When the court asked with one voice how he dared breathe such an insult he answered that there were three things that proved that what he said was true."

"It would amuse me to know what the three things were," said M. de W.

"One was," I said, "that the Queen held up her dress while walking; another, that she threw a shawl over her head; and the last, that she picked her teeth and chewed the contents! I actually blush for the Danes when I read the account of that dinner."

"I confess," laughed de W., "that that *was* pretty bad. Tell me some more."

"The courtiers hurried to examine into affairs and found that everything that Hamlet said was true. The poor Queen was horribly mortified, for they discovered that her papa had been a peasant."

"I suppose," said M. de W., "that the court forbade the banns after that."

"No," I said, "Hamlet went home with his bride, and the royal Danish court of Jutland made an enormous feast for the home-coming of the princely couple. *This* was the thing that Hamlet had waited for all his life. Saxo hurries over this harrowing episode. Hamlet succeeded in getting all the guests dead drunk, then he pulled the tapestries all down on top of them and set fire to the palace and burned them all up. What do you think of your adorable Hamlet now?"

"I think," said M. de W., curtly, "all things considered, that Hamlet was a damn fool!"

"I thought so too until I read the speech he made to his subjects when he mounted the throne. It was the most beautiful bit of sentiment, the tenderest tribute to his dead father, and showed his undaunted love for his country. I am sorry that Shakespeare made no mention of this."

Mr. Story, who was with us, said he once heard a lady say she did not care much for Shakespeare, because he was "so full of quotations."

ROME, *1884.*

Dear ____,—The King drives every day in his high English phaeton through the crowded streets, not fearing to expose himself to his people, as some other sovereigns do.

When some one remonstrated with him, "Your Majesty ought not to run such risk," he answered, smilingly: "*Comment donc! C'est un des ennuis de notre métier.*" Everybody bows respectfully, and in return he takes off his hat and holds it at right angles, keeping the reins in the other hand. Sometimes he does not get the chance to put his hat back on his head the whole length of the *Corso*. His adjutant sits by his side and a lacquey sits behind, dressed in black. The King likes simplicity in all things.

The Queen drives in a landau (*à huit resorts*), accompanied by her lady in waiting; the servants in their brilliant red liveries can be seen from a long distance. Her Majesty recognizes every one, smiles and bows right and left; sometimes she will look back and give a person an extra smile. She says that she can see, while flying by, all the objects exposed in the shop windows, and often sends the servant back to buy what she has noticed.

When their Majesties meet in the drive in their respective equipages the Queen rises in her seat as if to make a courtesy, and the King responds in the most ceremonious manner.

Before Christmas the Queen goes about in the shops and makes her own purchases (the shops are then shut to the public). All the ladies of the court receive magnificent gifts, generally in the shape of jewels.

The King always keeps on his writing-table and within touch a quantity of rare unset stones. He likes to look at them and handle them; and then, when the occasion comes to give a present, he has the stones set in diamonds.

MILAN, *November 2, 1884.*

My dear Aunt,—We arrived here last night, and shall remain till to-morrow, when we are expected at Monza, where the King and the Queen have invited us to make them a visit.

Count Gianotti came this afternoon to tell us that we are to take the train leaving here at three o'clock. Johan and I went out for a stroll while the maid and valet were packing. We wandered through the Victor Emmanuel Gallery, then went into the ever-enchanting cathedral. I never tire of seeing this wonderful place. I pay my two soldi for a chair and sit there, lost in thought and admiration. The dimness and silence make it very solemn and restful. Every little while a procession of intoning priests shuffle by to go to some altar in one of the side-chapels for some particular service. Sometimes it is a baptism, and the peasants whose babies are going to be baptized stand in an awed group around the font. Everything is done in a most matter-of-fact way. I look at the splendid carvings and filigree of marble and wonder how any *one* mountain can have furnished so much marble, since it started furnishing hundreds of years ago. It is lucky that the mountain belongs exclusively to the Church!

On my return to the hotel I found a card from Countess Marcello, saying that the Queen had suggested our going to the Scala Theater, and that we were to occupy the royal box. She has just left Monza. She is lady in waiting to the Queen, and, her duties having finished for this month, she is replaced by the Princess Palavicini. She told us that there were at present no guests at Monza. She said that there are three categories of toilets: "*good, better,* and *best*" (as she put it), besides the unexpected which always arrived in the shape of court mournings, and one must be prepared for them all. When the King's sister (Princess Clothilde) is there, only severe, sober, and half-high dresses are worn. For the Queen's mother (the Duchess of Genoa) the usual evening dress, *décolletée,* with a train. But when the Queen of Portugal comes everything must be extra magnificent, with tiaras and jewels galore and the last things of modernity.

We arrived in the theater just as the curtain was going down on the first act. The audience stared steadily at us with and without opera-glasses. I suppose people thought that we were members of some royal family. As the performance was not interesting and I was tired, we left at an early hour. I scribble this off to you just before going to bed.

MONZA, *November 3d.*

You see that I am writing on royal paper, which is a sign that we are here. Now I will tell you about things as far as we have got. At the station in Milan, Count Gianotti met us and put us safely in the carriage, which bore a kingly crown; Princess Brancaccio accompanied us. On arriving at Monza station we found Signor Peruzzi waiting for us, and an open barouche drawn by four horses mounted by postilions from the royal stables. We drove through the town and through the long avenue leading to the *château* at a tremendous pace, people all taking off their hats as we passed.

THE PALACE, MONZA (FRONT)
Occupied in the summer by the King and Queen of Italy.

PALACE AND GARDENS
Here the King and Queen entertained their friends. Apartments in the second story, the entire right half as seen in the picture, were occupied by the De Hegermann-Lindencrones.

In the courtyard (which is immense) the carriage stopped at the entrance of the left wing, and we entered the *château*, where the Marquise Villamarina met us and led the way to our apartment, telling me, as we walked along, that her Majesty was looking forward with much pleasure to seeing us, and said that we were expected at five o'clock for tea in the *salon* and that I was to come dressed as I was, adding that she would come for us to show the way.

I had time to admire our gorgeous set of rooms, which is finer than anything I had ever seen before—finer than Compiègne, and certainly finer than our apartment at Fredensborg.

We passed through an antechamber which led to my *salon*, the walls of which are covered with red damask, the curtains and furniture of the same; many beautiful modern pictures hang on the walls, and there are pretty vitrines filled with *bric-à-brac*. My dressing-room is entirely *capitonné* in blue satin from top to bottom—even the ceiling. It has long mirrors set in the walls, in which I am reflected and re-reflected *ad infinitum*. My bathroom is a dream with its tiled walls and marble bath. (My maid's room is next this.) My bedroom is as large as a ballroom; the curtains, *portières*, divans, and comfortable arm-chairs are of white satin, and in the middle is a glass chandelier fit for a Doge's palace. A hundred candles can light me when I go to bed. My bed stands on a rather high platform and has white-satin curtains hanging from a *baldaquin* with fringe and tassels, and a huge Aubusson carpet covers the whole floor.

Next to my bedroom is J.'s bedroom, which is also very large, with two windows, furnished in red brocade; great gilt consols support the elaborate-framed Italian mirrors. Then comes his dressing-room, which connects with his bath-room and his valet's room. Then another antechamber giving on to a corridor which leads to the great gallery.

The Marquise came to my door, and we followed her through two or three drawing-rooms before we reached the center room, which is a very large *salle* with a dome taking in three stories.

The Queen welcomed me most cordially and seemed very glad to see me. She kissed me on both cheeks and made me sit by her on the sofa. She was, as always, lovely and gracious.

The repast was a very sumptuous high tea—all sorts of cold meats, birds, confitures, cakes of various kinds, and sandwiches.

I asked the Queen if she had been singing much during the summer. "Alas, no!" she replied. "My voice has had a vacation, and Vera and Marchetti have also had theirs. I have been in Stresa with my mother, and in Turin, but, now you are here, we shall certainly have some music. Vera is here," and at that very moment the amiable old master appeared. We remained talking till nearly six o'clock; then we went up to dress for dinner. I had a better look at our rooms. They appeared more magnificent than before. My maid had unpacked everything, and a fire was burning brightly in my bedroom, making it look cozy, if one can make such a royal and luxurious apartment look cozy.

I looked at my bed on its platform and wondered how in the world I was ever to get in it when the time came. The sheets and pillow-cases were of the finest linen trimmed with exquisite Valenciennes, like huge pocket-handkerchiefs. Instead of blankets there was a large white-satin perfumed, sachet with a cord sewed round it, completely covering the bed.

Johan was told not to be in evening-dress suit. The King always wears a *redingote* and a black tie. The other gentlemen, of course, do the same. The dinner was at seven o'clock. Every one was assembled when we entered the *salon*. The Prince of Naples was talking with some ladies. His *Gouverneur*, Colonel Osio, stood near him. After a few moments the King and the Queen came in together. The King greeted us with great kindness. The Prince kissed his mother's hand, made a military salute to his father, and left the *salon*. He is fifteen years old now, but looks younger. He wears a uniform which makes him look even smaller than he really is. The King gave his arm to the Queen, and every one followed into the dining-room, going through the Japanese room. I should say that there were twenty people at table, J. and I being the only guests. I sat on the right of the King, and Johan sat on the right of the Queen. The dinner was delicious. We had the famous white truffles from Piemonte supplied exclusively for the King. These truffles exist only in certain forests belonging to the Crown in Piemonte. And there is only a certain kind of pigs that have the particular kind of nose that can find them and rout them out from under the ground. A pig and his nose are not enticing caterers, but nevertheless the truffles are delicious. When they are served they have rather a strong odor of garlic, but they do not taste of it in the least.

"Well," said the King, as we sat down to the table, "what have you been doing?"

"Your Majesty would be soon tired if I told you all I have done," I said.

"*Bien!* that is a good commencement. We will have enough for the whole dinner.... I listen...."

"To begin with, we spent two months in Denmark. Then I went to America to see my mother; then to Paris; then to the Riviera; and from Monte Carlo here."

"Monte Carlo," remarked the King. "That is a bad place. I have never been there. It is out of the circuit of my official duties," he added, laughingly.

"It is a very bad place, your Majesty, if you are unlucky in play; otherwise it is a lovely place."

"Of course you played at the tables?" the King said.

"Of course," I replied.

"And lost all your money," said the King, and laughed.

"No, your Majesty. I won. I won enough to bring away a hundred-franc gold piece which I keep as a fetish."

"Lend it to me! I need a fetish badly," said the King.

"Certainly I will," and prepared to unhook it from the chain it was on.

"No, no! I am only joking. I do not need anything to bring me luck." Then he changed the conversation suddenly.

After dinner we returned to the *grande salle*. The King and the gentlemen remained with the ladies a little while, then went to smoke in the billiard-room. As the King hardly ever sits down—or, if he does, sits on the edge of the billiard-table—the gentlemen were obliged to stand during the hour before the King joined the Queen. We ladies sat with the Queen, who entertained us with her impressions of the novels she had just been reading.

She has such a wonderful way of absorbing and analyzing that she can give you in a few words a complete and concise synopsis of the plot and all the situations, besides making clever criticisms.

It was eleven o'clock before his Majesty and the gentlemen returned from their billiards and cigars. The Queen got up, bade us good night, and left the room with the King.

I was appalled when I was ready to occupy my royal bed. It seemed to have become more imposing and more majestic than when I last saw it. I tried to put a chair on the platform, but the platform was too narrow. The only way was to climb on a chair near the bed and from it make a desperate jump. So I put the chair, said, "*One, two, three,*" and jumped. The white-satin hangings, fringes, and tassels swung and jingled from the rebound. Once in bed, I cuddled down under the scented linen. I brought the sachet up to the level of my nose, where it hovered for just a little moment before it slid off me and off the bed.

Then commenced a series of pulling up and slipping down which lasted until I was thoroughly waked up for the night. The only way I got the better of the sachet was to balance it warily and pretend I slept.

In the morning we were served a real Italian breakfast in our room: thin Pekoe tea, a little cream, and much powdered sugar, and an assortment of sweet cakes replacing the customary English buttered toast.

MONZA, *November 4, 1884.*

Dear Mother,—I want to tell you what we did, though we did not do anything of great interest. It was such horrible weather that we could not drive out, as is the Queen's custom every day. After luncheon Signor Vera (the Queen's singing-master who accompanied us in Rome) was called in, and her Majesty and I sang our duets.

All the music from the Quirinal seems to have been transported here, and Vera knows exactly where to put his hand upon everything as it is needed. There is a new edition of Marcello's psalms which are very amusing to *déchiffrer*. Sometimes the Queen takes the soprano part, at others she takes the contralto.

At three o'clock the Queen went to her apartment, and I took that occasion to pay some visits to the other ladies in their different *salons*. We met in the *grande salle* for tea. M. and Mme. Minghetti arrived from Milan by the same train we came on Monday, and came straight from the carriage into the *salon*. The Queen seemed enchanted to see them. They are charming people. He is as delightful as he is unpretentious, which is rare in a man so celebrated as he is, and she has lost none of her fascinations, although she is a grandmother. They brought the last news from Rome, and the conversation was on politics and war; they talked so rapidly that neither my brain nor my Italian could keep pace with them. I might have told you something of interest if I had been able to understand what they said.

At seven o'clock there was a military dinner. As there were about sixty people present, the dinner was served in the large dining room. The King and the gentlemen of the household were, as usual, in *redingotes* and black ties, but the generals and the officers were in all their war-paint, most gorgeous to behold. I sat on the left of the King (Madame Minghetti was on his right), and next to the dearest old general in the world, who was politeness itself, and, though I suppose we shall never see each other again, he gave himself much trouble to entertain me. He told me that he had been with the King when he fought in the battle of Custozza (in the Austrian war), where the King had shown so much bravery and courage. The King, hearing what my neighbor was saying (he probably raised his voice a trifle), leaned across me, and, laughingly holding up a warning finger, said:

"If you go on like that I shall leave the table."

"Oh, your Majesty! that would never do," said my general. "Now, madame," turning to me, "shall we talk of the weather?"

After dinner there was *le cercle*. Their Majesties went about and talked to everybody. The King seemed in the best of spirits, laughing continually, and familiarly clapping the officer to whom he was talking on the back. Every one stayed in the *salon* until it was time for the military guests to take their leave.

November 5, 1884.

Dear ____,—This morning I received a little word from the Marquise Villamarina: "Please put on a warm dress, as her Majesty intends taking a long drive after luncheon, and it will be chilly and damp before we get back."

We came into the *salon* just in time not to be too late, for their Majesties entered almost immediately.

The Prince of Naples (they call him the *Principino*) sat next to me at luncheon. He is very clever—unusually clever—and has a memory that some day ought to stand him in good stead. Mine by the side of it felt like a babe in arms. The questions he asked, *à brule-point*, would have startled a person cleverer than I am. He is very military and knows all about the different wars that have been fought since the time of Moses, and when he wished to know how many officers were killed in the battle of Chattanooga I had to confess that, if I had ever known, I had forgotten. But he knew everything concerning Chattanooga and all other battles.

When the white truffles were served (they were temptingly buried in a nest of butter) the Prince said, "How can you eat those things?"

"You mean, your Highness, these delicious truffles?"

"Yes," he answered; "they don't taste bad, but they stink so."

"Oh, Monseigneur," I cried, "you must not say that word. It is a dreadful word."

"Oh no, it is not. It is in the Bible."

I could not contradict him. I hope he will find out later that there are some words in the Bible that are not used in general conversation.

After luncheon the Queen said: "We are going to take a very long drive. You must dress very warmly." I went to my room. I had a little time before the rendezvous in the *salon*, and I thought perhaps I could finish my letter begun yesterday, but, alas! I could not.... I returned to the *salon* with everything I owned in the way of furs and wraps, and found all the guests waiting for the Queen.

The equipages here are always *a la Daumon*—that is, open landaus—seats for four people inside, a rumble behind, and a seat for the coachman, if there Is a coachman, but the two postilions on the four horses are seemingly all that are required. In front of the garden-side *perron* were the two landaus waiting. The Queen, Madame Minghetti, and Johan sat inside of the first landau. General Garadaglia and I sat on the coachman's box and manoeuvered the brake. It happened rather often that we forgot to manoeuver. Then we would get a very reproachful glance from the postilions, and we would turn the brake on to the last wrench; then we would get another look because the wheels could not move. Somehow we never got the right tension. The Queen enjoyed our confusion.

When we passed through the small villages the whole populace would run out into the streets to gaze at us.

I thought it strange that the villagers, who must have seen the Queen hundreds of times, did not seem to recognize her, and sometimes bowed to me, thinking, I suppose, that I, being on the first seat, must naturally be the first person. How different it is in Denmark! When any royal carriage passes, people courtesy, sometimes even when the carriage is empty.

The Queen ordered the postilions to go slowly through the narrow streets of the village to avoid the risk of running over the crowds of children. I never saw so many. Eight or ten at each door! They all seemed to be of the same age, and all were dressed in red calico, which made a very pretty note of color against the shabby houses. There are a great many manufactories about here, and I suppose red calico must be cheap.

We reached the *palazzo* before sunset. I was quite chilled through in spite of all my wraps (heavy and warm as they were) and thankful to get out of them and get a hot cup of tea.

We found the Marquise Dadda and the Countess Somaglia, who had arrived for tea. The Queen always receives her friends at this time.

Another military dinner this evening! Evidently, Monza is polishing off the military just now. It is very amusing for us, as it gives us the chance to see all the celebrities. I sat to the left of his Majesty, and he told me in a loud voice who every one was and what each one had done. He did not seem to mind their hearing. Pointing to one of the generals, he said, laughingly: "He is *tout ce qu'il y a de plus militaire*; even his night-gowns have epaulettes on them, and he sleeps with one hand on his sword."

MONZA, *6th of November.*

Dear ____,—Signor Bonghi, the great Italian savant, arrived for luncheon to-day. He is a personality! I will describe him later. I will only say now he is most learned and very absent-minded. After luncheon the Queen wanted us to see the old cathedral of Monza, where, as you know, the famous iron crown of Charlemagne is kept. So after lunch the landau was ordered for us. Marquise Trotti (*dame d'honneur*) accompanied us. The Queen asked Signor Bonghi to go with us to explain things. Quite a crowd collected about the church door to stare at the court equipages. The handsome tall servants, in their brilliant red liveries, were alone worth looking at.

It is very much of a ceremony to see the iron crown. After having visited the cathedral thoroughly we were conducted down some steps to the little chapel which contains the crown. The priest is obliged to put on the robes of high mass, and is assisted by another priest and a boy who swings the censer all the time. The *cappellano* collected the money (twenty lire) from our party before the proceedings. (It is always well to be on the safe side.) The money question settled, the priest read some prayers, knelt many times, then ascended a little step-ladder, opened a gilded cupboard which was fastened to the wall, unlocked it, said some more prayers, and then with great reverence took out a casket, which he held high above his head, intoning a special prayer. He came down from the step-ladder, bringing the casket with him, which he opened, and we were allowed to look at, but not touch, the celebrated relic. The same ceremony was gone through when it was replaced.

Do you know that this crown was born in the year 593, and is made out of a nail supposed to be taken from Christ's cross and hammered into a ring, and is encircled by a gold band about eight centimeters wide? Outside the iron is a gold band set with *soi-disant* precious stones. Not much to look at, and certainly not heavy to wear.

While we were there Signor Bonghi, at the request of the Queen, copied a Latin inscription on a tomb. He translated it from the Latin and gave it to the Queen when he returned, also to me. (I inclose it.)

INSCRIPTION ON A TOMB IN MONZA CATHEDRAL

Quod fuit, est; erit peril articulo brevis horae
Ergo quid prodest esse fuisse fore
Esse fuisse fore trio florida sunt sine flore
Cum simul omne peril quod fuit est erit.

That which is, that which has been, that which shall be

Perishes in one short hour.

To what use is it to exist, to have existed,

Or to exist in time to come?

The Present, the Past, the Future

Are three flowers without perfume,

Since all perish together,

The Present, the Past, the Future.

Princess Pia di Savoya, Princess Trivulzio, Count Greppi, and others were invited to tea. After they had gone the Queen had a fancy to run out in the park without a hat, in spite of the cold and drizzly rain, and with only a light cloak. She did not mind, so no one else minded. Of course, we all did as she did, except Princess Palavicini (*dame d'honneur*), who had just arrived, and who asked permission that she might retire to her room in order to rest before dinner.

MONZA, *November 7th.*

Dear Mother,—I try every day to get a moment to write, as you desire, but the days go so quickly and the evenings come so soon that I hardly have time to do anything but change from one dress to the other.

After luncheon this morning the King ordered some large scales to be brought into the *salon*, and we were all weighed. Our kilos were written in a book, and each person was asked to write his name under his kilo. This took a long time. The Queen weighs twenty kilos less than Johan. There was a twinkle in the eye of the King when General Pasi got on the scales. General Pasi is enormously tall, and big in proportion, being a good deal more than six feet and very stout. They piled on all the weights they had, but nothing sufficed. Pasi looked aghast (Could the royal board be so fattening?) ... and wondered if it were not time for heroic action. And when it was found that the King had had his foot on the scales all the time every one was convulsed with laughter, especially the King, who enjoyed his little joke. The Queen's drive to-day was to the Marquise Dadda's (one of her ladies in waiting), who has a pretty villa and park near here.

We had thought of leaving Monza to-day, but the Queen wished us to stay longer, and of course we did not refuse, though my toilets were at a rather low ebb, having thought to remain only a few days.

I sat to the left of the King at dinner. He seemed very melancholy, and told me that never in his life had he had such a painful experience as he had this afternoon. A few days ago a quite young soldier had struck his superior officer and had been sentenced to death. The King said: "He is to be shot to-morrow in the barracks near the park, and this afternoon his poor mother, accompanied by the priest, came to the palace to make a last and supreme effort to obtain pardon. His mother clung to my knees and wept her soul out: 'He is my only child and only nineteen years old—too young to die. Take me instead. *Sono vecchia, egli tanto giovine!* ['I am old, and he so young!'] The priest added that the boy had always been such a good son—kind and gentle to his mother—and begged that he should be pardoned." The King repeated all this with tears in his good eyes.

"I am sure that your Majesty did pardon him. Did you not?"

"No," he said, "though it broke my heart to refuse. In military affairs one must not interfere with the discipline."

"But this one," I urged, tearfully; "could there not be extenuating circumstances? Do pardon him, your Majesty. Just think what that would mean for the poor mother."

But the King, true to his ideas of military discipline, said: "No! He is condemned to die. He must die."

The King could not shake off the impression this interview had made on him, and J., who passed the evening in the smoking-room with his Majesty, said that he never saw the King so depressed as he was this evening.

The Queen came up to me directly after dinner, saying: "What *were* you and the King talking about? You both looked so serious and sad."

I told her.

She said, "The King has such a good heart."

The thought of the poor young fellow who was to be shot kept me awake, and I thought at five o'clock that I heard the report of guns, but I was not sure. My imagination was so keen that I could have pictured anything to myself.

The first thing the King said to me at luncheon was, "Did you hear this morning?"

I told him I heard something, but I dreaded to think what it might have meant.

"Alas!" he said, as his eyes filled with tears, "it is too true, I hate to think of it."

We left Monza at three o'clock this afternoon, I cannot tell you how kind their Majesties were to me! The Queen kissed me good-by and said, "*Au revoir à Rome.*"

The King gave me his arm and went down the steps of the grand staircase of the principal entrance with me and put me himself in the landau. "You do not know what an honor this is," said Signor Peruzzi—as if I did not appreciate it!

We drove to the station in state and traveled in the royal compartment to Milan.... We intended to leave for Rome and home this evening, but I feel too tired to do anything but send to you these few lines and go to bed.

To-morrow night will find us in the Palazzo Tittoni, where the children already have arrived.

ROME, *January, 1885*.

Dear Aunt Maria,—Just now we are reveling in Liszt. Rome is wild over him, and one leaves no stone unturned in order to meet him. Fortunate are those who have even a glimpse of him, and thrice blessed are those who *know* and hear him. He is the prince of musicians—in fact, he is treated like a prince. He always has the precedence over every one; even Ambassadors—so tenacious of their rights—give them up without hesitation. Every one is happy to pay this homage to genius.

We met him the first time at M. de Schlözer's dinner. Schlözer, with his usual tact, plied him well with good food, gave him the best of wines and a superlative cigar. (Liszt is a great epicure and an inveterate smoker.) M. de Schlözer never mentioned the word "music," but made Liszt talk, and that was just the thing Liszt wanted to do, until, seeing that he was not expected to play, he was crazy to get to the piano. Finally he could not resist, and said to Schlözer, "Do play something for me!"

"Never!" said Schlözer. "I would not dare."

Then Liszt turned to me and asked me to sing. I also said, "I would not dare." Whereupon he said, "Well, since no one will do anything, I will play myself."

(The Minghettis, von Keudell, and Count Arco, Schlözer's secretary, were the guests.)

How divinely he played! He seemed to be inspired. Certainly the enthusiastic and sympathetic listeners were worthy to be his audience.

"Do you still sing Massenet?" he said to me. "Do you recollect my dining with you in Paris, and your singing those exquisite songs?"

"Recollect it!" I cried. "How do you think I could ever forget?"

"Will you not sing? I will accompany you," he said. "Have you any of Massenet's songs?"

"I have nothing with me to-night. I never dreamt of singing," I answered.

Schlözer said: "That is no obstacle. I will send a servant to your house directly to fetch the music." And in a very short time the music was in my hands.

Then Liszt sat down and, turning over the pages, found what he wanted, and I sang. Schlözer was radiantly happy. There was not one disturbing element. Every one was as appreciative as he was himself—those who listened as well as those who performed.

NOTE FROM F. LISZT

Liszt was at his best; I mean that he could not have been better. Knowing that Count Arco sang, he insisted on hearing him. Arco at first declined, but finally yielded—there was no resisting the arch-charmer. Liszt played the "*Suoni la tromba*" (Arco's *cheval de bataille*), by heart, of course, singing himself, to help the timid singer, and adding variations on the piano.

Liszt was in such high spirits that we would not have been surprised if he had danced a jig. He threw his long hair back from his forehead, as if to throw care to the winds. Later he spread his large hands over the keyboard in protest and said, "*No more from me*, but we must hear Schlözer before we go." Therefore Schlözer was obliged to play. He can only improvise, as you know. Liszt sat by his side and played a helpful bass.

Schlözer ordered some champagne, and we all drank one another's healths. It was after one o'clock when we bade our host adieu. Johan and I took Liszt in our carriage and left him at his apartment in the Via Margutta on our way home.

We saw a great deal of him afterward, and he dined with us twice. The first time we asked Grieg, the Norwegian genius, thinking it would please Liszt to meet him. Perhaps this was a mistake. However, it was a most interesting evening. Mrs. Grieg sang charmingly (Grieg's songs, of course); and Liszt, with his hands folded in front of him, was lost in thought—or was he asleep? Let us say he *dozed*—only waking up to clap his hands and cry "Brava!" But it was perfectly wonderful when he read at sight a concerto of Grieg's, in manuscript, which Grieg had brought with him. Liszt played it off as if he had known it all his life, reading all the orchestra parts. Both these great artists were enchanted with each other, but after a while Liszt became tired of music and asked if we could not have a game of whist. To play a banal game of whist with Liszt seemed a sacrilege, but we played, all the same. I was very *distraite*, seeing Grieg and his wife (who do not play cards) wandering restlessly around the room, and sometimes I put on an ace when a two would have done the deed.

Liszt plays the piano better than he plays whist. I don't know how many times he revoked. Every one pretended not to notice, and we paid up at the finish without a murmur. He was delighted to win four lire and something, and counted out the small change quite conscientiously. Johan drove him home—a very tired and sleepy Liszt—and only left him at the sill of his door.

I received a very queer letter the day Liszt dined here. I copy it for you. It was from the Princess W____, a lady whose friendship he renounced when he took holy orders.

I hear that you are going to have the Master (*le Maître*) to dine at your house. I beg of you to see that he does not sit in a draught of air, or that the cigar he will smoke will not be too strong, and the coffee he drinks will be weak, for he cannot sleep after, and please see that he is brought safely to his apartment.

Yours, etc., etc.

All these instructions were carried out to the letter. On another occasion Liszt wrote to me that he would bring some of his songs to try over at five o'clock. I inclose his letter. What a chance, thought I, for me to give pleasure to some of my friends who I knew were longing to see him. Although he had said *entre nous* in his letter, and I knew that he really wanted to look through the songs alone with me, I could not resist the temptation—though it was such rank disobedience—and said to them:

"Liszt is coming to me at five o'clock. If you would like to hear him, and consent to be hidden behind a door, I will invite you." They all accepted with rapture, and were assembled in the little *salon* before the time appointed. The door was left open and a large screen placed before it.

Johan fetched Liszt in our carriage, as he always does. I received him and the book of *Lieder*, which he brought with him. (Only Johan and Nina were present.) He opened the book at "*Comment disaient ils?*"—one of his most beautiful songs, which has an exquisite but very difficult accompaniment. He played with fairy fingers, and we went over it several times. I could see the screen swerving and waving about; but Liszt's back was turned, so he could not see it.

After we had finished tea was served, and then he said, "Have you heard my 'Rigoletto'?"

"Yes," I said, "but not by you."

"Well," he said, "I will play it for you. Your piano is better than the one I have. It is a pleasure to play on it."

The screen, now alive with emotion, almost tipped over. After "Rigoletto" he played "*Les soirées de Vienne*," and this time the screen actually did topple over and exposed to view the group of ladies huddled behind it. I shuddered to think how the Master would take this horrible treachery.

He took it better than I expected—in fact, he laughed outright. The ladies came forward and were presented to him, and were delighted. I am sure that Liszt was, too; at any rate, he laughed so much at my ruse and contrition that the tears rolled down his cheeks. He wiped them away with his pocket-handkerchief, which had an embroidered "F.L." in the corner. This he left behind, and I kept it as a souvenir.

Some days after this there was a large dinner given by the German Ambassador (Herr von Keudell) for the Princess Frederick Carl. Liszt and many others, including ourselves, were present. The Ambassador allowed the gentlemen only a short time to smoke; he gave them good but small cigars. I do not know how the great Master liked this, for he is a fervent smoker. However, as *le charbonnier est maître chez lui*, our host had his way and the music commenced, as he wished, very soon after dinner. Both the Ambassador and his wife are perfect pianists.

They play four-hand pieces on two pianos. On this occasion, to do honor to the famous composer, they grappled with a formidable work by Liszt, called "Mazeppa." (I fancy that Liszt is a little like Rossini, who used to say, "*Jouez pour moi toute autre chose que ma musique.*") Mazeppa's wild scampering over the two keyboards made our hair stand on end, but the Master dozed off in peaceful slumber and only waked up and cried "Bravo!" when Mazeppa had finished careering and the two pianists were wiping their perspiring brows. Liszt begged the Princess to whistle, and opened his book of *Lieder* at "*Es muss ein wunderbares sein*" (a lovely song) and said, "Can you whistle that?" Yes, she could; and did it very carefully and in a *wunderbares* manner. Liszt was astonished and delighted.

Then Liszt played. Each time I hear him I say, "Never has he played like this." How can a person surpass himself? Liszt does. He had the music of "*Comment disaient ils?*" in the same book and begged me to sing it. "Do you think," he said, "you could add this little cadenza at the end?" And he played it for me.

"I think so," I said. "It does not seem very difficult," and hummed it.

"I had better write it for you," he said, "so that you will not forget it." And he took out his visiting-card and wrote it on the back. (I send it to you.)

FROM F. LISZT
Handwritten music score.

Liszt is not always as amiable as this. He resents people counting on his playing. When Baroness K. inveigled him into promising to take tea with her because he knew her father, she, on his accepting, invited a lot of friends, holding out hopes that Liszt would play. She pushed the piano into the middle of the room—no one could have possibly failed to see it.

Every one was on the *qui vive* when Liszt arrived, and breathless with anticipation. Liszt, who had had many surprises of this sort, I imagine, saw the situation at a glance. After several people had been presented to him, Liszt, with his most captivating smile, said to the hostess:

"*Où est votre piano, chère madame?*" and looked all about for the piano, though it was within an inch of his nose.

"Oh, Monseigneur! Would you, really...?" advancing toward the piano triumphantly. "You are too kind. I never should have dared to ask you." And, waving her hand toward it, "*Here* is the piano!"

"Ah," said Liszt, who loves a joke, "*c'est vrai. Je voulais y poser mon chapeau.*"

Very crestfallen, but undaunted, the Baroness cried, "But, Monseigneur, you will not refuse, if only to play a scale—merely to *touch* the piano!"

But Liszt, as unkind as she was tactless, answered, coldly, "Madame, I never play my scales in the afternoon," and turned his back on her and talked with Madame Helbig.

As they stood there together, he and Madame Helbig, one could not see very much difference between them. She is as tall as Liszt, wears her hair short, and is attired in a long water-proof which looks like a soutane; and he wears his hair long, and is attired in a long soutane which looks like a water-proof. As regards their clothes, the only noticeable difference was that her gown was buttoned down the front and his was not. Both have the same broad and urbane smile.

One of the last dinners with Liszt before he left Rome was at the Duke and Duchess Sermonetas'—the Minghettis, the Keudells, Schlözer, and ourselves. Lenbach, the celebrated painter, was invited, but forgot all about the invitation until long after the dinner. Then he hurriedly donned a *redingote* and appeared, flurried and distressed. Liszt was in one of his most delightful moods, and began improvising a tarantella, and Madame Minghetti jumped up suddenly and started to dance. Schlözer, catching the spirit of it, joined her. Who ever would have thought that the sedate German Minister to the Pope could have been so giddy! He knelt down, clapping his hands and snapping his fingers to imitate castanets. Madame Minghetti, though a grandmother, danced like a girl of sixteen, and Liszt at the piano played with Neapolitan gaiety! It was a moment never to be forgotten. Keudell's kind eyes beamed with joy. Lenbach looked over his spectacles and forgot his usual sarcastic smile. We all stood in an enchanted circle, clapping our hands in rhythmical measure.

Our good friend Ludolf, as Liszt's ambassador, asked the abbé—who has a great respect for "the powers that be"—to a beautiful dinner, to which we were invited, the Minghettis, the Keudells, and four others—making twelve in all. Madame Minghetti accepted for herself, but excused her husband, who she said was not to be in Rome that evening. Count Ludolf asked M. de Pitteurs (the Belgian Minister) to fill Minghetti's place.

Five minutes before dinner was announced, in came Madame Minghetti with Monsieur Minghetti.

"What!" cried the Count. "I did not expect *you*! Why did you not send me word that you were coming? We shall be thirteen at table, and that will never do."

Both M. and Mme. Minghetti were very much embarrassed.

"There is nothing easier," answered Signor Minghetti. "I can go home."

You may imagine that this was not very pleasant for the great Minghetti, who had probably never had such an experience in all his life.

Count Arco, seeing the situation, and as a solution to the difficulty, went across the street to the club, thinking that some one could be found. Fortunately, he succeeded, and you may be sure the emergency guest was only too delighted to make the fourteenth at *that* table.

The Minghettis kindly and magnanimously overlooked the Count's want of tact.

Liszt, as if he wished to make us forget this untimely incident, played after dinner as he had never played before. But nothing could suppress Count Ludolf—never mind where the *plats* were, his feet continued to get into them. Right in the middle of Liszt's most exquisite playing our irrepressible host said, in a loud voice:

"If any one wishes to have a game of whist, there are tables in the other room."

Liszt stopped short, but, seeing all our hands raised in holy horror at the thought of exchanging him for a game of whist, consented amiably to remain at the piano.

Liszt honored me by coming to my reception, brought by M. de Keudell—Liszt is always brought. Imagine the delight of my friends who came thus unexpectedly on the great Master. They made a circle around him, trying to edge near enough to get a word with him. He was extremely amiable and seemed pleased to create this manifestation of admiration. (Can one ever have enough?) There are two young musical geniuses here at the Villa Medici, both *premier prix de Rome*. One is Gabriel Pierné, surnamed "*Le Bébé*" because he is so small and looks so boyish—he really does not seem over fourteen years of age—and another, Paul Vidal, who is as good a pianist as Pierné, but not such a promising composer.

I asked Liszt if he would allow these two young artists to play some of their compositions for him. Liszt kindly consented, and the appointed day found them all in the *salon*. Liszt was enchanted (so he said); but how many times has he said, clapping the delighted artist on the shoulder, "*Mon cher, vous avez un très grand talent.... Vous irez loin; vous arriverez*," a great phrase! And then he would sit down at the piano, saying with a smile, "Do you play this?" and play it and crush him to atoms, and they would depart, having *la mort dans l'âme*, and overwhelmed with their imperfections. Instead of encouraging them, he discouraged them, poor fellows! Speaking of young artists in general, he said once, "*Il n'y a personne qui apprécie comme moi les bonnes intentions, mais je n'en aime pas toujours les résultats*."

You may believe that my artistic soul is full of joy when I can collect about me such artists as Liszt, Grieg, Sgambati, Pierné, Vidal, Mme. Helbig, and Countess Gigliucci, not to mention the Queen's *Gentilhomme de la reine* (Marquis Villamarina), who has the most delicious barytone voice I have ever heard—but he seems to think as little of this divine gift as if it were his umbrella. Vera (the singing-master) was prevented from coming to-day to the Queen's lesson, and Signor Marchetti replaced him. He is a very well-known composer, and has written an opera called "Ruy Blas," which has had quite a success here in Italy. The Queen and I sing a duet from it which is really charming.

Baron Renzis had some theatricals at his pretty villa in Piazza Indipendenza, in which Nina acted the principal *rôle*, in "L'été de St.-Martin." Senateur Alfieri (son of the celebrated Alfieri) took the part of the uncle. One of the thirteen pictures Lenbach painted of Nina was put on the stage and afterward brought before the curtain, but it created no enthusiasm—people did not think it did her justice.

One actor (a young Frenchman) had such a stage-fright that when he had to say this phrase (it was all he had to say), "*Le peintre vous a diablement flattée*," he said, "*Le diable vous a peintrement flattée*," which caused a roar of laughter and hurt Lenbach's feelings....

Massenet has just sent a complete collection of his songs—all six. I like the first two best—"*Poëme d'Avril*" and "*Poëme de Souvenir*." This last he dedicated to me. There stands on the title-page, "*Madame, Vous avez si gracieusement protege le Poëme d'Avril...*", etc. The "*Poëme d'Hiver*," "*Poëme d'Octobre*," and "*Poëme d'Amour*" have pretty things in them, but they are far from being so complete as the first ones. Massenet wrote the date of its composition on each title-page, and a few bars of music.

I took them to the Queen, and we looked them over together. She was enchanted, and thought them the most graceful and refined things she had ever heard. She said, "I envy you having them."

"Would your Majesty like to have some?" I asked.

"Yes, indeed; very much," she replied. "But I could never sing them. You would have to teach me how. They suit your voice, but would they mine? No one can sing them as you do."

"I learnt them with Massenet; that is why," I replied.

I wrote to Massenet and begged him to send the same collection to the Queen, as she had been so delighted with his songs, and added, "Don't forget to put your name, the dates, and a bar or two of music just like what you sent to me."

Most amiably he did what I asked for, and the Queen was more than pleased, and immediately thanked him through the Marquise Villamarina.

Massenet has become a great celebrity now. Twenty years ago, when he was struggling to get on in Paris, Auber and I helped him. I used to pay him five francs an hour for copying manuscripts. Now one pays twenty francs *just to look at him*!

Mr. Morgan, of London, has hired our good friend George Wurts's magnificent apartment in the relic-covered Palazzo Antici-Mattei. Wurts is secretary to the American Legation in Petersburg, but comes occasionally to see his friends in Rome, who all welcome him with delight. Mr. Morgan gives beautiful dinners, and, although he has as many fires as he can possibly have, the huge rooms are freezingly cold, and sometimes we sit wrapped in our mantles.

ROME, *1st of January, 1886.*

My dear Aunt,—All Johan's and my most affectionate greetings: "May the year which commences to-day bring you every joy." I am selfish enough to wish that it will bring *us* the joy of seeing you. You promised to make us a visit. Why not this spring?

It is six o'clock. I am sitting in my dressing-gown and feeling good for nothing. The diplomatic reception this afternoon was as brilliant as the others which I have described so often. The Queen was, *if possible*, more beautiful and gracious than ever. (I think the same each time I see her.) Every eye followed her. Does there exist in the world a more complete and lovely woman? To-day the Queen's dress was exquisite—a white satin covered with paillettes and beads, the court train of blue velvet heavily embroidered in silver. The tiara of diamonds, with great upward-pointed shaped pearls which her Majesty wore, was the King's New-year gift. "My Christmas present," the Queen told me.

The King seemed more talkative than usual; he spoke a long time with each person and smiled and laughed continually. Politics must be *easy*—like honors in whist. There is evidently no trouble in that quarter.

March.

Dear ____,—I have permission to tell the great secret. Nina is engaged to the young Dane I wrote to you about—a Count Raben-Levetzau. He is very charming and belongs to one of the best families in Denmark. We went to the German Ambassador's (Herr von Keudell's) ball last evening at the Palazzo Caffarelli, which the King and the Queen honored with their presence. As soon as I could, I approached the Queen, who was sitting in one of the gilded chairs on the *estrade* which does duty for a throne, and told her of Nina's engagement. She came forward to the edge of the platform and, beckoning Nina to come to her, held out her hand and kissed her on both cheeks before the whole assemblage. Of course, the news circulated as quick as lightning. When the King heard it he came straight up to us, and I presented Frederick to him. His Majesty was most affable, and said, smilingly, to Nina:

"Are we really going to lose you? We shall miss our beautiful stella" (star). And turning to Frederick, he said: "I do not give my consent *at all*. I think that I will forbid the banns."

Every one crowded around Nina, eager to congratulate her. Frederick was as radiant as a new-blossomed *fiancé* could possibly be.

March.

We are as busy as bees. The trousseau is being made by the nuns in the Trinita de Monti convent. The Queen sent Nina a beautiful point-lace fan with mother-of-pearl sticks. The Queen of Denmark sent her a bracelet with diamonds and pearls. Count Raben's family and all the colleagues have given her beautiful presents.

April 10th.

It is all over—Nina is married and gone.

Day before yesterday was a day of emotions. In the morning we went at ten o'clock to the Campidoglio, where the magistrate's offices are and where the *sindaco* (the Marquis Guiccioli, a great friend of Nina's) performed the civil marriage. He particularly wished to do this *en personne* as a special favor. He made a charming and affectionate speech and gave the pen we signed the contract with to Nina. Then we drove home, changed our dresses, and were ready at two o'clock for the real marriage at the church.

The church was filled to the last pew. When Nina came in on Johan's arm there was a murmur of admiration. She looked exquisitely in her bridal gown, and as she turned round before descending the altar steps and threw back her veil she was a vision of beauty, and I am sure she will be a "joy for ever." All Rome came to the reception at our house.

While at Sorrento we went one afternoon to take tea with the Marion Crawfords. They have a charming villa on the rocks. They seemed very glad to see us, and showed us all over the villa and their pretty garden. "My den," as Mr. Crawford called his sunny and comfortable library quite worthy of the lion he is. They are a very handsome couple. She is as sympathetic as he is, and they both talk in the most entertaining and lively manner. We had a delightful afternoon.

I was asked to sing at a charity concert to be given in the magnificent *Salle de Gardes* in the Barberini Palace. The concert was arranged by all the most fashionable ladies in Rome, who with the ladies of the court were *dames patronesses*.

I accepted, as the Queen expressed the wish that I should. She even selected the songs she thought best for the occasion, and was present with all the court, which, of course, gave great *éclat* to the concert.

Every place was taken, and, enormous as was the *salle*, it was crammed to its limit, people standing up by hundreds. Sarah Bernhardt, being in Rome, promised to lend her aid; she recited a monologue in her soft, melodious voice, but so low that it could hardly have been heard farther than the first few rows of seats.

I sang the "Rossignol" and Liszt's "*Que disaient ils?*" to Sgambati's accompaniment. Madame Helbig played the accompaniment of the "Capriciosa" of Blumenthal, the one that has all those wonderful cadenzas which run rampant through the different keys. Madame Helbig is a marvelous musician. I must tell you what she did. When I was soaring all alone up in the clouds without any earthly help in that long cadenza, she foresaw that I was not coming down on the right note and changed the key from four sharps to four flats without any one noticing it, thereby saving me from dire disaster.

Any musician can change from sharps to flats, but she was reading this very difficult accompaniment almost at first sight and before a large audience. I think that it was a tremendous *tour de force*.

AALHOLM, *August, 1886*.

My dear Aunt,—Did you receive the newspaper cuttings I sent you describing the home-coming of Frederick and Nina? Did they not read like fairy tales?

Aalholm Castle is situated on the sea. It is one of the most historic places in the country, and seems to have been bandied back and forth to pay the different kings' debts.

Christopher II. was imprisoned here (the prisons still exist), and two more moldy and unpleasant places to be shut up in cannot well be imagined. The guards used to walk up and down in front of the aperture through which food was passed to the unfortunate and damp monarch.

Later Aalholm came into Count Raben's family (in the eighteenth century). There are, of course, all sorts of legends and ghostly stories which, as in all ancient castles, are, with the family specter, absolutely necessary. Women in gauzy drapery have been seen roaming about in dark corridors, horses have been heard rattling their chains in the courtyard. Mirrors also do something, but I forget what. However, no phantoms, I believe, have been noticed during this generation; probably the building which is going on now has discouraged them on their prowling tours and routed them from their lairs. I have watched with interest for the last three weeks the workmen who are making a hole in the massive walls in a room next to mine. The walls are about ten feet thick and are made of great boulders, the space between being filled with mortar which time has made as hard as iron.

Every king or owner of Aalholm since the time it has stood on its legs seems to have had different ideas about windows. One sees on its tired old exterior traces of every kind and every period. Some round, some a mere slit in the wall, some with arches all helter-skelter, without any regard to symmetry or style.

Each owner made his window, and each successor bricked it up and put his window in its place. The building is very long, with two towers. It looks at a distance like a huge dachshund with head and tail sticking up. There is a chapel in one wing, which no one ever enters, and there is a theater in another wing, where in old times there were given plays.

The park is beautiful beyond words. You come across some old graves of vikings, of which nothing is left save the stones they used for the making of them. The treasures that they contained have long since been removed by a wise government in order to fill the national museums. Many gold and silver coins have been picked up *in the grounds*, and are turned to use by making tankards and bowls, and very pretty and interesting they are. On the walls of the large hall there are inscriptions which were made in the sixteenth century to commemorate the visits of different monarchs. King Frederick II., 1585, must have had many friends with him. Like our modern guest-book, each guest left his name and motto, which was painted on the walls, with his motto and his particular sign, such as a mug or a rake (I hope these did not refer to his personal attributes). One that King Frederick wrote seems to me to be very pathetic, and makes one think that his friends must have been ultra-treacherous and false. It reads: "*Mein hilf in Gott. Wildbracht allein ist treu.*" ("God is my help. Wildbracht [the name of his dog] alone is faithful.") Don't you think that has a sad note in it?

AALHOLM. BUILT IN 1100
In 1585 some changes were made and from time to time windows have been cut through the walls.

INSCRIPTIONS IN ONE OF THE ROOMS AT AALHOLM, BEARING THE DATE 1585

Those at the top are:

Left: "My hope is in God. Wildtbragt [his dog] alone is faithful.—Frederick II., King of Denmark and Norway."

Right: "God forgets not His own.—Soffia, Queen of Denmark."

Those below were made by members of the court, who attached their individual marks instead of signatures.

MILAN, HOTEL MILAN, *October 17, 1886.*

Dear Aunt M____,—Just think what luck I have had. They say that everything comes to those who wait, and what I have waited for has come at last. I have seen and made the acquaintance of Verdi, the famous. He always stops at this hotel, because he is a friend of the proprietor's, Mr. Spatz, who, knowing my desire to meet Verdi, said that he would arrange an interview. This he kindly did. Verdi received me in his *salon*. He looks just like his photographs—very interesting face with burning eyes. His welcome was just warm enough not to be cold. The conversation opened, of course, on music. I said that I admired his music more than that of any other composer in the world. This was stretching a point, but it brought a pale smile to his verdigris countenance (this is unworthy of the worst punster). I told him that I often had the honor of singing with the Queen, and that we sang many duets from his operas. He did not seem to be much impressed by this miracle and received it with amiable indifference.

I longed to hear him talk, but with the exception of a few "*veramentes*" and "*grazies*" he remained passive and silent. By way of saying something he asked me if I had heard Tamagno in "Othello."

"Yes," I said. "I cannot think of anything more splendid. I never heard anything to equal him, and Monsieur Maurel is equally fine, is he not?"

"His singing is well enough," answered Verdi, "but his accent is deplorable."

After this the conversation languished, and I feared it would die for want of fuel. I felt that I had been spinning my web in vain—that I might catch some other fly, but not Verdi, when suddenly he said:

"You tell me that you sing often with the Queen. Which duets of mine do you sing?" he asked with seeming interest.

I named several.

"What voice has the Queen? Soprano or contralto?"

"The Queen's voice is mezzo-soprano," I answered.

"And yours?" he asked.

"Mine is about the same, equally mezzo-soprano."

This seemed to amuse him.

"Do you think the Queen would like to have me write something [quite jocosely] equally mezzo-soprano?"

"I am sure that the Queen," I answered, gushingly, "would be overjoyed."

"*Bene*," said the great *maestro* with a smile. "Then I win."

"How enchanting!" I cried, crimson with enthusiasm. "But may I beg one thing?"

"Beg! *Je vous en prie.*"

"*Fa dieze* [F sharp] is a weak point in both our voices."

"*Bene*," he said, waving his hand toward his piano. "I will write a duet for you, and only put one G minor in it."

"G minor!" I exclaimed. "Why, that is—"

He interrupted, "Have you ever noticed that G minor is much easier to sing than P sharp?"

He did not wait for my assurance that I did not notice any difference, but said, suddenly, "When do you go to Monza?"

"We are waiting to hear. Perhaps to-morrow."

"Ah," he said, thoughtfully, as if turning over in his mind whether or not he could have the duet ready.

MONZA, *October 19th.*

Bonghi came yesterday. At the request of the Queen he read aloud my sketch of the Hamlet legend before the *promenade en voiture*. The Queen thanked me and said that she was going to keep the manuscript, but Bonghi cut my literary wings by pronouncing in his brusque way that, although it was interesting and he liked the contents, it was badly written.

"*Chère madame*," he said, "you write very well, but you do not know the art of punctuating. You write as the water runs, as the arrow flies; therefore, in reading what you have written I have no time to breathe. I cannot separate the different ideas. A comma means a *point d'arrêt*, a moment of repose. Every period should be an instant in which to digest a thought."

I felt crushed by this, but tried to defend myself by saying that I had only written it for one indulgent eye, and ended lamely by promising that the next time I wrote anything I would be more careful. "I will do as Mark Twain did—put the punctuations at the end, and one can take one's choice."

We had some music again this evening. The Duke played some solos on his violoncello. He has a beautiful instrument. If Amati made cellos (perhaps he did), he must have made this one.

At dinner I sat next to him.

He said, "I was very much interested in what you wrote about Hamlet."

"In spite of the lack of commas?" I asked.

"Yes, in spite of the lack of commas. But I wonder if all you wrote was true?"

"How can we ever find out?"

"I hate to think of him as a myth."

"Please don't think of him as a myth. Think of him as you always have; otherwise you will owe me a grudge."

Looking across the table to Signor Bonghi, he said: "He is a wonderful man. I like his name, too—Ruggiero Bonghi, *tout court*."

"It sounds," I said, "so full of strength and power and straight to the point, with no accessories, doesn't it?"

"You say that to *me*, who have twenty-four names."

"Twenty-four! Dear me! Do you know them all?"

"I must confess that I do not, but I will look them up in the Gotha and write them out for you."

"Twenty-four," I repeated. "How out of breath the priest who baptized you must have been!"

"Oh," cried the Prince, "he did not mind; he got a louis [twenty-franc piece] for each name."

ROME, PALAZZO SFORZA-CESARINI, *January, 1887*.

My dear Aunt,—After the reception of the Diplomats on the 1st of January we moved from Palazzo Tittoni to this, our new home.

We have in the largest *salon* an enormous and gorgeously sculptured chimneypiece which has a tiny fire-place that, when crammed full of wood, and after we have puffed our lungs out blowing on it and prodded it with tongs, etc., consents to smile and warm the chair nearest to it, but nothing else.

The ceiling (a work of art of some old master) is way up in the clouds; I am almost obliged to use an opera-glass to see which are angels' or cherubs' legs up there in the blue.

The figures in the corners, I suppose, represent Faith, Hope, and Charity; the fourth must be the Goddess of Plenty. She is emptying an enormous cornucopia over our heads of the most tempting fruit, which makes my mouth water and makes me wish she would drop some of it in my lap.

This palace used to belong to that nice hospitable family you've heard about—*the Borgias*. I dare say they did a good deal of their poisoning in these very *salons*.

We were rather agitated the other day when a hole was discovered in one of the walls. I put my hand way down in it as far as I could and pulled out a little bottle which contained some dark liquid. Poison, for sure! It looked very suspicious. Giuseppe, our Italian butler, who is as Italian as an Italian can be, was frightened out of his senses (the few he possesses) and held the bottle at arm's-length.

To test the contents of the vial he put half of it in some food he gave to a thin and forlorn cat who hovered about our kitchen, and for whom Giuseppe cherished no love. However, the cat survived with eight of its lives. Then a rabbit a friend of Giuseppe's wanted to get rid of was given the rest. He also lived and thrived. After these experiments we don't think much of Borgia poisons.

One of the rooms behind the *salon* (so large that it is divided into four) has the most beautiful frescoed ceiling. It is a pity that it is so dark there that one cannot see it properly. Perhaps originally it was a chapel and the frescoes were easier seen when the altar-candles were burning. But can one imagine a Borgia needing a chapel or a Borgia ever praying?

Just around the corner from us is the *campo di fiori* (field of flowers), where one might expect to buy flowers, but it is the one thing you do not find there. Everything else, from church ornaments to umbrellas, from silver candlesticks to old clothes, you can buy for a song not so musical as Mendelssohn's "without words"; on the contrary, the buying of the most insignificant object is accompanied by a volume of words screamed after the non-buyer in true Jewish style.

Then around another corner you come across the Torso, made famous by that witty tailor called Pasquino, where he placarded his satirical witticisms; his post-office for anonymous letters!

We have just come home from the Pantheon. There is held every year for the anniversary of King Victor Emmanuel's death a memorial service *pour le repos de son âme*. If it had been my soul it would never have reposed; it would have jumped up and clapped its wings to applaud the music, which, though always beautiful, to-day was divine.

I even forgot to freeze during the long two hours we stayed in the icy-cold building, open to wind and weather above and full of piercing draughts below. The marble pavement, which has collected damp and mold since 27 B.C., has long since become so wavy and uneven that you walk very unsteadily over it; the costly marbles of which the pavement is made in fine mosaic-work have sunken away from their contours centuries ago, so that now you only realize how beautiful it must have been in its prime.

The high and imposing catafalque, erected for this occasion, which filled the whole center of the large *basilique*, reaching almost to the dome, was surrounded by enormous candelabra containing wax candles as big as birch-trees.

The ministers of state and the diplomats had a *loge* reserved for them next to the orchestra, and, although there were carpets and rugs under our feet, the humidity and cold penetrated to the marrow of our stateful and diplomatic bones.

There were tiers of seats for people who were fortunate enough to procure tickets.

Gayarré, the wonderful Spanish tenor, sang several solos, each one more exquisite than the other. I have never heard a more beautiful voice, and certainly have never heard a more perfect artist. The way he phrases and manages his voice is a lesson in itself.

Tamagno, the famous Italian tenor, sings wonderfully also, but very differently. He gives out all the voice he has, and you are overcome with the strength and power and the compass of his unique voice. He is the *tenor robusto par excellence* of the world.

One cannot compare the two singers. Gayarré has the real quality of a tenor, exquisitely tender, suave, and still powerful. He has a way of keeping his voice bottled up until a grand climax; then he lets it swell out in a triumphal burst.

This funeral service is a very long and fatiguing affair. I pity the *carabinieri* (the soldiers) who are on service that day. Although they are men chosen for their powerful build, some of them cannot endure the fatigue of standing "at arms" the two hours that the service lasts. I suppose the poor things are put there from early dawn, and there they must stand, stiff and straight, with uplifted sword, without moving a muscle. We saw one (not this year, but last) faint dead away and drop in a heap on the marble steps of the altar. His sword and casque made a great clatter when they fell and rattled over the pavement. Four of his comrades rushed in, picked him up, and carried him out, staggering under his weight. He was replaced by another *carabinier* noiselessly and so quickly that you hardly knew that anything had happened.

The Argentina Theater attempted to give Wagner's Ring. It was a dismal performance. Wagner is not at his best in an Italian setting, with all the gas turned on and the scenery half tumbling down and the orchestra fiddling in full view.

In the first act of "Rheingold," where the three maidens are swimming, the poor girls, with hair of unequal lengths, sprawled about, their arms clutching at air, and held up to the roof by visible and shaky ropes, half the time forgetting to sing in their wild efforts to keep themselves from falling, separated from the audience only by a gauze curtain which was transparency itself.

DENMARK, *July, 1887.*

My dear Aunt,—Denmark in July is ideal. It is never too warm in the day and always cool at night.

I have been spending a few days with Howard on his farm.

On the Fourth of July Howard wished to give the peasants in the neighborhood an entertainment to celebrate his country's "glorious Fourth." He hoped to inspire them with due enthusiasm and give them a good day's sport.

The Danish peasant's idea of amusement is to walk leisurely to the place of rendezvous, to sit quietly and rest from his week's hard work, eat plenty of Smörrebrod (sandwiches), drink barrels of beer, have tobacco *ad libitum*, and finally to leave as lazily as he came.

This feast was going to be otherwise. Everything was to be done *à l'Américaine*. The Fourth fell on a Sunday, and the farmers all accepted and came on the stroke of the clock, dressed in their Sunday-best clothes, which are of heavy broadcloth, made in the fashion of Louis Philippe, voluminous over the hips, thick, heavy-soled boots, and with long snake-like pipes hanging from their mouths.

Howard had arranged all sorts of *gymkhana* sports, for which prizes were to be given. There were to be the long jump, the high jump, a running-race, catching the greased pig, pole-climbing, a race in a bag, and so forth.

"They shall have a high old time," said Howard.

Their dismay only equaled their astonishment when they were told what was expected of them. What! Jump, run, and be tied up in bags and climb poles? Was this the way that they were going to amuse themselves on this hot day? Were soiling their clothes, perspiring, and suffering tortures in their tight boots the delightful, reposeful feast they had been invited to? Their inborn politeness would not allow them to do otherwise than obey the wishes of their host. They tried their best to perform the feats put down on the program.

Their week's work of mowing, cutting trees, plowing, threshing, and the different things belonging to a farmer's life seemed child's play compared with this so-called enjoyment.

They did not understand why they got prizes for deeds they had not done, and received the box of cigars or silver mug with unperturbed serenity.

Consternation and resignation were the only expressions on their faces. Neither did they understand when they were told to cry "Hurrah!" and wave their hats after Howard should finish his oration. That he made standing on a table. He expatiated on the beauty of liberty and the soul-inspiring feeling of independence, and became quite eloquent. They cheered in a spiritless and cheerless manner. For them liberty was a high-sounding word which meant nothing. An enlightened government provided them with all they needed. Why have the bother to choose your doctor or your priest when all that is done for you? Only to pay taxes. Can anything be more simple?

The games H. tried to teach them were not successful. They stood in a circle and were told (Howard rubbed his hands in a dainty manner) that "this is the way we wash our clothes." This did not appeal to them; they knew too well how they washed theirs, and they saw no fun in imitating such every-day affairs as washing and ironing.

Every way "we did" things had to be explained at length and translated into Danish. And the most inexplicable of all the games was "Oranges and lemons." When they were asked if they wanted oranges or lemons; they all answered, truthfully and conscientiously, "Oranges." Who in his senses would prefer a sour lemon to a juicy orange? The result was that the battle was very one-sided—all oranges and only one lemon.

The dance was also rather dismal. The musicians played some national waltzes, and the guests shuffled about on the sanded floor, treading a slow measure and on one another's toes; the women held on to their partners by their shoulders, and the men clutched the women round their bulky waists. However, they all kept the measure, and some of the men really danced quite well.

The *finale* was the fireworks. It ought to have been a grand display, but the rockets were damp, the "wheels," which ought to have wheeled up in the air, merely whizzed on the ground and seemed to make for the nearest guest in an absolutely vicious manner. All the things that ought to have gone off stayed and sputtered.

As an entertainment it was a failure. The guests, however, had plenty to eat and drink, and carried away pockets full of tobacco and cigars, but it was rather pathetic to see the worn-out and weary farmers dragging their tired limbs slowly and ponderously down the avenue with a look of "Why all this?" depicted on their faces.

MONZA, *October 17th.*

After luncheon to-day we went out on the terrace to drink our coffee. The sun was warm and the air deliciously cool, a typical Italian autumn day. As we sat there we heard some mysterious noise which came from the side of the park where the avenue terminates and is divided from the deer-park by a large iron gate.

Looking down the avenue, we saw a man peering through the bars of the gate. He had a bear with him. Her Majesty was curious to see them and ordered the gate unlocked and the man and the bear permitted to enter. The man was quite young, with soft black eyes and dazzling teeth. He led the bear by a heavy iron chain passed through a ring in its nose. The Queen went down the steps and talked with him.

"Will he bite me if I pat him?" she asked.

"No, signora; he is very good" ("*E molto buono*"). He hesitated a moment, and then said, "Signora, will you tell me which of the ladies there is the *Regina?*" The Queen was immensely amused, and answered, "I am the Queen" ("*Son io la Regina*"). The young fellow was quite overcome, and threw himself on the ground and kissed the hem of her dress.

"How did you tame the bear?" inquired her Majesty.

He answered in a very agitated voice: "*Maesta*, it was very easy. Bears are not difficult to tame. One must only be kind and patient."

"You look," said the Queen, "as if *you* were very kind and patient."

The young Italian passed his hand lovingly over his companion's shaggy head, and as he looked up at the beautiful and smiling Queen his eyes filled with tears. "I love him," he said, simply; "he is my only friend." We, who stood near enough to hear, were trembling on the verge of weeping. He added, "We never leave each other; we eat and sleep together, and all I have I share with him."

I saw tears in the Queen's eyes, which she quickly wiped away; and, turning to the man, she asked, "Can he do any tricks?"

"*Si, maesta*, he can lie on his back and put his paws up in the air and hum."

This did not seem much of a trick, probably being a bear's customary attitude.

"Well," said the Queen, "let us see what he can do."

But, although the bear was addressed in terms of tenderest endearment and although we hoped that he would obey his master and do honor to the occasion, he did nothing of the kind. On the contrary, instead of lying down and humming he stood up his full height on his hind legs and began to waltz, swaying his long, plump body and shaking his thick, brown fur.

He opened his mouth wide, showing his white teeth and his great red tongue, and looked as if he were laughing and as if it was the funniest thing in the world that he was doing.

"He does not seem to be very obedient," smiled her Majesty.

"He is afraid," said the man, trying to make excuses for his pet.

"You must come again," said the Queen, "when your bear is better trained," and, turning to Signor Borea (her chamberlain), told him to give the man some money and direct him to the forester's lodge, where some food should be given to him.

The young Italian's face beamed with joy when he beheld the vast sum (twenty lire) he had received, and led his disobedient companion away in disgrace; but the bear, quite unconscious of being in disgrace, turned his head for a last friendly glance, walked on his hind legs in his clumsy and swaggering manner, but with a certain dignity, down the avenue.

The King, who was with us on the terrace, had been a silent witness of the whole scene, and, not being able to resist the promptings of his kind heart, followed the couple. We saw him put a gold piece in the brown palm of the poor fellow, whose "only friend" had failed him on this unique occasion. He seemed quite overcome by this Danaë-like shower of gold, and hesitated before taking the piece, thinking, perhaps, that on this occasion honesty might be the best policy, and said:

"The Queen has already given me much."

"That does not matter," said the King. "You must take what *I* give you. Do you know who I am?"

"No, signor. Are you Garibaldi?"

The King laughed. "No, I am not Garibaldi; I am the King."

This second surprise was too much for the little man, and he almost fell down in his emotion.

What his dreams were that night must have been like one of the Arabian Nights.

REGGIO, *October 17th.*

Dear ____,—Count Spaletti has a very fine *château* (a large park and a beautiful forest), where he and his family live in patriarchal style. It is the true Italian traditional home-life in every respect.

There is on the farm a large building in which the famous Parmesan cheese is made. We were shown the entire process from the milking of the cows down to the great wheels (which look like millstones) and the completed cheese. Milking is a process with which you are, perhaps, not familiar. It is done with the help of a maiden and a three-legged stool, while the cow goes on chewing the worn-out cud of her last meal, occasionally giving a Cenci-like glance of approbation.

But I won't tell you about that; I will let you in the secrets of Parmesan-cheese making, so that when you are eating it grated on macaroni you may know what an old stager you have to do with. The milk is put in great vats just as it comes from the *mesdames les vaches*; there it remains, occasionally turned around, not churned, with a wooden paddle, until it becomes a solid substance.

When it is hard enough to handle it is put into large round wooden forms and allowed to remain untouched—for how long do you think? *One year!* Then they put it under the oil *régime*—that is to say, olive-oil is poured through the cheese at regular intervals until the rind is as black and thick as leather. In four years it is ready to be sold. Each cheese weighs several hundred pounds, is a foot thick, and is as big as a cart-wheel. We eat it every day for luncheon and dinner. I like it so much better, fresh and straight from the farm (if anything four years old can be called fresh), than when stale and grated.

ROME, *1888.*

My dear Aunt,—Leo XIII.'s jubilee has been the means of bringing the world to Rome. Every day during these last weeks we have watched the carts passing our house piled with huge cases which contained the presents destined for the Holy Father.

The streets are filled with pilgrims from everywhere. One cannot look in any direction without seeing processions of nuns, priests, and monks of all nations and denominations, from the dingy brown Franciscans, the Capucines with their white mantles displaying their bare legs, to the youthful disciples of the Propaganda in their brilliant scarlet cassocks, not to speak of the *forestiere* armed with their red Baedekers, who are doing Rome and at the same time *doing* the Pope's Jubilee.

Everything and every one on the way to the Vatican.

We went to see the gifts, which are exposed in many rooms on the ground floor of the Vatican. There was an enormous quantity of things of every description, useful, ornamental, and superfluous. The windmills, bells, every sort of vehicle, rowboats, sailboats, and every modern invention had been put out in the Vatican gardens.

You can have no idea of the incredible amount of slippers sent (thousands of them); church *vêtements* by the hundreds, embroidered by millions of women who must have worked themselves blind; the most exquisite articles of needlework, incrusted with pearls and precious stones which have probably cost a mint of money.

The Princess del Drago's gift was a large diamond cross with an enormous emerald in the center, an heirloom from her mother, the Queen of Spain. There were many other private gifts which were equally valuable. Almost a ship-load of canned fruits and vegetables sent from America; these were arranged in a gigantic pyramid. Just to look at them made my mouth water and me homesick.

Ridiculous objects from *naïf* donors, such as babies' socks and jackets, and silver things for a lady's toilet-table, and other equally inappropriate things, must have surprised the Pope when he saw them. I have not mentioned the millions of francs the Pope received in money; he can easily dispose of that; and he intends, I believe, to make presents to every church in Italy of the different objects which can be useful. But what can he do with the babies' socks?

On last Thursday the Pope said mass in St. Peter's. It was the great event of the year.

As we are accredited to the Quirinal, of course I never can have the opportunity to be received by his Holiness; therefore I was very glad when the monsignore who is still *Dantefying* us offered to give me a *carte d'entrée*.

I was obliged to be at St. Peter's at a very early hour, and succeeded, owing to having a "friend at court" (the Swedish chamberlain to the Pope, Marquis de Lagergren), in getting an excellent place where I had a good view of the Pope and the whole ceremony. Ladies are dressed entirely in black, with black veils instead of hats, on these occasions.

There was a great deal of noise in the church—much scraping of chairs, rather loud talking, people being shown to their seats, and, above all other noises, *the organ*.

I cannot honestly say that the music was beautiful. With the exception of the days when the best singers of the Pope's choir sing, the music in St. Peter's is not good. The organ is as antiquated as the organist, who plays with all the stops pulled out.

The center of the church was filled with wooden benches and chairs. The altar was brilliantly lighted with hundreds of wax candles; the columns around it were hung with tawdry red damask curtains, which, in my opinion, rather took from the dignity of this magnificent church.

The Swiss Guards ushered people to their seats. They looked very picturesque in their costumes of bright red and yellow, slashed sleeves, and brass helmets.

In due time the serious and somber chamberlains, in their black satin and velvet costumes, appeared; next came the bishops, in their purple robes; and directly preceding his Holiness the Pope were the cardinals, in red. Then came the twelve men carrying the gold pontifical chair in which the Pope was seated; they walked very solemnly and slowly.

Every one dropped on his knees, and the Pope raised his thin white hand to bless the kneeling crowd.

He mounted the steps of the high altar and began reading mass. His voice was very feeble and scarcely audible.

It was very impressive. It would be impossible to give you an idea of the intense solemnity of this scene, especially for me, as I have no talent for description. Women wept and waved their wet handkerchiefs; the sterner sex would have done the same, I dare say, if they had not been ashamed to show so much emotion.

March 10, 1888.

The Emperor Wilhelm of Germany died yesterday. Though he was so very old, the news of his death was unexpected and cast a gloom over Rome. Of course, all gaieties are ended, and court mourning ordered for three weeks. King Umberto left directly for Genoa to meet the new Emperor, who started from San Remo on his way to Berlin. The dinner for King Umberto's birthday, which was to have been on the 14th, has been *décommandé*.

The Prince of Naples has already left for Berlin to represent the King at the Emperor's funeral—his first official act since he has become of age.

May 1, 1888.

My dear Aunt,—My letters are very uninteresting. I cannot help it. There is nothing going on in society. In fact, many of the Italians have left Rome, and the colleagues are resting on their oars—those who have any to rest on. I am resting on my "Pinafore" oars. How lucky we had it when we did!

Taking advantage of this moment of inactivity, the Roman ladies arranged a charity performance, for which Marquise Del Grillo (Madame Ristori) promised to give her services. She chose the famous play "Marie Antoinette," which is supposed to be one of her best. The tickets were to be procured only from the ladies of the committee (of which I was one), and, though they cost a fabulous price, the theater was crammed to suffocation.

Madame Ristori's acting was, of course, perfect, her voice musical, her Italian delicious, and her gestures were faultless. If one might dare criticize such an artist, one could say that her movements might have been a little more queenly, but a queen's grace and dignity must be very difficult to acquire from sheer imagination. Also her dress was far from what it ought to have been. I am sure no French dressmaker had the making of *that* gown. In the first act Marie Antoinette, in the *apothéose* of her glory, wore voluminous skirts and crinoline, according to the famous picture. Madame Ristori wore a crinoline, to be sure; but her dress was too short in front and showed her low-heeled shoes of white satin, and when she moved about her gown of heavy brocade swayed from side to side like a pendulum.

One recognized the great artist in the scene in the prison, where she bade the king and her children adieu. This was very touching, and there was not a dry eye in the audience. I know that *I* sniffed and wept and blew my nose, and was quite ashamed of showing my feelings so explosively.

I went to see her on her reception-day (the next Friday) and found her in her every-day surroundings, her pretty daughter hovering about with teacups and cakes, everything looking very home-like and prosaic, and Marie Antoinette eating sandwiches with a healthy appetite and talking of the latest gossip. I could hardly believe that I had shed so many tears over her sad fate a few nights ago.

The sad news of the death of Emperor Frederick came day before yesterday from San Remo. Every one had been expecting his death for months. The Italians loved him, and mourn him as if he had been their own. There is court mourning for three weeks.

MONZA, *October 1, 1888.*

My dear Aunt,—You ought to have a map of Europe continually under your eyes, and little pins to stick in the places where we last were. Space and distance are nothing to your "wandering jew(el)s." Going from Italy to Denmark and back again twice a year, we are obliged to traverse the whole of Europe, and, as "all roads lead to Rome," we can choose the one we like best.

Wherever we go we are enigmas to our fellow-travelers, who can never decide what nation we belong to. Johan talks Danish to me; we talk French to the governess, German to the valet, Italian to my maid, and English alternately. I think we would have puzzled the builders of the tower of Babel at that confusing moment when they all burst forth in unknown tongues.

ROME, *October 15, 1888.*

My dear Aunt,—We are having a series of entertainments in honor of the new Kaiser. This is his first official visit since he has become Emperor. He arrived here on the 11th at four o'clock.

We were invited by M. and Mme. Huffer to see the *entrée*. They being Germans, their decorations surpassed all others. Carpets out of every window, flags flying, and the German coat of arms placed in every available spot on their beautiful palace in the Via Nazionale. The King, accompanied by the Prince of Naples, followed by the Duke of Genoa, Duc d'Aosta, M. Crispi, Marquis Gravina, and Marquis Guiccioli, and other notabilities, drove to the station through a double line of troops on both sides of the street.

The usually dirty waiting-room in the station was hung with tapestries taken from the Quirinal and the splendid Louis XV. furniture taken from the beautiful Palace of Caserta.

The train which preceded the Emperor's, decked out with garlands and flags, came in sight, the traditional red carpet was laid down, the final orders shouted, and the Imperial train appeared. The soldiers presented arms, and the military bands struck up the German national hymn. The King wore the uniform of a general. He advanced to meet his Imperial guest. They embraced and kissed each other on both cheeks, then they presented the princes and the different members of their suites.

The Emperor was in the red uniform of the Hussars and looked very young and handsome.

In the first *berline* (as they call the demi-gala blue landaus) were the Emperor and the King; in the second were the Prince of Naples and Prince Henry of Prussia (the Emperor's brother); in the third the Duc d'Aosta and the Duke of Genoa; in the fourth, Count Herbert Bismarck and the German Ambassador (Count Solms). The other carriages, of which there must have been ten, contained the military and civil members of both the sovereigns.

There was a great demonstration in front of the Quirinal Palace. The Emperor and the King came out on the balcony amid screams of "*Eh! viva!*" One old man—a German, I suppose—who was covered with medals shouted at the top of his lungs. "*Hoch!*" hoping to make a sensation, but the Emperor made no sign that he heard it.

The next day (Friday), as had been arranged long beforehand, the Emperor made his visit to the Pope; the carriage from the Quirinal brought him to the residence of Herr von Schlözer (the German Minister to the Vatican), where the Emperor lunched and changed his uniform.

Schlözer's account of the luncheon was very amusing. His household was apparently not arranged for the reception of emperors. He and his secretary were in great straits to provide the proper luxuries for their august guest. Schlözer possessed nothing so frivolous as a mirror, therefore he sent to borrow ours. We sent him the one we thought best suited to the occasion. It was so different from Schlözer's modest belongings that the Emperor's quick eye guessed instantly that it was a stranger, and said, "Where did this come from?"

I give you Herr von Schlözer's account in his own language.

"I had no extra toilet things to put into the Emperor's room, but, fortunately, I had bought a cake of soap in Berlin; this I put on a piece of marble I had picked up in the Forum, which I thought would do for a soap-dish. The Emperor went into the adjoining room to change his uniform, and suddenly appeared in the doorway, holding out his wet hands, and said, '*Mein liebe* Schlözer, can't you give me a towel?' *Donnerwetter!* said Schlözer, that was the one thing that I had forgotten."

The luncheon was (excepting the famous wines on which he prides himself) of the simplest kind of Italian repasts, of which macaroni, frittura mista, and cutlets with saffron (*à la Milanais*) formed the chief feature. The Emperor was in the best of spirits and enjoyed it all, interlarded as it was with Schlözer's unique remarks.

The Emperor's own horses and carriages and *piqueurs* (brought expressly from Berlin for this one visit to the Pope) were waiting before the German Legation to convey his Majesty and Herr von Schlözer to the Vatican. The whole route through which they drove was lined with a double row of the national troops to the very steps of the Vatican. Every window was filled with people anxious to catch a glimpse of the handsome and youthful Emperor as he passed by in his open victoria; Prince Henry and Count Bismarck followed in another of the Emperor's carriages.

At the early hour of half past nine the *haute société*, the Ministers, the Senators and Deputies—in fact, *all Rome*—were summoned to meet the Emperor at the Campidoglia. It was to be lighted for the first time with electricity—a great event. People were to meet in the statue-gallery. After all were assembled, the King, the Queen, and the Emperor entered, followed by the princes and their different suites. The Emperor was dressed in the uniform of the *garde de corps* (all white) with a silver breastplate and silver helmet. He was an apparition! and did not look unlike one of the statues. Or was he a Lohengrin who had come in a swan-drawn skiff down the Tiber to save some Italian Elsa?

There were some presentations made. I, for one, was presented to his Imperial Majesty, and was charmed with his graciousness. We talked English, which I think rather pleased him, for he made some facetious remarks on things and people and actually laughed.

The next evening, the 18th, the fireworks and the illumination of the Forum, the Colosseum, and the Palatino, were the entertainment after a *dîner de famille*.

The Diplomatic Corps was bidden to the Villino. The place was rather too small to contain all the guests. Fortunately, it was a pleasant evening; there was a full moon which lent charm to the scene. Bengal lights, to my mind, are the cheapest form of illumination, but the fireworks—for which the Italians are so renowned—were splendid. Rockets of all colors, bursting in mid-air and sending down showers of lighted balls, were never-ending, and everything belonging to pyrotechnics was in profusion and perfection.

The *bouquet* (which is the French for the *apothéose*) surpassed everything I had ever seen before. It lasted several minutes. When everything has burned out, only the brilliant "W" with an Imperial crown remained, and faded gradually away.

ROME, *March, 1889.*

Dear Aunt,—Rome is placarded all over with blood-curdling pictures of "the Wild West Show" and portraits of our friend Buffalo Bill. I call him "our friend," although I can't say I know him very well. We traveled in the same car with him for a whole week on our way to California ten years ago. That is not enough, is it?

I had never seen a Wild West Show and was most eager to go; besides, I wanted to see "our friend" in his professional character. We made up a large party and went there *en bande*.

The tents were put up not far from the Vatican gardens, behind Castel St. Angelo. None of us had ever been to such a performance, and we were all delighted at the marvelous feats of lassoing by the cowboys and the rifle-shooting of the cowgirls, who looked so pretty in their short leather skirts and leggings. One of them threw pieces of silver in the air and shot them in two with her rifle. Everything was wonderful.

Duke Sermoneta, who went with us, having read on the posters that Buffalo Bill professed to tame any wild or vicious horse, wished to test Buffalo Bill's ability, and perhaps with a little maliciousness had ordered some of the wild horses from his estate to be brought to Rome.

These untamed horses are like those that used to run in the *corsi dei Barberi* during the carnival in Rome when Rome had carnivals. The Duke was very sure that no one could tame them, much less put a saddle on them; the audience, no doubt, thought the same. There was quite an excitement when the frightened things came rushing into the arena and stood looking about them with terrified eyes. But the cowboys knew very well what to do. They quickly lassoed them, and somehow, before we could see the whole process, they were forced to the ground, plunging about and making desperate efforts to get up. Finally, after many attempts, a saddle was placed on them, and lo and behold! the ferocious wild horses were conquered and, as meek as Mary's little lamb, were ridden around the arena to the accompaniment of great clapping, screaming, and applause. Every one was as enthusiastic as the Duke Sermoneta over the stubborn and agile young Wild-Westers. Then Buffalo Bill's herald came forward and proposed that the Italian *campagna* boys, who had brought the Duke's horses, should mount the American bucking horses. The Duke gave his consent readily. He was very willing that his men should show what they could do. Well, they showed what they could *not* do; they could not keep on the horses a minute, even if they managed to get on; they turned somersaults in every direction, fell off, and rolled about on the ground. The audience roared.

Buffalo Bill appeared on a beautiful horse, holding his gray sombrero in his hand, acknowledging the applause. He looks very handsome with his long, fair hair falling on his shoulders and his Charles-the-Second fine face.

The Duke said, "How I should like to speak to that man!"

We said that we knew him and that perhaps we could get him to come to us. I wrote on my card: "It would give M. de Hegermann and myself much pleasure to speak with you. We traveled in the same train with you to California some years ago, if you remember." I sent the card by a little page who was selling popcorn. At the first opportunity Buffalo Bill came, preceded by the boy. He said he "remembered us perfectly." I introduced him to the Duke, who, after having complimented him on his "show" and laughed over the awkward attempts of *his* boys, asked him if we might see the camp.

No gentleman from the court of Louis XV. could surpass Buffalo Bill's refined and courteous manners. He said if we would wait until the performance was over he would "show us about."

We did wait, and went all over the camp with him, and saw everything that was to be seen, and smelled the different fried things which lurked in every corner. Buffalo Bill beckoned to some of the cowboys to come forward and named them to us. I think they were delighted. They had such good, honest (and even handsome) faces. My heart warmed to them.

One said to me, "Why, you talk English as good as an American!"

"That is not wonderful," I answered; "I am an American."

"Is that so?" he asked. "Well, America's a pretty good place, ain't it? A good sight better than over here—that is what I think," and, pointing to the Duke Sermoneta said, "Is that gent American, too?"

"No," I answered. "He is an Italian. Those were his horses you tamed this afternoon."

"Is that so? Well, I would not like to tell him that them boys of his can't ride worth a cent and the horses ain't worth their hide."

I hoped that Duke Sermoneta had not overheard this conversation.

Buffalo Bill showed us a young Indian woman who had had a baby a few days ago.

"It was baptized this morning," he added. "What do you think it was called?"

"Is it a boy or a girl?" asked the Duke, looking at the brown, wizened face of the little thing, which was swaddled in an old shawl.

"A girl," answered the young mother, in English.

"Then I suppose you called it Roma," I said.

"No," said Buffalo Bill. "It is the custom among the Indians to give to the baby the name of the first thing the mother sees after its birth."

"Then they must have named it Tent," I said.

Buffalo Bill laughed. "No, you must guess again. It was called Saint Peter's."

"Poor little girl!" said the kind-hearted Duke, and put a gold piece in the ready and delighted hand of the mother.

ROME, *1890*.

Dear ____,—Signor Sonsogni, the promoter of music and art, gave several librettos of operas to different composers in Italy, and promised a large reward to the victorious competitor.

Signor Crispi kindly offered me his *loge*, thinking that it would interest me to be present at one of the performances. There had been many of these before, but nothing remarkable had so far been produced.

We arrived in the theater while they were playing a short opera of two acts, which was unfavorably received and quickly condemned with contempt and hisses.

The judges looked bored to death and discouraged, and the audience seemed ready to growl and grumble at anything.

Mugnoni led the orchestra in his usual excitable manner. If any of the operas had been good for anything they would have shown at their best under his masterful baton.

Then came the "Cavalleria Rusticana."

Already when the overture was played the audience was enchanted, and as it progressed the enthusiasm became greater and greater, the excited audience called for the *autore* (author).

Mascagni, urged and pushed forward from the sidewings, evidently against his will, appeared, looking very shabby in an old gray suit with trousers turned up, as if he had just come in from the street. His hair was long and unkempt, his face haggard and thin—evidently he had been starved and unwashed for weeks. This really was the case.

He bowed modestly and with a *naïf* awkwardness which was very pathetic. The Italian public, just as wild in its enthusiasm as it is merciless in its disapproval, rose as one man with a bound and cheered vociferously. But when the Intermezzo was played there was a burst of thundering applause, clapping of hands, and shouts of enthusiasm. I never heard anything like it.

Mascagni was called at least twenty times before the curtain. Any other composer would have beamed all over with joy and pride at such an ovation, but Mascagni only looked shy and bewildered. The tears rolled down my cheeks as I looked at the poor young fellow (he is only twenty years old), who probably that very morning was wondering how he could provide food for his wife and baby. Fancy what his emotions must have been to wake up so unexpectedly to glory and success!

FRANCESCO CRISPI
Prime Minister of Italy. From a photograph taken in 1887.

Mascagni, his wife, and his baby lived in a garret, and had not money enough to buy even a candle. The only instrument he had when he wrote the opera was an accordion. His little wife is nineteen, and the baby is one year old.

Italy thought it possessed another Verdi. The next day after his triumph Leghorn (his birthplace) gave him the citizenship of the town. Sonsogni handed him a large sum of money (the promised prize), and Mascagni had orders to begin on another opera. Will that be as good? One says that necessity is the mother of invention; it seems that in this case poverty was the father of "Cavalleria Rusticana."

1890.

Dear ____,—Johan is named to Stockholm, and we must leave Rome. Needless to say that I am broken-hearted to leave Italy and the Queen.

MILAN, *September 16.*

Dear ____,—We went yesterday to bid good-by to their Majesties, who are at Monza, and for J. to present his letters of *rappel.*

We arrived in time for luncheon; there were no other guests.

After luncheon we sat out under the trees by the side of the pretty lake; there was an awning put there, and we stayed all the afternoon in the shade of the large trees which bordered the lake. The King was very gay; he wanted every one to row out in the small boats that were there; then he and the Prince took another boat and tried to collide. The King pretended that he could not row, and made such hopeless attempts that all those in the other boats were splashed with water.

On taking leave of her Majesty, which was done with a great deal of weeping on my part, she handed me a beautiful sapphire-and-diamond brooch and a very large photograph signed by her dear hand *en souvenir.* The King gave Johan his photograph and the decoration of *la couronne d'Italie.* The day passed only too quickly. I cannot tell you how miserable I was to take leave of their Majesties, who had always been so kind and gracious to me.

But what use is it to mourn my fate. Nothing can change the fact that we are bidding good-by to Italy.

STOCKHOLM, 1890-1897

STOCKHOLM, *October, 1890*.

Dear L.,—We arrived here (our new post) at an early hour in the morning. We found the secretary and carriages waiting for us, and drove to the hotel, where we stayed until our apartment was quite ready. Our furniture from Rome has already arrived, so all we have to do now is, like coffee, to settle.

We have taken the same house that has been the Danish Legation for the last forty years, and where Johan used to live when he was secretary here twenty years ago.

The apartment is very large. It has twenty-four rooms, ten windows on Drottning Gatan, and thirteen on the side-street. The ballroom has five windows (three on one street and two on another); a large *salon*, two smaller *salons*, a library, and a spacious dining-room; and it has (quite rare in Stockholm) a *porte-cochère*. The Chancellery is in the courtyard, having its separate entrance and staircase.

The evening before we left Copenhagen we had the honor of dining with the King and Queen of Denmark, at Amalienborg. It was a family dinner, J. and I being the only guests. After dinner the Queen talked a long time with me and handed me the letter she had written to the Queen of Sweden.

"I told her," she said, "that I was very fond of you, and I knew that she would be equally so. And how the Duke of Nassau [her brother] admired you and your singing."

"If your Majesty hadn't said it, I never would have believed that the Duke liked my singing. I was under the impression that he would have liked me better without the singing."

"Yes," the Queen said, "I confess that he is not musical, and does not like *all* music, but he really did like to hear you sing. He told me so."

"Of course he knows," I answered, "but he is the last person from whom I expected to receive a compliment."

As their Majesties retired, the Queen held out her hand, and when I stooped to kiss it she kissed me affectionately on both cheeks. The King, on shaking hands with me, said, "*God Reise*" which is Danish for *bon voyage*.

The first days in a new post are always very busy ones. My first visit was to *the doyenne* of the *Corps Diplomatique*, Baroness Ph. She gave me a list of visits to be made, and a quantity of her own cards with *pour présenter* with mine.

Yesterday J. was received by the King, and presented his *lettres de créance*.

Although J. had been Secretary of Legation, and had been groomsman at the marriage in Stockholm of the Crown Prince of Denmark to Princess Louise (niece of King Oscar), and was very well known to the King, all the regular formalities had to be gone through with. J. made his traditional official speech to the King, both standing; and the King solemnly answered with an elaborate assurance that the relations between Sweden and Denmark had always been of the best and that they would remain so.

When the ceremonious utterances were ended, the King put his arm on J.'s shoulder and said: "Now let us sit down and have a good talk together of old times." The King "thee-and-thoued" Johan, and said, "*Her, du. Naar kommer din husfru?*" which in English means, "Listen thou. When is thy wife coming?" It is so strange that the Swedish language has no word for *you*. One must either address people by their title, which is sometimes very awkward, or else say *thou*.

I was dreadfully puzzled when I first came here. Right opposite my window was a sign, "*Dam Bad Rum!*" I said: "How queer! People generally cry up their wares, not down. Who ever heard of a seller saying that his rum was as bad as that?" I found out afterward that the sign was merely to let people know that a ladies' bath-room was to be found there.

The next excitement was my audience with the Queen, and thereby hangs, if not a tale, a teapot with a tempest in it. I must tell you all about it. I hope you will appreciate the tremendously complicated position in which I was placed.

It seems that in the time of Queen Christina of Sweden, one hundred and fifty years ago, the ladies of her court wore black silk or satin dresses and sleeves of a certain pattern. The court has seen no reason to make any change of dress since that time. To-day it wears the same style of dress and the same *sleeves*—the cause of the tempest!

In answer to my request for an audience I received a letter from the *grande maîtresse*, saying that the Queen would receive me on Thursday next; the *doyenne* of the *Corps Diplomatique* would present me. Then followed instructions: my dress was to be a black satin ball-dress, a train of four meters, lined with black silk, *décolleté*, white *glacé* gloves, *et les manches de cour*. I had no idea what *les manches de cour* were, and, naturally, I went to the *doyenne* to find out.

If I had announced that I intended to throw a bomb under the King's nose the effect could not have been more startling than when I said those fatal words, "*Les manches de cour.*"

Madame la doyenne was so overcome that for a moment speech left her. She proceeded to tell me that in order to keep on the right side of the colleagues it would be advisable *not* to wear the sleeves.

"Why not?" I asked, perplexed. "My husband says it is only on this one occasion that a foreign minister's wife is required to wear the sleeves."

She acknowledged that this was true, but the diplomatic ladies had refused to wear them, and it was as much as peace and happiness were worth to displease the colleagues.

"How can they refuse?" I asked.

She explained that the idea of wearing the sleeves was disagreeable to them; therefore the court had passed over the point and made a compromise: the Queen received them at the summer palace, Drottningholm, *en toilette de ville*. In this way the difficulty had been temporarily overcome, but now it seemed they wished me to draw the chestnuts out of the fire.

"What am I to do?" I asked. "The only thing I can see is to leave Stockholm, my home, and my family, and come back in the summer when I can wear a bonnet."

I meant this as a tremendous satire, but she took it quite seriously and said, "That would be wiser."

I smiled and, handing her the letter I had in my hand, I said, "In this letter from the *grande maîtresse* she said you were to present me."

"Of course I am to present you, but I refuse to wear the sleeves."

"If such is the case," I said, "what would you advise me to do?"

She answered: "I would advise you to avoid wearing the sleeves. You will make a precedent which all the *Corps Diplomatique* will resent."

"Why should the ladies object to the sleeves?" I ventured to ask. "Are they so unbecoming?"

"It is not that they are unbecoming, but the Ministers' wives dislike being dictated to. They say that they represent their sovereigns, and object to be told what they shall wear and what they shall *not* wear."

I remarked that at the Court of St. James's no lady ever dreamt of objecting to wear the three plumes and the long tulle veil prescribed by *that* court, and I could not see any difference so long as it was their Majesties' wish.

To this she replied, "I think you will regret it if you offend the whole *Corps Diplomatique*."

On this I took my leave and drove straight to the *grande maîtresse*. My back was up, and even if the *Corps Diplomatique's* back was up, too, I was determined to do nothing to displease the Court of Sweden. I explained the situation to the Baroness Axerhjelm, who already knew it, of course, better than I did. I could see it was a sore point.

When I asked her to explain to me about the sleeves she offered to send for them that I might see them, and to lend me her sleeves that I might copy them.

When I looked at the offending sleeves I did not think they were so appalling—only two white satin puffs held in with straps of narrow black velvet ribbon. On a black corsage they could not be so dreadful, especially as the fashion now is sleeves puffed to exaggeration. How silly!

We received visit after visit and many letters from the now irate Corps—so many that we were quite bewildered. J. looked through the archives of the Legation to see if he could find anything bearing on this subject, but in vain. The mighty question does not seem to have troubled my predecessors. They seem to have worn the sleeves and gone on living.

J. remembered that the wife of his former Minister, on the occasion of the marriage of the Crown Prince, wore them. I decided to write to the Queen of Denmark to ask her advice, telling her of the threatened antagonism against me.

This is her letter in reply:

I advise you, dear Lillie, to do as their Majesties desire. The Crown Princess always wears the sleeves when in Stockholm, and I think it would be more polite and less awkward if you wore them also.

Therefore I had them made. Thursday came: my dress was ready and the obnoxious sleeves in their places, I quite admired them, and would not have minded wearing them every day. Still, I could not but think how a whole ballroom of ladies with them on must have appeared in Queen Christina's time.

Although it was the duty of the Baroness to accompany me, I was not surprised when I received a long letter explaining how a severe headache had suddenly swooped down on her and would deprive her of that pleasure.

That was her way of getting over this *impasse*.

The situation was awkward. This refusal at the eleventh hour was very annoying. I was not expected alone, but alone I should have to go. There was no alternative, and the absence of the *doyenne* must explain itself as best it could.

I arrived in solitary grandeur, and was conducted in state to the *salon*, where the *grande maîtresse*—with the sleeves, of course!—was ready to receive me. She did not seem in the least surprised at seeing me alone; possibly the *doyenne* had written her own account of the headache. I could see that she applauded the stand I had taken, so I felt that if I had lost favor with my colleagues I had gained it at court.

We went together to the *salon*, where we found the Queen. She rose and gave me her hand, and I bowed low over it. She was dressed all in black, with the white satin sleeves conspicuous under a long lace veil which hung from her head. She is very fine-looking, tall, and imposing, with a quiet and serious manner. She looks the personification of goodness.

I gave her the letter the Queen of Denmark had sent her. Then she talked of her brother (Duke of Nassau), and said he had written about me and my singing, when we were both guests at *Château Furstenberg*. The Queen added, "My brother is not musical" (indeed he was not), "but he said no singing had ever pleased him like yours." I bowed and tried not to look incredulous. "The King," she said, "is looking forward with great pleasure to seeing you again. He remembers a certain song you sang. Was it not 'Beware,' or something like that?"

I did not think it unlikely. I had sung it often enough, goodness knows.

I replied I did sing a song called that.

The dire step had been taken, and as far as sleeves were concerned the incident was closed.

When I reached home I changed my dress and drove to the house of the "suffering" *doyenne*. She had not expected such quick inquiries, for she looked the picture of health; and I met on the staircase a court lackey evidently bent on the same errand. She stammered a great many things about her headache, and how, when she had that particular *kind* of headache, she was incapacitated from any effort. I sympathized deeply with her.

Her first question was, "Did the Queen have on the sleeves?"

"Certainly," I answered, curtly.

January, 1891.

Dear L.,—King Oscar is a king after one's ideas of what a king ought to be. He looks the king every inch of him, and that is saying a good deal, because he is over six feet. He has a splendid physique, is handsome and of much talent. He is a writer and a poet, and speaks all languages. You must be told that some kings are kings; but King Oscar, there is no doubt about what he is!

At a concert the other evening he came and sat by me, and began talking of music, of *his* singing, and *my* singing, and so forth, and finished by saying, "Would you like to have me come to you some day and sing?"

"Of course, your Majesty," I said. "I should be delighted. When may we have the honor of expecting you?"

"How would next Thursday be?" he asked. "And would half past two be agreeable to you?"

I replied, "Any day or any hour will suit me," although it was in fact the only day which did *not* suit me, as it was my reception-day.

"I hope that we may be quite by ourselves," said the King. "Only you and the members of your Legation."

This I could easily promise, as I should have, in any case, closed my doors.

"Your Majesty will stay and have a cup of tea. I hope."

"With pleasure," he answered, "if that will not make my visit too long."

"Too long, your Majesty! How could it be too long?"

"Well, then, you may expect me."

How prepare for *les détails*? Madame de Sevigny writes somewhere, "*que les détails sont aussi chers à ceux que nous aimons, qu'ils sont ennuyeux aux autres.*"

The servants laid the traditional red carpet on the staircase. Palms and plants were put in every possible place.

At two o'clock the servants were already on the watch. The *porte-cochère* was wide open and the *concierge* all in a flutter. The piano-tuner, who had just spent an hour tuning my Bechstein, had departed when a cart drew up in front of the door. What do you think it was? Nothing less than the King's own piano, an *upright* one, though it did connive at *deception*, as you will see. It was one of those pianos with which one could, by turning a key, lower the whole keyboard by half-tones, so that a barytone could masquerade as a tenor and spare the pianist the trouble of transposing the music, and no one would be the wiser.

This was emotion No. 1.

Emotion No. 2: a carriage which stood before the door brought Mr. Halstrum, the pianist.

Emotion No. 3 was another carriage full of things—a music-stand, a quantity of music-books, his Majesty's spectacles, and a mysterious basket.

Emotion No. 4: the servants, with all their heads out of the window, spied a carriage coming full tilt up the street. In it was M. Odman, the best tenor from the Opera.

Finally the royal equipage, of which there could be no doubt this time, was seen from way down the street. J. descended the stairs to receive his Majesty as his carriage entered the *porte-cochère*. I stood at the door of the apartment, and the King in his usual friendly manner said a hearty, "*God dag, god dag, Fru Hegermann!*"

He was attended by only one chamberlain. We went into the *salon*. After a little while the King said, "What shall I sing for you?" and handed me a list of songs.

"Anything your Majesty sings will be delightful," I answered, eagerly.

"Yes, but you must choose," the King said.

I chose one I wanted to hear, but the King had already decided beforehand what he wanted to sing. (I might have spared myself the trouble.) He went toward the piano, but before he sang he took out of the mysterious basket an egg, which he broke and swallowed raw, to clear his voice. He began at the first song on the list, "Adeleide" (Beethoven), and sang that and one after another of those on the list. It seemed queer to have the *rôles* reversed in this way. I generally sang for royalty, but here royalty was singing for me.

KING OSCAR
From an autographed photograph taken in 1896.

The King and I sang the duet from "Romeo and Juliet" and his brother's romance, "*I Rosens doft*," which I had sung with the King in Paris many years ago. I sang some of my songs—"Beware," of course. I wondered when the tenor, whom I was longing to hear, would come on the program. He only came once, and that was when he sang a duet with his Majesty, a duet which the King had had arranged from the Jacobite song called "Charlie is my Darling."

The tenor, whose English was not his strong point, sang with great pathos "Cha-r-r-r-r-r-lie es my tarling," as if a love-sick maiden were calling her lover. When the King sings he throws his whole soul into the music. If Providence had bestowed a beautiful voice on him he would have done wonders, but one cannot expect a sovereign to give much time to cultivating his talents.

Our music finished, tea was served, and his Majesty, apparently pleased with his visit, left at five o'clock.

Here is something the King wrote in my, album which is very characteristic of him: "If you do anything, do it without delay and with your whole heart and mind."

January, 1891.

Dear L.,—I am going to give you a detailed account of the visit of the Crown Prince and Princess of Denmark, their annual visit for the King's birthday. Johan left the evening before to go to Kathrineholm, the last station before Stockholm, in order to meet their Highnesses, and from there to take the train and arrive here with them. Several of the King's household did the same.

I was at the station at eight o'clock. It is pitch-dark here at that hour. I pitied J. when I thought of his having to dress in full uniform in the little hotel at Kathrineholm.

The King and his four sons and gentlemen and ladies belonging to the court and society quite filled the room appropriated to royalty in Stockholm station.

The train steamed in, and steps were placed at the door of the car. The Crown Princess descended, followed by the Crown Prince, Prince Christian, Princess Louise (the eldest daughter), and Prince Hans (the King of Denmark's brother).

There was a great deal of kissing. The Princess was beaming with joy, and said a word to every one.

The dinner at court was at six. It was a family dinner, and as such the Queen was able to be present. As a rule, she is not present at large dinners, because of her health. The King gave his arm to our Princess, the Crown Prince took the Queen. Prince Carl gave me his arm and put me on the left of the King.

During the repast the King asked me if I had read his book of travels. I regretted to say that I had not. Then he called his *chasseur*, who always stands behind his chair, and told him to beg the adjutant to see that a copy of the book should be sent to me.

He talked a great deal of Paris, of his admiration for the Empress Eugénie, and how he had enjoyed his visit during the Exposition of 1867. He said, "Do you remember our excursion in my little boat when you, the Princess Mathilde, and Marquis Callifet did me the honor to come with me?"

"Yes, I remember very well, but I think the honor was on our side."

"Do you remember," he said, "the guitar, and those delightful songs you sang—'Beware?' Do you remember?"

I remembered, certainly, and wondered if I had ever sung anything else in my life.

"And our going to the Rothschilds' place near Boulogne," he continued, "where the porter refused to let us enter the park?"

"Yes," I replied. "But when he heard who you were all the doors were thrown wide open."

"Those were pleasant days," the King said with a sigh of recollection. "I was a good friend of yours, and never will I change."

"I hope you never will, your Majesty."

"Never," he said. "When once I am a friend, I am a friend for always, and I shall always be a good friend to you." And, taking up my hand from the table, he kissed it—a most embarrassing moment for me!

Our ball was a great success. Perhaps you don't know how festivities belonging to royal visits are managed. Entertainments are prearranged three or four weeks before the arrival of the royal guests.

I had never entertained royalty before, therefore I was naturally rather nervous. I sent to Nice for kilos of flowers, and to Rome for mosaic brooches and little *fiaschettis*, which I filled with perfume. I sent to Paris for canes and card-cases and silver pencils, and arranged a surprise for my guests. This was a fancy-dress quadrille, to be danced by sixteen young people at the beginning of the cotillon. Four couples were dressed as shepherds and shepherdesses in different-colored satins, with powdered hair and bright ribbons. The other four were dressed as *incroyables*.

The great problem was how to arrange the different suppers, of which there must be five or six. The royalties must have a room to themselves. There must be three separate suppers for the other guests, two for the dancers, and two buffets going on all the evening.

In the ballroom a dais was arranged with a red brocade for a background, on which were two red chairs for the King and the Crown Princess.

After giving the last orders J. and I stood at the doors to receive our guests, who soon began pouring in. People in Sweden are always very punctual, and arrive precisely at the time for which they are invited. Of course, when royalty is present one should be a little earlier.

Here the host always names the hour when the carriages are to be ordered. I think this is very wise, because if the poor horses had to stand out in the cold, waiting until their masters chose to go home, they would freeze to death. Fortunately, my dress, ordered from Paris, arrived just the day before.

At half past nine the servant announced the arrival of the royal carriages. J. and the secretaries flew downstairs, two servants raced after them, each carrying a candelabrum of six lighted candles. After J. had helped the King from the carriage he took the candelabra from the servants and preceded the King up the stairs to where I stood, according to custom, on the threshold of the door. I presented to the Crown Princess a large bouquet of red and white roses (the Danish colors), with long streaming ribbons to match, and a smaller bouquet to the Princess Louise.

The *tambour*, a curious name given to an antechamber in Sweden, seemed overflowing with dazzling uniforms and showy liveries. It was a very cold night, and all the guests were muffled up to the tips of their noses when they came in. The display of india-rubbers was stupendous. You can see how necessary were the twenty-two large porcelain stoves which, in Sweden, are built into the walls. For my ballroom I was obliged to add an American stove of the kind one fills once a day from the top.

The King gave me his arm, and as we entered the *salon* every one courtesied to the ground. Then the Crown Princess came in with J.

Tea was passed, and when the usual ceremonies like presentations and greetings were finished, the *quadrille d'honneur* commenced.

The King took his place on the dais and watched the dancing.

At eleven o'clock supper was announced. In entering the supper-room the King gave me his arm, the others following.

We were fifteen at our table, ten of whom were royalties.

J. did not sit down to supper with us, as it is not the custom in Sweden for the host to absent himself from the rest of his guests.

Now came the moment for the surprise!

When the royal guests were seated on the dais, sufficient space was made in front of them, the door opened from a side-room, and the dancers entered.

I think those sixteen young people showed much self-denial to be willing to forego the early pleasures of the ball, as they had to do, and give up the time when others were dancing to being dressed, wigged, powdered, and painted. I had to put four rooms at their disposal, two for the ladies with their maids, one for the gentlemen and their valets, and one for their refreshments and supper.

The shepherds and shepherdesses looked and danced their quadrille charmingly. The music for this was the mazurka from "Romeo and Juliet." When the *incroyables* came in there was a murmur of admiration. They were beautifully dressed. They wore black satin costumes, and the ladies had white ruffs round their necks. The gentlemen wore high collars and lace jabots. Each had a long stick in his hand and a monocle in his eye. The shepherds stood back while the *incroyables* danced their quadrille. The music of this was the "Gavotte Louis XIII." As I had chosen the eight prettiest girls in Stockholm, the effect was perfectly enchanting. After the second quadrille they joined forces and danced a *ronde* to the music of "*Le Galop Infernal*" of "*Orphée aux Enfers*" (Offenbach). It was a great success, and the King desired them to dance it over again.

The King thought it must have been a tremendous undertaking, but I told him that it was no trouble to me, as the ballet-master from the theater had taught them.

These young people stayed in their pretty costumes for the cotillon, which commenced directly after their dance.

In Sweden people are not *blasé* as to cotillon favors. They are not accustomed to receive anything more elaborate than flowers and little bows, so I think they all went home happy with their gifts.

There is such a queer custom here. During the cotillon, at the same time with the ices, beer is served, and something they call *mandel-melck* (milk mixed with almond essence). The young ladies also have to be sustained every little while by huge glasses of the blackest of porter.

The royal guests left at two o'clock; then we had a sit-down supper for those remaining. At five o'clock I found myself in my bed, tired out but happy that everything had gone off so well.

The next day the Crown Prince of Sweden had arranged a tobogganing party at Dyrsholm. We were a very gay company of twenty-four, meeting at the station to take the little local train to Dyrsholm, and arriving about twelve o'clock.

Here we found an excellent luncheon which his Royal Highness had ordered, and which was, oh, so acceptable to us hungry mortals! On excursions of this kind in this cold latitude one is obliged to be very careful not to eat and especially not to drink too much, as there is always danger of congestion.

It was a glorious day, the sun shining brilliantly in a clear sky, but bitterly cold. The thermometer, I was told, was eighteen below zero; I would have said thirty. We ladies were muffled up to our ears in fur, our feet buried in *pomposhes*, which are long, india-rubber boots lined with fur, and when we stood in the snow we had great shoes lined with straw.

Everything about us was white; the trees, were loaded with icicles and snow. The hill down which we toboganned was very steep, ending in a long slide over the frozen lake. The snow on both sides of our path was piled up four feet high at least. The fun of toboganning is the bunker. The sudden rise gives you such an impetus, and on the other side you get such a tremendous bump that generally one, if not *both*, of you fall off head first in the snow.

One must be an adept to manage these sleds. The Crown Prince toboganned, as he did everything else, to perfection. Of course, each prince had his own sled and invited some lady to go with him. The lady generally sits in front, with her legs stretched out, and holds on to everything she can, her clothes in particular. The gentleman sits behind, steering with his feet.

The Crown Prince went often alone, and then he would lie flat on his stomach and steer with his long legs, as if he were sculling a boat. I did not feel the least nervous when I went with him, but I confess I did feel a little shy when I had to put my arms round his neck and clutch him for dear life when we jumped the bunker. He preferred having his companion behind him.

The *revers de la médaille* was the toiling up the long slope in the intense cold. I wondered if the pleasure was worth the toil, but if one did not go down on the sleds one would have to stay on the top of the hill and freeze.

We enjoyed this sport till darkness put an end to it; then we returned, tired, cold, and hungry to town, to dine hurriedly and be ready for the theater at eight o'clock—a gala performance.

THE KING OF SWEDEN
From a photograph taken when he was Crown Prince Gustav. The crown and robe were worn at the formal opening of the Riksdag by his father, King Oscar.

J. and I were invited to sit in the royal box. The opera was "Orphée," by Glück. The Crown Princess suffers agonies when she hears music (everything sounds false to her sensitive ears). Therefore, to spare her, they had chosen the shortest opera.

In the *entr'actes* refreshments were served in the small *salon* which is kept in reserve for the King. It is the same room where King Gustave III. retired when he attended the ball which proved so fatal to him on the night of his assassination. The libretto of "*Ballo in Maschera*" by Verdi, is made on this subject, and the scene laid in Boston.

STOCKHOLM, *1892*.

Dear L.,—The opening of the Rigsdag is a great event in Stockholm. The *Corps Diplomatique* met in the room in the palace called Kronesal. The walls are covered with the three gold crowns of the Swedish coat of arms painted on a blue background. They passed on through the rooms of the Order of the Sword, which had just as many swords on its walls as the other had crowns. You can never make a mistake as to where you are! The ladies were told to wear *toilette de ville*, and the gentlemen to dress in gala uniform.

Just before the time the King was to come in we were ushered down a little narrow staircase which led into the Rigsdag, passed in front of the throne, and went up a still narrower staircase to the gallery reserved for the diplomats, which seemed very shaky. Some day when the Rigsdag is opening there will be a collapse of diplomats.

The body of the hall was filled with the gentlemen, all the members of the two Chambers in evening dress and the court officials in their uniforms.

When the Queen is present, which is not often, she sits opposite the *Corps Diplomatique*, surrounded by the ladies of the court, who wear little white fur capes over their shoulders.

The galleries on both sides were filled with the nobility and society. The throne on which King Oscar sat is on a raised platform filling the whole end of the hall. The throne is unique, made of silver, silver lions supporting it on both sides. Back of the throne was a long blue velvet curtain hanging from the canopy.

Everything was ready and every one in his place. A deep silence reigned throughout. There was a blast of trumpets; every one stood up, and the King came down the same little staircase we had. He looked very majestic in his splendid robes of ermine, over which hung the blue Order of the Seraphim, the highest order in Sweden, and of course all his other decorations. The crown he wears is magnificent, made of costly jewels, and, I should think, very heavy, causing the King to hold his head very straight and steady. He looked up at the *loge* of the diplomats, made a slight inclination of the head, then mounted the few steps of the throne and sat in his silver chair.

The Crown Prince came next, followed by Prince Carl and Prince Eugen. The three are as tall as the King. They wore blue velvet mantles trimmed with ermine, their uniforms showing underneath, and as if they had been handed down, but not let down, from former and shorter Princes.

They wore crowns which seemed difficult to balance on their heads.

The King took the Proclamation from the hands of his *Rigskanzler* and, standing up, read it in a loud and clear voice. He did not use his eye-glasses, because the letters were made so large that he could read without them. It was a fine and thrilling moment.

The Rigsdag being opened, the King left as he had come.

STOCKHOLM, *1892.*

Dear L.,—Prince Chira, one of the sons of the King of Siam, came to see us to-day. He has just returned from St. Petersburg. We were very glad to see him again. We knew him so well in Copenhagen, where he has been living for some years. He has been in the Danish army, and, although only nineteen years old, has passed the most difficult examinations, and is now an officer. He talks English, French, and Danish with equal facility. When at Aalholm he entered into all our games and charades with enthusiasm.

He did not mind at all being dressed up as a Sambo, and favored particularly a yellow wig. He has very yellowish skin, almond eyes, and beautiful white teeth. He came to see us straight from the castle, where he had been to see the King. He was very enthusiastic about his Majesty (who is not?). He told us how the King had taken the grand cordon of the Seraphim Order off his own shoulders and hung it on his. The King being a giant, and Prince Chira about the size of a boy of ten, you can imagine how the cordon fitted him. Chira said, "I reached up to about the King's waist, and when the King put the cordon on me it trailed on the ground, and I kept tripping over it when I left the room. It is most awkward," he added, laughing, "and I must wear it to-night at the big dinner at court which the King gives me."

"Leave it with me, and I will have a tuck made in it and send it to you before dinner." This he did. We measured off how much of a tuck should be made, and sent it to him in time. He came the next day to thank me and bid us good-by. He said, "I looked splendid last night *in my cordon.*"

In June and July it is never really dark in these latitudes. The sun shines till eleven o'clock, the birds sing and bustle about during the so-called night, and the cocks begin to crow at absurd hours. They must be perplexed as to what they are doing all these months. The early bird has to be very early to get off with the worm.

BAYREUTH, *August, 1893.*

Dear L.,—At last my dream of dreams has become a reality—under what enchanting conditions! Mrs. L., my beloved friend, invited me to stay three weeks with her in the apartment which she has taken, 28 Opernstrasse, which was the habitation of Wagner's special doctor. Mrs. L.'s other guests were her sister, her niece, and Mr. and Mrs. Brimmer from Boston. Johan promised to join us later. Mrs. L, had her own cook and servants, and we lived like princes of the blood. A walk about the streets in the morning, then a sumptuous lunch, and then a little *siesta* to fit us for the rest (or rather fatigue) of the day.

At a little before four the carriages were at the door and we drove up the hill to the Shrine, passing the foot-sore and weary pilgrims toiling on their way. The servant took our hats and coats, for no one must wear a hat in the audience, and no one needed a coat in this awful heat.

THE RIKSDAG OF SWEDEN
From a photograph showing the opening of the Riksdag at Stockholm, January, 1897. The De Hegermann-Lindencrones were *doyen* and *doyenne* of the diplomatic corps; he stands in the gallery on the left, fourth from end.

The signal to enter the auditorium is given by a blast of trumpets, generally the four bars of the most well-known melody in the to-be-given opera. The only boxes in the theater are in the rear, and Madame Wagner sits with her family in the middle one. After the people have taken their seats the house becomes pitch-dark, and from the depths of the unknown one hears the first notes of the overture. Then the curtains are noiselessly drawn up. After this no one dares to breathe—woe to the unlucky one who gets a fit of sneezing or a tickling in the throat; better die at once than be the recipient of all the inward curses that are hurled at you! The first act generally lasts an hour, and the people emerge from the stifling auditorium into the fresh air with a sigh of relief. The Germans make dashes of kangaroo leaps toward the casks of beer, and then rush for the tents where they get something to eat at the price of blood.

The *entr'acte* lasts an hour; then we hear the blasts of the four heralds again, which is the signal for the second act to commence, and so on until ten o'clock at night. Then *home*, where we find a gorgeous *diner-soupertoire* which triumphantly ends a day of emotion.

Wagner's operas, which lay about on our tables, all seem to have been given by him to *meinem lieben Freund*, the doctor. How I regret that dishonesty did not get the upper hand! How easy it would have been for me to have purloined a book and its signature, but I am proud to say that I resisted, and my collection of autographs is to this day devoid of anything from Richard Wagner, showing that virtue is not always its own reward, since I regret having been virtuous.

The off days were also delightful. We drove to the Hermitage, lingered in the grounds belonging to the gentle and clever Margräfin, and wondered if her tiny little court was not a trifle *ennuyenx*! One could fancy her sitting under the shady trees of the *charmille*, sewing beads on some bags, specimens of which were exhibited to us by an officious menial, and were of the most hideous description. I say hideous because I hate beads and all their works. I have just finished reading her memoirs, and I can only think how small their talk must have been—how narrow their visions!

We drove to the other pretty resort, Bellevue, and meandered about the rococco gardens, and sat on the stone benches surrounding the lake, and watched the graceful movements of the swans as they tried to avoid the spray from the fountains. We tried not to see the native music-lovers who clustered in crowds about the tables, which were covered with red checker-board table-covers and drinking-mugs. They sit under these lovely shady groves for hours, in their thick coats, which they wear in any season and in any climate, their ponderous field-glasses slung over their fat shoulders and their pockets bulging with guide-books and postal cards, swallowing by barrelfuls the cool and beloved beer and eating *Butterbrod* by platefuls.

On Saturday evenings Madame Wagner—called familiarly Frau Cosima—opens her *salon*, and every one goes who can get an invitation. There is generally music, and the best-artists from the Opera-house are delighted to sing. Also the inevitable pianist who is "the finest interpreter of Chopin." (Did you ever know one who was not?)

Very interesting evenings, these, because one sees all the notabilities that flock to Bayreuth. Princes, plebeians, and artists meet here in the limitless brotherhood of music.

Madame Nordica has been singing throughout this season. Her Lohengrin is Van Dyke, and Gruning plays Tristan to her Isolde. Her voice is charming, and she acts very well, besides being very good to look at. She has a promising *affaire de coeur* with a tenor called Dohme, Hungarian by birth, and, I should say, anything by nature. He is handsome, bold, and conceited, and thinks he can sing "Parsifal." Madame Nordica has, I believe, sung for nothing, on the condition that her *fiancé* should make his *début* here previous to taking the world by storm, but Madame Cosima, with foresight and precaution, has been putting him off (and her on) until the last day of the season, which was yesterday. Then Frau Cosima allowed him to make his appearance, upon which he donned his tunic, put on the traditional blond wig, took his spear in hand, and set forth to conquer. His first phrase, "*Das weiss ich nicht*" which is about all he has to say in the first act, was coldly received. However, his bare legs and arms were admired from the rear as he stood his half-hour looking at the Holy Grail. In the second act, where he resists Kundry's questionable allurements, he did passably well, though he gave the impression that even for a *reiner Thor*—the German for a virtuous fool—she had no charms. She was a masterful, fat, and hideous German lady, and when she twisted a curl out of her yellow wig and sang, "*Diese Loche*" and cast her painted lips at him with the threat, "*Diese Lippe*" he remained hopelessly indifferent, with a not-if-I-know-it expression on his face. He was neither a singer nor an actor, and did not have a shadow of success. But he thought he had, and that was enough for him. It is not allowed in Bayreuth to show any sign of approval (or the contrary) until the curtain falls on the last act of the last performance. Then the public calls the artists out *en masse*. Parsifal came with the others, and looked more like an Arab beggar than anything resembling a Parsifal. Madame Nordica took her *fiancé* off the next day. She received from Madame Cosirna a lace fan, with thanks, for her exertions during the Bayreuth season, but she was repaid enough by the satisfaction of seeing her *fiancé* make his *début*, his first and last appearance, I fancy.

They went to Nuremberg the next day and had rooms near ours. We could hear her trilling with joy during their dinner duets, and when I went to see her in her apartment the Conquering Hero told stories about himself which I accepted at a fifty-per-cent. discount. Madame Nordica has certainly the loveliest of voices. What a pity the tenor of her life should not have a better chance to run smooth, for run smooth it will not with such a *Thor* in her possession.

STOCKHOLM, *June, 1894.*

Dear L.,—You will wonder why you have not heard from me for such a long time, but we have just returned from a trip to Norway. You know J. is accredited there as well as in Sweden, and he has to put in an occasional appearance, and we thought while he was putting that in we would put ours in with it. Our party included Nina and Frederick.

For five days we careened over mountains and dales, driving, sailing, riding Norwegian ponies, and always enjoying ourselves to the utmost. One who has not seen the Norwegian *fjords* does not know how beautiful and picturesque the scenery is. You must come some day and see it for yourself.

We reached Bergen the 24th of June, the longest day of the year. There is no question of its being really dark, only between 1 and 2 A.M. you cannot see to read. It is a lovely time to travel, because you can travel the whole twenty-four hours.

Bergen is a very pretty town, with clean streets and nice shops. The jewelry, silver, and fur shops are really quite wonderful, but—there is always a thorn to every rose—the smell of fish pervades the town. Go where you will, you cannot escape it. You don't wonder at this when you visit the fish-markets and see the monsters which are brought out of the deep every morning. They look like small whales.

Nina and I, with the energy of the American woman who knows what she wants and knows how to get it, were determined to see Grieg in his surroundings. We hired a carriage in Bergen and started on our pilgrimage. It needed not only the energy of an American, but the tongue of a Dane and the perserverance of Danaides. The Griegs live in the most unget-at-able place that you can imagine, because he does not want any one to get at him.

However, after driving for miles and worrying the life out of our driver by poking him in the back with our umbrellas and asking him if we had not arrived and when we should arrive, and such useless questions, our poor tired steed climbed a long hill where the road suddenly ended its course. We were obliged to leave the carriage and make the rest of the hill on foot, only to encounter, on arriving at a gate bearing these large and forbidding letters: "*Her boer Edward Grieg, som önsker at vaere fri for folk.*" ("Here lives Edward Grieg, who wishes to be let alone.")

But Nina and I were not to be balked by such a trifle as Edward Grieg's wishes, and with some difficulty we managed to unfasten the hasp of the wooden gate. We expected to see a dragon or a ferocious bulldog fly at us, but all was peaceful within, and we walked into the lair without being molested, and marched boldly to the front door of the villa. There Mrs. Grieg opened the door to us and was (she said) delighted to see us. "And," she added, "how happy Grieg will be, too!" This, we thought, was doubtful, but Grieg pretended to be very "happy."

We stayed as long as we dared, and, on being offered tea and cakes and urged to stay longer, we were shown, as a great privilege, the little summer-house at the bottom of the hill where Grieg retires when he wishes to compose, and where Mrs. Grieg or any other angel dare not to tread. He has a grand Steinway. This is about the only American thing which Grieg does not hate. He said that he would have been a rich man if America had given him a royalty on his music, which is, as he said, played in every house in America. They bemoaned that they were overrun by American lady reporters. That was the reason they had put that notice on the gate—to keep them off the premises. They would beg, he said, "just to look at the garden and pluck a little *ukrut* [weed], and then go away and write all sorts of nonsense, as if they had dragged all my secrets out of me. They are terrible," he added, "your lady compatriots."

FACSIMILE OF LETTER FROM GRIEG

A LETTER FROM GRIEG
[Translation.]

CHRISTIANA, *Nov. 30, 1891.*

My wife's and my own heartiest thanks for your kind telegram. I received it eight days too late by a perfectly incomprehensible and unfortunate mistake, but the joy over your greeting was none the less therefor. We remember so often and so willingly the beautiful time in Rome where you showed us so much kindness. We hope and wish to have a glimpse of you at not a too distant day, perhaps in Stockholm. With best greetings to your husband from us both.

Your devoted

EDWARD GRIEG.

Grieg played some of his latest compositions, which were perfectly exquisite, and played them as only he can. He was full of fun, and told us of an American songstress who had been one of those who had "got in." She insisted on singing for him "*Jeg elsker dig*" and made a cadenza of her own at the end. He said Mrs. Grieg almost fainted, and that his own hair had not finished standing on end ever since. He played this awful cadenza for us, and I must say it was ridiculous. Mrs. Grieg sings delightfully— *nothing but Grieg, of course.* She has not a strong voice, but sings with exquisite pathos and charm.

Grieg loves to talk of his rude behavior and dwell with pleasure on his brusque speeches. He said a young American lady asked him to teach her one of his songs, and after she had sung it he turned round on the piano-stool and said:

"Are you singing for your living?"

"No," she answered, "I sing for my pleasure."

"Don't you think that dancing would be pleasanter?" he asked.

It was evident that they saw us go with regret; we certainly left them with regret. They looked, as they stood there together waving farewell, like two little gray elves; she with her short gray dress and short gray hair; and he with his long gray coat and long gray hair—a Grieg study in gray.

STOCKHOLM, *September, 1894.*

Dear L.,—Just as I was going to get a little rest, who should come to Stockholm but the Prince of Naples? I begged him to give us one evening before he left, which he promised to do. He seemed as glad to see us as we were to see him.

"What would your Highness like best," I asked him, "an official dinner followed by a reception, or a little dinner with a dance?"

"Oh, madame, the little dinner and a little dance, by all means."

So a little dinner it was. He does not care for dancing, but he knew the lancers and quadrilles, and we danced those. We played "Fox and geese"; I fancy, from seeing his amusement, that he had never had a real romp in all his life. To finish, we danced a Virginia reel. This was new to him and pleased him immensely. He insisted upon going through the entire dance until every couple had done its part.

A few days later King Oscar sent me the decoration of *Litteris at Artibus*, which I shall wear on great occasions. This decoration is a gold medal, and the ribbon that goes with it is blue. Queen Christina of Sweden instituted the order. The medal is only given to women of merit, artistic or literary. Jenny Lind, Frederika Bremer, and Christina Nillson, and others have it.

I have become the *doyenne* of the Diplomatic Corps. I intend to make my colleagues walk very straight. So far my duties consist of dancing in *quadrilles d'honneur* and always being taken into supper before every one else, and having the first place everywhere; I take precedence of all guests. These honors do not turn my head.

STOCKHOLM, April, 1897.

Dear L.,—We have been named to Paris.

Never did people have such a time getting away from a place.

All our furniture except a sofa and two chairs had been packed, and was already on the way to Paris.

The entire morning I was busy receiving notes and bouquets of all dimensions, tied with every imaginable national color.

We breakfasted with our colleagues from Germany, who had the apartment above us. While still at table a royal chamberlain announced that King Oscar was coming in half an hour to bid us good-by. Heavens! How could we receive his Majesty without carpets or curtains, only the sofa and two chairs! What a predicament! But our good and kind friends came bravely to the rescue. They offered to send down rugs, palms, and flowers, so that we could receive our royal guest in the curtainless room. Well, the palms and plants did certainly make the room look more inviting. J. camped on the one chair, and the King and I sat on the sofa. The King stayed half an hour. We were as sorry to leave him as he was to have us go. He kissed me on my forehead, and kissed J. on both cheeks, and said, "I shall come to Paris to see you."

J. escorted the King down-stairs and put him in his carriage, while I wiped away a tear.

The royal visit over, our borrowed plumes were returned. Hardly was the apartment bare again when there came a court lackey telling our bewildered valet that the "Crown Prince would be at the house in a short moment." Our colleagues most amiably sent the rugs, etc., down again, and we sat in state and waited.

The Prince came, bringing a large photograph of himself, and said many nice things, expressing his sorrow that we were going to leave Stockholm, and bade us good-by.

The time was gradually approaching when I should put on my hat to depart.

There were still a lot of things to be attended to at the last moment. Our people had to be bid good-by and paid, and thousands of trifles, as you may imagine, to be thought of, and I began to despair of getting away. I seriously proposed to J. to pretend to leave, bidding people good-by at the station, and stop at the first place, to return the next morning and finish quietly what seemed so impossible to do then.

What was our dismay, then, at receiving a telephone message from Prince Carl, asking if I could receive him. Of course, I answered I would be proud, and our colleagues above, learning of this new complication, sent, without begging, the useful and ornamental things which had adorned our *salon* before.

Prince Carl came. He brought me a little bunch of lilies-of-the-valley, intending a gentle allusion to my name. We were very sad at the idea that we were to part, but part we must, and pretty soon. The tired rugs were taken back once more.

Prince Eugen kindly telephoned that he wished to say good-by. It was already so late that there was no question of the rugs, for it was within an hour of our departure; therefore we were obliged to receive the Prince without any accessories. He came with a little offering of flowers. However, that did not make any difference, because we all stood up. It is the custom here in Stockholm that every one goes to the station to speed the parting guest. The station was overcrowded. We were showered with the good wishes of two hundred and fifty people, and flowers were in such quantities that we had to have an extra compartment for them.

Dear Lady Hegermann!
I beg to include with this note according to my promise yesterday, your photograms's, hoping that they will be found according to your so amiably expressed wishes? The fourth is my sons, in His state dress, like mine, at the openings of the "Riksdag". If you should wish some exchange as to the others, you will only have to say a word, and your wish shall immediately be fulfilled by yours most truly devoted old friend

Oscar.

t.t.t.t.

Stockholm, Palace,
on the 18th of May 1895

A LETTER IN ENGLISH FROM KING OSCAR

PARIS, 1897-1902

PARIS, *May, 1897.*

Dear L.,—I can hardly believe that we have been here a month. The time has slipped by, as it has a way of doing when one is frightfully busy; in my case it was particularly exasperating.

Johan's secretary took rooms for us at the Hôtel Chatham, which was not a very good choice, as you will see.

The day for Johan to present his *lettres de créance* was fixed for the 20th of April. M. Crozier, the gentleman who introduces Ambassadors and Ministers to the President, appeared with two landaus, escorted by a detachment of the *Garde Nationale*.

The little courtyard of the hotel could not contain more than the carriages; the horsemen were obliged to stay in the very narrow rue Daunou, which they filled from one end to the other.

While the two gentlemen were exchanging their greetings I slipped out and walked down the rue de la Paix, which I found barred from the rue Daunou as far as the rue de Rivoli.

I felt very proud when I thought from whom it was barred.

I went into a shop while the brilliant *cortège* was passing and, feigning ignorance, asked the woman at the counter:

"What is this procession?"

"*Oh! C'est un de ces diplomates*" she said, shrugging her shoulders.

I left the shop without buying anything—a paltry revenge on my part; still it was a revenge.

We have found a suitable apartment in the rue Pierre Charron, and I have just now begun to look up some of my old friends. Alas! there are not many left, but those who are seem glad to see me. My first official visit was to Madame Faure. This was easily managed. I simply went on one of her reception-days. An Elysian master of ceremonies was waiting for me, and I followed him into the *salon* where Madame Faure sat, surrounded by numerous ladies. A servant wrestled in vain with my name, "Crone" being the only thing he seized, but the master of ceremonies announced to the President that I was the Danish Minister's wife, after which things went smoothly. To leave no doubt in the other guests' minds that I was a person of distinction and the wife of a Minister Madame Faure asked me innumerable questions about *Monsieur le Ministre*.

We were scarcely settled when there came the awful catastrophe of the burning of the *Bazar de Charité*, about which you have probably read. I had promised to go to it, and I can say that my life literally hung on a thread, for if my *couturière* had kept her word and sent my dress home at the time she promised I should certainly have gone and would probably have been burned up with the others. Marquise de Gallifet also owed her life to my not going. She came to make me a visit and lingered a little. This *little* saved her life. She entered the fated bazar just a moment before the fire broke out, and therefore managed to escape.

Frederikke and I drove to the offending dressmaker. (How I blessed her afterward!) When we passed the Cours la Reine we were very much astonished to see a man without a hat, very red in the face, waving two blackened hands in the most excited manner. He jumped into a cab and drove away as fast as the horse could gallop. Then we saw a young lady, bareheaded, in a light dress, rushing through the street, and another lady leaning up against the wall as if fainting. The air was filled with the smell of burning tar and straw, and we noticed some black smoke behind the houses. I thought it must come from a stable burning in the neighborhood. We had been so short a time in Paris that I did not realize how near we were to the street where the bazar was held.

At half past five we drove through the rue François Ier on our way home and saw a few people collected on the Place, otherwise there seemed nothing unusual. When we passed through the avenue Montaigne we met Monsieur Hanotaux (Minister of Foreign Affairs) in a cab, looking wildly excited. He stood up and screamed to me, "*Vous êtes sauvée.*" What could he mean?

I thought that he was crazy. I screamed back, "*Que dites vous?*" but he was already out of hearing. It was only when we reached home that we learned what had happened and understood what he had meant.

How dreadful were the details!

The bazar was in a vacant lot inclosed by the walls of surrounding houses, from which the only exit was through the room where a cinematograph had been put up. This, being worked by a careless operator, took fire.

The interior of the bazar consisted of canvas walls, of which one part represented a street called *Vieux Paris*.

The bazar was crowded; the stalls were presided over by the most fashionable ladies of Paris, and there were many gentlemen in the crowd of buyers.

When the fire broke out a gentleman whose wife was one of the stall-holders stood up near the door and cried out, "*Mesdames, n'ayez pas peur. Il n'y a pas de danger,*" and quietly went out, leaving people to their fates.

Then came the panic.

Young ladies were trampled to death by their dancing-partners of the evening before. One of them was engaged to be married, and when her *fiancé* walked over her body, in his frenzy to escape, she cried to him, "*Suivez moi, pour l'amour de Dieu!*" He screamed back, "*Tout le monde pour soi,*" and disappeared.

She was saved by a groom from the stables opposite. She was horribly burned, but probably will live, though disfigured for life. Under the wooden floor were thrown all the *débris*—tar, shavings, paper, etc. This burned very quickly, and the floor fell in, engulfing those who could not escape; the tarred roof and the canvas walls fell on them. What an awful death!

The kitchen of a small hotel, which formed one side of the vacant lot, had one window about four feet from the ground. This was covered with stout iron bars. The cook, when he realized the disaster, managed to break the bars and, pushing out a chair, was able to drag a great many women through the window. He and the stable-boy were the only persons who seemed to have done anything toward helping.

Of course, around the uprooted and demolished turn-stile was the greatest number of victims, but masses were found heaped together before the canvas representing the street of *Vieux Paris*. The poor things in their agony imagined that it really was a street. It was all over in an hour. It seems almost incredible that such a tragedy could have taken place in so short a time. And to think that the whole catastrophe could have been averted by the expenditure of a few francs! When the architect heard that there was to be a cinematograph put up he pointed out the danger and begged that some firemen should be engaged. The president of the committee asked how much this would cost and, on being told twenty francs for each fireman, replied, "I think we will do without them."

The Duchesse d'Alençon and the wife and daughters of the Danish Consul-General were among the victims. The dead were all taken to the Palais de l'Industrie and laid out in rows. Through the whole night people searched with lanterns among the dead for their loved ones. It was remarked that, though there were many men's canes and hats, there was not one man found among the burned. Not one man in all Paris acknowledged that he had been to the Bazar.

Within an incredibly short time subscriptions amounting to over a million francs were collected. From America came many messages of sympathy and a great deal of money. But no one could be found except the cook and the stable-boy who had done anything to merit a reward. After giving them large sums the rest of the money went to form a fund for the building of a chapel in commemoration of the disaster.

PARIS, *1897.*

Dear L.,—Social life here is very confusing and fatiguing; physically, because distances are so immense. People live everywhere, from the Île St.-Louis to the gates of St.-Cloud. Hardly a part of Paris where some one you know does not live. The very act of leaving a few cards takes a whole afternoon.

In reality there are three societies which make life for a diplomat, whose duty it is to be well with every one, very complicated and unending. The official season for dinners, receptions, and *soirées* is in the winter; French society, just returned from the Riviera and Italy, has its real season in spring, when Longchamps and Auteuil have races and Puteaux has its sports. The autumn is the time when strangers flock to Paris; then commence the restaurant and theater parties. How can any lady have a reception-day where people of all countries, all politics, and all societies meet? Impossible! I have tried it, and I am sorry to say that my receptions are dead failures. Still, I persevere, as I am told it is my duty to receive.

When our first invitation to the ball of the Élysées came I was most anxious to see what it would be like. Is it not strange that the cards of invitation are the same used in the Empire. "*La Présidence de la République Française*" stands instead of "*La Maison de l'Empereur.*" I have the two before me, the old and the new, and they are exactly alike, color, paper, and engraving!

The Diplomatic Corps has a separate entrance at the Élysées. We were met and conducted by a master of ceremonies to the room where the President and Madame Faure were standing. M. Faure is called *un Président décoratif.* He is tall, handsome, and has what you might call princely manners. The privileged ones passed before them and shook hands, quite *à l'Américaine.* I was named by M, Crozier and got from M. Faure an extra squeeze by way of emphasizing that I was a new-comer.

We then passed into the *salon* where our colleagues were assembled, and did not move from there until the presidential pair came in at eleven o'clock. At these balls there are a great many—too many—people invited.

I have been told that there are six thousand invitations sent out. To one gentleman is assigned the duty to stay in the first *salon* and pass in review the toilets of the promiscuous guests and judge if they are suitable. When he sees a lady (?) in a high woolen dress with thick and soiled boots in which she has probably walked to the ball, he politely tells her that there must be some mistake about her invitation, and she walks meekly back to her *comptoir*.

When M, and Madame Faure had finished receiving, they came into the room where the diplomats were; and the President, giving his arm to the lady highest in rank (the *protocole* arranged the other couples) we marched through the crowd of gazers-on, through the ballroom, where some youths and maidens were whirling in the dance, through the palm-filled winter garden, where the people were crowded around a buffet, and through all the *salons* until we reached the last one, quite at the end of the palace, where a sumptuous buffet awaited us. At one o'clock we returned home. It amused me to see old Waldteufel still wielding his *bâton* and playing his waltzes as of old. I wanted to speak to him, but, being in the procession, I could not stop.

Yesterday I had a visit from Adelina Patti. I had not seen her for a long time. It seemed only the other day that I had written a letter condoling with her on the death of Nicolini, her second husband. This time she was accompanied by her third husband, Baron Cederstrom, a very fine-looking Swede whose family we knew well in Sweden. The *diva* looked wonderfully young, and handsomer than ever. When they came into the *salon* together one could not have remarked very much difference in their ages, though he is many years younger than she is.

Massenet comes often to see me. He is a great man now. He and Saint-Saëns are the most famous musicians of France at the present moment. Massenet has never forgotten old kindnesses; and, no matter where he is, whether on a platform at a concert, or in a drawing-room full of people, he always plays as a prelude or an improvization the first bars of a favorite song of his I used to sing. He sends me a copy of everything he composes, and always writes the three bars of that song on the first page.

Among others we find our friend Marquise de Podesta. She is a sort of lady in waiting to Ex-Queen Isabella of Spain. I went to see her at the Queen's beautiful palace in the avenue Kléber. I was delighted when she asked me if I would like to make the acquaintance of the Queen. I went two days later to what she called an "audience." The Queen received me in a beautiful room lined with old Gobelin tapestry and furnished with great taste. She is rather heavy and stout and wears a quantity of brown hair plastered over her temples, which does not give her the height a Queen ought to have. She was very amiable, asked many questions about places and people I knew, and before I was aware of it I found myself spinning out lengthy tales. I should have much preferred she do the talking.

JULES MASSENET AT THE HEIGHT OF HIS CAREER
From an autographed photograph taken in 1894.

The Empress Eugénie is now here. And fancy! living at the Hôtel Continental, right opposite the gardens of the Tuileries. I have not seen her for six years (since Cap-Martin). Baron Petri, who always accompanies her, answered my note asking if I might come to see her, saying that the Empress would receive me with pleasure. You may imagine my emotion at seeing her again. I found her seated at the window facing the Tuileries. How could she bear to be so near her old home? As if reading my thoughts, she said: "You wonder that I came here to this hôtel. It is very sad. There are so many memories. But it seems to bring me nearer *mon fils bien aimé*. I have him always before me. My poor Louis! I can see him as a little boy, when he used to drive out in his carriage, always surrounded by the *cent gardes*." She told me of the terrible journey she had made to South Africa. She had wished to go over the same route that the Prince had taken on his way to Zululand. How dreadful it must have been for her! Can one imagine anything more tragic? Her only child, whom she loved beyond anything in the world, whom she hoped to see on the throne! The future monarch of France! a Napoleon! to be killed by a few Zulus, in a war not in any way connected with France. The Empress appeared weighed down with grief; nevertheless, she seemed to like to talk with me. I wish I could have heard more, but the arrival of the Princess Mathilde interrupted us, and I left.

The papal *nonce* (Ambassador of the Pope) had his official reception last week in his hotel, rue Legendre, which is far too small to hold all the people who went there. All Paris, in fact. No one is invited to these receptions, but every one thinks it a duty and a politeness to attend; consequently, there are a great number of people who walk in, are presented, and walk out.

The *nonce* is a charming man, simple in his manner, kind and gentle. I felt very proud the other evening to be on his arm after the dinner at the Minister of Foreign Affair's, and walk about with him. When we passed by some of the unclothed Dianas and Venuses the dear old man held up his hand to cover his eyes: "*Non devo guardare!*" Nevertheless I caught him peeping under his eyelids. He came on my Thursday to see me, accompanied by Monsignore Montagnini, his secretary, and sat a long time lingering over his teacup, and made himself very agreeable to the many ladies present.

The *nonce* accepted our invitation to dine on the 26th (he fixed the day himself). That evening I received a note from the secretary to say that the *nonce* had forgotten that the 26th was Ash Wednesday, and, naturally, could not have the pleasure, etc.

Prince Valdemar, the youngest son of the King of Denmark, and Princess Marie, his wife, were dining yesterday with us, with Prince George of Greece, who is extremely agreeable and handsome. She (the Princess Marie) when in Paris stays with her parents, the Due and Duchesse de Chartres, in their beautiful palace, known In Paris for its artistic architecture and its onyx staircase.

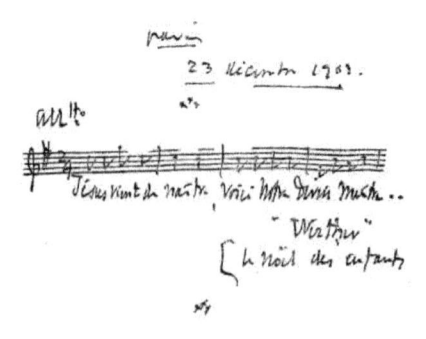

A NOTE FROM MASSENET
This was a reply to a letter of introduction which Madame de Hegermann-

Lindencrone had written Miss Geraldine Farrar to Massenet. He taught her subsequently *Manon*.

The Princess desired to meet President Faure for some reason, and, as she could not do that In her father's house, she desired us to arrange a meeting on the neutral ground of the Legation. On the day fixed they met here In the afternoon. I remained out of the *salon*, and only returned when the tea-table was brought in. The President partook of his tea with graceful nonchalance.

PARIS, 1897.

Dear L.,—You ask, "What are you doing?" If you had asked what are we *not* doing I would have told you, but what we *are* doing covers acres of ground. We are in a whirlwind of duties and pleasures, dinners, *soirées*, and balls. It would bore you to death to hear about them. Many of my old friends are still in Paris; those *you* knew are Countess Pourtales (just become a widow); Marquise Gallifet, who is more separated from her husband than ever. She remains Faubourgeoise St.-Germain, and he favors the Republic.

I find Christine Nillson here. From Madame Rivière she has become Countess Casa-Miranda. She has a pretty little hôtel near us, where she sings not, "neither does she spin." I meet her at dear old Mrs. Pell's Sunday-afternoon ladies' teas. Nillson and I are the youngest members of the club. You may imagine what the others must be in the way of years. Mrs. Pell gives us each (we are twelve) a gold locket with a teacup engraved on its back, and a lock of her once brown hair inside, and we assemble and eat American goodies made in an ultra-superior manner by her *chef*.

Our occupations or amusements depend very much upon whom we are with. A whole army of doctors has just descended on us, and we are doing the medical side of Paris. One day we went to see Dr. Doyen, the celebrated cutter-up of men. He said that operations other doctors spent an hour over *he* did in ten minutes. It sounds a little boastful, but after what I saw I am sure that it is true. He has a very large hospital where he preaches and practises and gives cinematographic representations of his most famous operations. It was very interesting, because at the same time that we were looking at him in the pictures he was sitting behind us explaining things. Strange to say that one or two of the doctors with us fainted away. The ladies did not faint, neither did they look on. The operation which took the most time was the cutting apart of the little Indian twins, Radica and Dodica. This last one (poor little sickly thing) was dying of tuberculosis, and the question was whether the well one should be separated or die with her sister. While this was going on the little survivor came to the door and begged to be let in (she was tired of running up and down the corridor); therefore we knew that the operation had succeeded, which helped to make it less painful to witness.

We visited, in company with these same doctors, the Pasteur Institute, young M. Pasteur accompanying us. We began at the rooms where they examined hydrophobia in all its developments. Persons who have been bitten by any animal are kept under observation, and they have to go to the Institute forty times before they are either cured or beyond suspicion. There are two large rooms adjoining each other, one for the patients and the other for the doctors. Every morning the unhappy men and women are received and cared for.

May 15, 1898.

My dear L.,—We have just come home from bidding our Crown Prince and Princess good-by at the station.

On Thursday Madame Faure and her daughter came to see me. On bidding them adieu I said I hoped the President had not forgotten the photograph of himself which he had promised me. Madame Faure answered, "*Vous l'aurez ce soir même, chère Madame.*" That very evening while we were dining with Count and Countess Cornet we heard that Félix Faure had suddenly died. To-day we learned how he had died. Not through the papers, but secretly, in an undertone and with a hushed voice.

I think that the French papers ought to take the prize in the art of keeping a secret. One could never imagine that a whole nation could hold its tongue so completely! There appeared no sensational articles, no details, and no comments on the President of the French Republic's departure from this world. Everything in the way of details was kept secret by the officials. In our country, and, in fact, in every other country, such discretion would have been impossible; the news in all its details would have been hawked about the streets in half an hour. Here was simply the news that Félix Faure had died.

A week later the President's funeral took place at Nôtre Dame. Seats were reserved for the *Corps Diplomatique* by the side of the immense catafalque which stood in the center of the cathedral. Huge torches were burning around it. After every one was seated, in came the four officers sent by the German Emperor. Four giants! The observed of all observers! Their presence did not pass unnoticed, as you may imagine. They seemed more as if they were at a parade than at a funeral. The music was splendid;

The famous organist Guilmant was at the organ, and did "his best." I believe Notre Dame never heard finer organ-playing. I never did.

The streets were full of troops; the large open square in front of the cathedral was lined with a double row of soldiers. The diplomats followed on foot in the procession from Notre Dame to Père la Chaise, traversing the whole of Paris.

PARIS, *1899*.

My dear Sister,—You may think what a joy it is to me to have my dear friend Mrs. Bigelow Lawrence staying with me here. Every day we go to some museums and do a little sight-seeing. She is interested in everything.

The new President (Loubet) gave us for one night the Presidential *loge* at the Grand Opéra, and I cannot tell you how delighted we were to hear Wagner's "Meistersinger" given in French, and marvelously executed. All the best singers took part. The orchestra was magnificent beyond words. The artists played with a delicacy and a *culte* not even surpassed at Bayreuth. In the *entr'actes* we reviewed—seated in the luxurious, spacious *loge* where the huge sofas and the *fauteuils* offered their hospitable arms—our impressions, which were ultra-enthusiastic. Near us was Madame Cosima Wagner, whom one of our party went to see. She expressed the greatest pleasure at the performance, not concealing her surprise that a representation in French and in France could be so perfect. If that most difficult of ladies was satisfied, imagine how satisfied *we* must have been!

FÉLIX FAURE WHEN PRESIDENT OF FRANCE
From a photograph taken shortly before his sudden death and sent by his widow to Madame de Hegermann-Lindencrone.

As a *bonne bouche* we took Mrs. Lawrence to Madame Carnot's evening reception. These receptions are not gay. They might be called standing-*soirées*, as no one ever sits down. The guests move in a procession through the *salons*, the last one of which is rather a melancholy one. In the middle of it is a square piece of marble lying flat on the floor, and a quantity of withered wreaths and faded ribbons piled up on it. They are the souvenirs of the late President's funeral. Madame Carnot, a most charming lady, wears a long black veil as in the first days of her widowhood, and receives in a widowed-Empress manner.

Mrs. Lawrence's visit is the incentive for active service in the army of musicians. The President often sends me the *ci-devant* Imperial *loge* at the Conservatoire. In old times I used to think how splendid it would be to sit here! Now I have the twelve seats to dispose of—six large gilded Empire *fauteuils* in front, and six small ones behind. There is always a bright coal-fire in the *salon* adjoining, but it does not take away the damp coldness from a room where a ray of light or a breath of fresh air never can penetrate. The concerts seem exactly the same as they used to be; they do not appear to have changed either in their *repertoires* or in their audiences.

Beethoven, Haydn, and Bach are still the fashion, and the old *habitués* still bob their heads in rhythmical measure.

The chorus of men and women look precisely as they did when dear old Auber was *directeur* (twenty-five years ago). I think that they must be the same. The sopranos are still dressed in white, and the contraltos in black, indicative of their voices' color.

Pugno with his pudgy hands played the Concerto of Mozart in his masterful manner. One wonders how he can have any command over the keyboard, he has such short arms and such a protruding stomach.

As a modern innovation Pierno's "*Création*" was given, beautifully executed, but received only with toleration.

Just to go up the familiar worn staircase brought the old scenes vividly before me. Then it was a great piece of luck to obtain a seat within its sacred walls, and such an event to go to a concert that I can still remember my sensations.

PARIS, 1899.

My dear Sister,—You ask me to tell you about the "Dreyfus affair."

It is a lengthy tale, and such a tissue of lies and intrigue that common sense wonders if the impossible cannot be possible, if wrong cannot be right. You probably know more of the details of the case than I do, if you have followed it from the beginning, as I am just beginning to follow.

I assure you it is as much as your life is worth to speak about it; and, as for bringing people together or inviting them to dinner, you must first find out if they are Dreyfusards or anti-Dreyfusards, otherwise you risk your crockery. The other day I was talking to an old gentleman who seemed very level-headed on the start. Perhaps I might learn something! I ventured to say, "Do tell me the real facts about the Dreyfus affair." Had I told him that he was sitting on a lighted bomb the effect on him could not have been more startling.

"Do you know that he is the greatest traitor that has ever lived? He gave the *bordereau* to the German government."

"What is a *bordereau*?" I asked.

He seemed astonished that I did not know what a *bordereau* was. "It is a list of secret documents. He gave this three years ago."

"Who discovered it?" I inquired.

"It was found in the paper-basket of the German Embassy, and Monsieur Paty du Clam knew about it."

"And then?"

"Well, then he was arrested and brought before the *conseil de guerre*, found guilty, and degraded before the army."

"Did he confess that he wrote the *bordereau*?"

"No! On the contrary, he swore he had not, but the generals decided that he had. So he *must* have!"

"The generals may have been mistaken," I said. "Such things have happened."

"Oh no. It is impossible that these officers could have been mistaken."

"What did he say when he was accused?" I continued.

"I hardly think that he was told of what he was accused."

"Do you mean to say," I cried, "that he did not know that he was suspected of high treason?"

"He must have known that he wrote the *bordereau*," he replied.

"*If* he wrote it," I interrupted. "Was he not condemned only on his handwriting?"

"Yes," replied my elderly friend, whose head I had thought level. "But to discover the truth one had to resort to all sort of ruses in order to convict him and convince the public."

"Why did the generals want to condemn him, if he was not guilty?" I asked.

"They had to condemn some one," said my friend, who was beginning to be dreadfully bored. "The generals found Dreyfus guilty, therefore Dreyfus was guilty without doubt."

"Do you think that if an injustice has been done it will create a great indignation in other countries and will affect the coming Exposition?" I inquired.

"Ah," said my wise friend, "*that* is another thing. I think myself that it would be prudent to do something toward revising the judgment; everything ought to be done to make the Exposition a success."

And there the matter rested.

I doubt if his friendship stood this test. Any one who takes Dreyfus's defense is looked upon as an enemy in the camp. I devour the papers. *Le Matin* seems to be the only unprejudiced one. J. reads the others, but I have no patience with all their cooked-up and melodramatic stories.

On the 11th of September the King of Siam gave the diplomats an opportunity to meet him at a reception in the new and beautiful Siamese Legation.

The King is good-looking, and tall for a Siamese. He talked English perfectly and showed the greatest interest in everything he had seen. When he left Paris a few days later he bought three hundred dozen pairs of silk stockings for his three hundred wives. Quite a sum for the royal budget! One can't imagine bigamy going much further than that, can one? And he is only forty-two years old!

I was very glad to meet Colonel Picquard at a dinner in a Dreyfusard house. All that I had heard of him made me feel a great admiration for him. I was not disappointed. He is a most charming man, handsome, with such an honest and kind face. I hoped he would talk with me about Dreyfus, and said as much to my hostess, who in her turn must have said "as much" to him, for he came and sat by me. I did not hesitate to broach the tabooed subject. He said: "I do not and have never thought that Dreyfus was guilty. He may have done something else, but he never, in my belief, wrote the *bordereau*. I had not known him before. I was the officer who was sent to his cell to make him write his name; they forced him to write it a hundred times. He was perfectly calm, but it was so cold in his room that his fingers were stiff and his hands trembled. He kept saying, 'Why am I to do this?' I was convinced then and there of his innocence. I could have wept with compassion when I saw how unconscious the poor fellow was. I was also on duty," he added, "when Dreyfus was conducted to the Ecole Militaire the day he was degraded before the troops: his epaulettes were torn from his shoulders and his sword was broken in two. I never could have imagined that any one could endure so much. My heart bled for him."

Dreyfus was imprisoned *two weeks* and subjected every day to mysterious questionings, of which he could not divine the purpose. Neither he nor his counsel knew on what grounds he was arrested.

Forzinetti, who was in charge of Dreyfus's prison, also believed him innocent, and said he had never seen a man suffer as he did. He kept repeating, "My only crime is having been born a Jew." He has been confined ever since on the *Ile du Diable* under the strictest surveillance. His jailer was not allowed to speak to him. When airing himself in the little inclosure, exposed to the awful heat, there was always a gun pointed at him. Sometimes he was chained to his bed with irons, and a loaded pistol was always placed by his side in case he became weary of life. Colonel Picquard said:

"It can only be the strong desire to prove his innocence that keeps his courage up." Colonel Schwartkopfen (the German military *attaché* in Paris) declares solemnly to any one who will listen that the German Embassy has never had anything to do with Dreyfus, and the *bordereau* is unknown there.

We are very anxious about the news we get from Denmark. The dear Queen is very ill, and there is little hope of her recovery.

PARIS, *29th September.*

Dear ____,—The Queen died last night.

Every one in Paris has come to us to express his sympathy. As is the custom in Europe, people write their names in a book placed in the antechamber. There are several hundred signatures. In Denmark there is mourning ordered for six months. As there is no Danish church in Paris, a memorial service for the Queen was celebrated in the Greek chapel. It was most solemn and beautiful. I love to hear the mournful chants of the white-robed, solemn priests.

It was very sad to hear of the assassination of the beautiful Empress of Austria. She was in Geneva and about to take the little boat to go up the lake. The assassin met her and, apparently running against her accidentally, stabbed her. She did not feel the thrust and continued to walk on. When she stepped on the boat they noticed the blood on her dress, and soon after, on being taken to the hotel, she died.

The French military *attaché* in Copenhagen was in Paris some days and invited us to dinner at his mother's, who has a charming home. We met a great many agreeable people, among whom was the poet Rostand (he is the brother-in-law of the *attaché*). Rostand was very talkative, and I enjoyed, more than words can tell, my conversation with him. He was most amusing when he told of his efforts "to be alone with his thoughts." He said that when he was writing *L'Aiglon* he was almost crazy.

"My head seemed bursting with ideas. I could not sleep, and my days were one prolonged irritation, and I became so nervous *que j'etais devenu impossible*. The slightest interruption sent me into spasms of *delire*. Do you know what I did?" he asked me.

"I suppose," I answered, "you went on writing, all the same."

"No. You could never guess," he laughed. "I sat in a bath-tub all day. In this way no one could come and disturb me, and I was left alone."

"Tubs," I remarked, "seem to belong to celebrities. Diogenes had one, I remember, where he sat and pondered."

"But it was not a bath-tub. I consider my idea rather original! Do you not think that the Great Sarah is magnificent in '*L'Aiglon*'?"

"Magnificent," I said. "You are fortunate to have such an interpreter."

"Am I not?" He was a delightful man.

He sent me a few lines of the Princess Lointaine, with his autograph.

At Mr. Dannat's, the well-known American portrait-painter, I met the celebrated composer Moskowski. One does not expect to find good looks and a pleasing talker and a *charmeur* in a modern artist. But he combines all of these. He said:

"I shall die a most miserable and unhappy man."

"Why?" I inquired. I feared he would confide in me the secrets of his heart, which is at present mostly occupied with his handsome and giddy wife. These, however, he kept wisely to himself.

"I am like Rubinstein," he said. "He was wretched because he could not write an opera. I also wish to write an opera, but I cannot."

"Who could, if not you?" I said. "I think your Concerto one of the most beautiful things I have ever heard."

"You flatter me," he said, modestly, "but, alas! you cannot make me a writer of operas. To-morrow afternoon is the *répétition générale* at the Cologne Concert of my Concerto. Teresa Careno plays the piano part. Would you allow me to accompany you, if you would like to go?"

Did I accept? Yes!

Teresa Careno surpassed herself, and the Concerto was enthusiastically received. Siegfried Wagner led the orchestra in a composition of his own. He was very arbitrary and made the artists go over and over again the same phrase without any seeming reason. One poor flutist almost tore his hair out by the roots. Wagner was so dissatisfied with his playing that he stopped him twenty times. At last, as if it were a hopeless task, he shrugged his shoulders and went on.

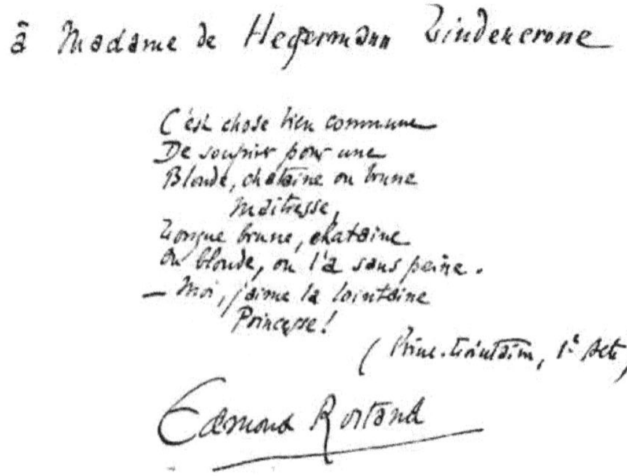

[Handwritten dedication:]

à Madame de Hegermann Lindencrone

*C'est chose bien commune
De soupirer pour une
Blonde, châtaine ou brune
    maîtresse,
Qu'une brune, châtaine
Ou blonde, on l'a sans peine.
— Moi, j'aime la lointaine
    Princesse!*
            (Princ. Lointain., 1ᵉʳ Act)

Edmond Rostand

LINES FROM "LA PRINCESSE LOINTAINE" WITH ROSTAND'S AUTOGRAPH

Count and Countess Castellane (Miss Gould) gave a great entertainment to inaugurate their hotel-palace in the Bois. The young King of Spain was their guest of honor, and the smiling hostess clung to his arm throughout the entire evening, introducing people as they passed. She did not know every one's name nor half of their titles.

The cotillion was short and the supper long, and both were costly. The King of Spain is not handsome, but he has charming manners and a determined jaw and a very sympathetic smile. We met him again at the Grand Prix in the President's pavilion. It was a most brilliant sight. Every one in Paris was there, and the toilets of the ladies were of the *dernier cri*.

The King of Sweden kept his word and really did come to Paris. A dinner for him at the Elysées included us (the only persons who were not French except the Swedish Legation). We are, as you know, what they call "*une legation de famille.*" I was more than enchanted to see the King again. He promised to come and take tea with me the next day.

"Who would your Majesty care to meet?" I asked him.

"My old lady friends whom I used to know here before," the King answered.

"Your Majesty does not mean all of them—that would be a legion."

"No, no," he laughed. "Not *all*, only ..." and named several.

Every one came, although invited at the eleventh hour. It was a merry meeting, and such *souveniring!*

The King walked to my house accompanied by Herr Ancacronra, and the gentlemen whom the French government attached to his Majesty during his visit. They were surprised that a King should prefer walking through the streets to being driven in a landau from the Elysées.

The King brought several photographs, which he distributed to his friends, and, wishing to write his name on them, desired me to give him "a nice pen with a broad point." Oh dear! Not a "nice" pen could be found in the house! And one with a broad point did not exist. As for the ink, it was thick at the bottom and thin on the top. He had to stir it about each time he put the pen in.

I was more than mortified.

PARIS, *1899.*

Dear L.,—Ambassador Eustis has been replaced by General Porter. It is fortunate for America that we have so clever and tactful a gentleman for our representative, especially in this moment of the Spanish-American War. The French sympathies are (or were) with the Spaniards, and the articles in the newspapers are, to say the least, satirical of the "Yankees."

When the reporters interviewed the Ambassador they got such a clear, straight, and concise view of the situation that they changed entirely their attitude, and *now* at last the papers tell the truth.

General Porter and his wife have taken the beautiful Spitzer Hôtel and are the personifications of hospitality. The marble staircase is draped with the American flag. They receive in the ancestral hall filled with knights in armor, and the guests sit in medieval chairs. The picture-gallery, which is famous, is lighted at *al giorno*. I fancy that most of the pictures have been taken away; however, there are a few in each of the small rooms, through which the guests wander with their heads at an angle giving an impression of subtle criticism.

General Porter always has a story *à propos*, no matter what you are talking about. I wish I could remember some of the best. This one I *do* remember. He said: "I never believe but half of what is told me, but," he added, laughing and pointing to a lady, who recently had twins, "this does not apply to *her*." He borrowed from Coquelin the following, "All American women are like pins—they go just as far as their heads allow them." Is this original? I think it good if it is.

Do you remember Countess de Trobriand?

Well, she is still flourishing at the ripe age of eighty, and gives *soirées* in her apartments in the Champs Elysées. Some one said of these entertainments that they were not *assez brilliant* to be called *trop brilliant*, but might be called *de trop*....

Zola is mixing himself up with *l'affaire* (that is what one calls the Dreyfus tragedy; there is no other "affair" that counts), and is making himself very unpopular. He does not mind what he writes, and his attacks reach far and wide and spare no one. If he stirs up mud at the bottom of the well he does it in order to find the truth. At any rate, he is honest, though he has had to pay dear for the best policy. I do not read his books, but I have a great admiration for him. The public feeling is so strong against him that crowds of the populace rush about the streets pushing, howling, and screaming at the top of their lungs, "*Conspuez Zola!*" which I cannot translate in other words than, "Spit on Zola!" Mrs. Lawrence and I met a mob while driving through the Place de la Concorde, and a more absurd exhibition of vindictiveness cannot be imagined.

Poor Zola has been condemned to pay a fine of—how much do you think? Twenty-five thousand francs! He would not or could not pay. The authorities put all his worldly goods, which they valued at twenty thousand francs, up at auction, and went, on the day of the sale, belted with their official scarfes and armed with pretentions, and commenced the farce of the auction. An old kitchen table was the first thing to be sold. Two francs were offered. "Going, going, go—!" when a voice struck in, "*Twenty-five thousand francs.*" This sudden turn nonplussed the authorities. The auction was called off and came to an untimely end because no one knew exactly what to do.

May, 1900.

Dear ____,—The opening of the Exposition was a grand affair. I never saw so many people under one roof as there were yesterday at the Salle des Fêtes. The order in the streets was something wonderful. The police managed the enormous crowd as if it had been composed of so many tin soldiers.

The ladies of the Diplomatic Corps and the wives of the foreign commissioners sat with Madame Loubet in a tribune, on very hard benches. The President stood on a raised platform overlooking the multitude, surrounded by his Ministers, his official suite, and the Ambassadors and Foreign Ministers in full uniform. It was a most brilliant sight.

M. Loubet made his speech in as loud a voice as he could command, but I doubt if it was very audible. Several orchestras played before and after the speeches.

Since then I have been many times to the Exposition, and the only fault I can find with it so far is that it is too enormous; but I admire the cleverness of the architects, who have brought Paris into the middle of it and made it a part of it. Both sides of the Seine are utilized in the most practical manner.

Every country has its own superb building in the rue des Nations. Frederick is the *commisaire* from Denmark. The Danish Pavilion is the first to be finished and is called a success. We baptized it with great *éclat*. There were speeches and champagne, and the Dane-brog was hoisted amid hurrahs of our compatriots.

The *tapis roulant* (moving sidewalk) is a very good scheme, as it takes you to every point. As yet people are a little shy about it and will stand and stare a long time before venturing to put their feet on it.

The *fêtes* at this time of the Exposition are overpowering. All the Ministers are outdoing themselves. They think nothing of inviting five hundred people to dinner and serving twenty courses. I sat next to M. L'Epine, *prefet de police*, and a more restless companion I never had, although when quietly seated in his place he is a most charming one. We had not been five minutes at the table before several telegrams were brought to him. A riot in Montmartre, a fire in the rue St. Honoré, or a duel at the Île de Puteaux, and he was up and down, telephoning and telegraphing, until finally before the end of the dinner he disappeared entirely. There were two concerts in different *salons* during the evening, one vocal and the other orchestral, each guest choosing that which he liked best.

I go every day to the Exposition. There is always something new and interesting. Yesterday it was a lunch with Prince Carl and Princess Ingeborg (our Crown Prince's daughter, who married her handsome cousin of Sweden) at a restaurant called *Restaurant bleu*, under the shadow of the Eiffel Tower. The Prince wished to make the acquaintance of Mr. Eiffel, and the Swedish Minister, who was present, secured the distinguished architect's company.

He went with us to the very top of his modern tower of Babel, even to his own particular den, which is the highest point, where he alone has the right to go. The sensation of being up in the clouds is not pleasant, and as you change from one elevator to the other and cast your eyes down the giddy space you tremble. The view of Paris spread out under you is stupendous, but I would not go up there again for worlds.

The princely pair dined with us the same evening *en toilette de ville*, and we went to the rue de Paris to see Sadi-Jako. The Japanese Minister, who sat in the box next to us, introduced her when she came in during the *entr'actes* to pay her respects to him. She is very small, and has the high, shrill voice which the Japanese women cultivate. She is the first woman who has ever acted in a Japanese theater. Otherwise the acting has always been done by men. Sadi's husband performs also, and in a dreadfully realistic manner. He stabbed himself with a sword, and with such vigor that real blood, so It looked, ran down in bucketfuls over the stage, and he groaned and writhed in his death-throes.

Paris would not be Paris if it did not keep us on the *qui-vive*. Every kind of celebrity from everywhere is duly lionized. Paris, never Republican at heart, still loves royalty in any shape, and at the merest specimen of it the Parisians are down on their knees.

We have had the heavy-eyed Krueger straight from the Transvaal. Paris made a great fuss over him, but he took his lionization very calmly. At the Opéra people cheered and waved their handkerchiefs. He came forward to the edge of the *loge*, bowed stiffly, and looked intensely bored. The *protocole* furnishes the same program for each lion. A dinner at the Elysées, a promenade, a gala opera, *et voilà*.

Fritjof Nansen, the blond and gentle Norwegian explorer, has just finished his visit here. As a Scandinavian friend he came for a cup of tea and made himself most agreeable, and was, unlike other celebrities, willing to be drawn out. He told us of some of his most exciting adventures. Starvation and exposure of all sorts belong to explorers.

No one would think, to look at the mild and blue-eyed Nansen, that he had gone through so many harrowing experiences.

"The worst were," he said, "losing my dogs. I loved them all. To see them die from want of food and other sufferings broke my heart."

I am sure that what he said was true, he looked so kind and good.

Among other personages of distinction Paris greets is the Shah of Persia. The Elysées gave him the traditional gala dinner, to which the diplomats were invited. The ballroom was arranged as a winter-garden, with a stage put at the end of it. The ballet from the Opera danced and played an exquisite pantomime, but the august guest sat sullen and morose, hardly lifting his Oriental eyes. People were brought up to him to be introduced, but he did not condescend to favor them with more than a guttural muttering—probably his private opinion, meant only for his suite. He merely glanced at us and looked away, as if too much bored for words. M.

Loubet stood on one side, and Madame Loubet sat in a *fauteuil* next to him, but he had nothing to say to either of them. The government had put Dr. Evans's beautiful and perfect villa in the Bois at his disposition. The persons belonging to the house say that it is swimming in dirt, and they never expect to get it clean again. The suite appear to have no other amusements than driving about the streets from morning to night. The Elysées must have a hundred carriages in use for them. Last evening there was a gala performance at the Grand Opéra for the *blasé* Shah. They gave "Copelia," with the lovely Mauri as *prima ballerina*. The audience made no demonstration, although it ought to have shown a certain amount of Te Deumness, on account of the Shah's escape from an attempt on his life. He was miraculously saved, and will go on living his emotionless life for ever and ever. May Allah protect him ... from us!

Speaking of Orientals, the Chinese Minister has taken a very large apartment in the Avenue Hoche. Evidently they expect to entertain on a large scale. The wife is called lady, but *he* is not called lord; the two pretty daughters look more European than Chinese, having pink-and-white complexions.

His Excellency was frightened out of his wits when M. Loubet, desiring a private interview, sent for him. He, not knowing European ways, thought his last hours had come, and, expecting speedy extermination, hid himself.

Milady, though half American, did not know exactly what Ascension day meant and asked her Chinese servant. He replied, "Great Churchman gone topside to-day."

Mr. Peck is the American commissioner to the Exposition, and Mr. Thomas Walsh is one of the members of the commission. He gave a colossal dinner at the restaurant at d'Armenonville, and begged Mr. Martin, who knows every one in Paris, to select the guests. It was only on the evening of the dinner he made the acquaintance of the one hundred people to whom he was host.

Nordica sang after dinner, and sang charmingly, as is her wont.

Mr. Walsh invited us to the American section. We sat on the tarred roof of a restaurant, where lunch was served *a l'Américaine*. My heart gladdened at the thought of hot griddle-cakes and corn fritters; but although everything was delicious, sitting on a tarred roof and being served by a loquacious black tyro was not appreciated by the foreign element.

A lady—I won't tell you her name, though you know it—showed the greatest interest in the house Mr. Walsh is building in Washington, and desired greatly to advise him and help him choose furniture for it. She thought Louis XVI. style very suitable for one *salon*, and proposed

Renaissance style for the library, and Empire for the gallery, and so forth. Mr. Walsh said, in his dry way, "You must really not bother so much, madame; plain Tommy Walsh is good enough for me." After which she lost interest in him and gave him up.

We were horrified to hear of King Humbert's assassination at Monza. He was such a good man and loved his country so devotedly. To be struck down by one of his own people seems too cruel. How dreadful for Queen Margherita!

Court mourning is ordered for three weeks.

PARIS, *1900.*

Dear L.,—Just a few lines from me to-day to answer your question, O merciless and adorable friend! Dreyfus has been brought back from the dreadful island where he has been confined these last five years. Five years of torture! He was taken to Rennes to be tried. His lawyer, Labori, has driven the judges almost out of their senses.

The sensational attacks of Zola and his sudden "*J'accuse*," the suicide of Henry, the repeated demissions of the Ministers and Généraux, *la femme Voilée*, the disappearance of Esterhazy (stamped as a first-class scamp), the attempt to get Labori's papers by shooting him—the ludicrous and tragic episodes have at last come to an end. Dreyfus is declared innocent, and people are beginning to realize what has happened.

Björnstjerne Björnson, the famous Norwegian poet, has, from the beginning, taken Dreyfus's defense and written article after article in the papers and proclaimed in every manner his belief in his innocence. He hurried to Paris when he heard that Dreyfus had returned. We were very glad when an invitation came from the Swedish Minister (Mr. Ackermann) to lunch with the great author. I wish that you could see him, for to see him is to know him. He has the kindest and noblest face in the world. I wept over his account of the interview between him and Dreyfus. The day and hour were fixed for his visit. He found Madame Dreyfus alone. She begged him to wait a moment, because her husband was so agitated at the thought of seeing him that he could not trust himself to appear. When at last Dreyfus came into the room Björnson opened his arms. Dreyfus fell weeping into them and sobbed, "*Merci! Merci! Vous avez crû en moi*"— Björnson replied: "*Mon ami, j'ai souffert pour vous, mon pauvre ami.*" Of course, this is only a very little part of what he told me, but it was all in this strain. He said that during the interview, which lasted an hour, Dreyfus did not utter a word of reproach against his tormentors.

BJÖRNSON
From a photograph taken in 1901.

Björnson gave a tea-party at his daughter's house in Passy, and invited us. I hoped that possibly Dreyfus might be there, but he was not. However, I had the pleasure of seeing Colonel Picquard again, and we had a long talk together. Afterward, when I bade Björnson good-by, he stooped down and kissed me on my forehead before the roomful of people. Imagine my embarrassment at this unexpected and gratuitous token of friendship, but, the kisser being Björnson, every one knew that the accolade was merely the outpouring of a kind and good heart.

PARIS, *August 15, 1900.*

The hottest day we have had! The thermometer was way up in the clouds. My maid, in doing my hair this morning, informed me of this fact. We conferred about my toilet for the afternoon *fête* in the Elysées Gardens. We heard that twelve thousand people were invited. Certainly I should be lost in a crowd like that and need not be dressed in my best. My maid thought a rather flimsy gown of about year before last would be good enough. Johan thought that he would be so entirely out of sight that he was on the point of not going at all. Well, we had a queer awakening. I was very much astonished when the master of ceremonies met me at the entrance and led me into the garden, where the vast lawn was one mass of humanity. He bade me take the first seat. I said to myself, "It is only for the moment; I shall have to move farther on later, when a higher-ranked lady arrives." Not at all! I remained in the place of honor, to the right of Madame Loubet, to the very end.

In the middle of the lawn were placed a dozen large red arm-chairs before which a strip of carpet was stretched, where we sat.

Three performances were arranged for the afternoon. To the right was a Japanese theater where Sadi-Jako and her troupe played their *répertoire*. In the center was a Grecian temple, before which a ballet of pretty girls danced on the grass in Grecian dresses. The effect was charming. To the left was a little Renaissance theater where people of different nationalities danced and sang in their national costumes. I never saw anything so wonderfully complete. Only the French can do things like that. When the moment arrived for the official promenade, you may imagine how I felt when I saw Monsieur Loubet approach me and offer me his arm. After all, I was the first lady! Why was I not dressed in my best?

Monsieur and I walked at the head of the procession. We made the tour of the gardens and through the whole palace, gazed on and stared at by the entire crowd of the twelve thousand spectators, until at last we reached the *salon* where the buffet was established.

PARIS, *1902*.

Dear L.,—You might think that we are nearly exhausted, but health and energy seem to assert themselves, and we bob up like those weighted playthings children have. We have turned heads-up from our journey to Denmark. We celebrated our silver wedding at Aalholm. I won't bother you with the usual phrase, "How the time has flown!" Twenty-five years! You have seen what an ordinary wedding in Denmark is like. You can coat this one with silver, and then you will but know half the excitement. The setting being Aalholm, the chief actors J. and I, the chorus being family and friends, you may imagine that this *fête* left nothing to be desired. Guests came from everywhere to the number of forty. Even our best man came from Norway. Deputations and telegrams dropped on us by the hundreds; presents of silver in every form and shape. My dress was silver, and silver sprays in my hair, and J. wore them in his buttonhole. The dinner arranged by Frederick on viking lines was splendid. Speeches at every change of plates. I wept tears of pathos. An address of five hundred names, adorned with water-color sketches of our different Legations, bearing a silver cover and a coat of arms, was presented by the Danish colony in Paris. It was all very touching and gratifying.

The famous beauty, Countess Castiglione, departed this world a few days ago. She was the woman most talked of in the sixties.

When I first saw her she was already *passée*. There is nothing that has not been said about her, but of this I know absolutely very little. She used to live in Passy, and was called "*La recluse du passé.*" She was so extraordinarily dressed and always created a sensation.

For the last thirty years no notice had been taken of her. I quote the *Figaro*:

"Countess Castiglione in her day was considered the most beautiful woman living. A classical beauty, but entirely without charm. For the last years she has lived, after having arrived at the age of eighty, in a dismal apartment in the Place Vendôme, friendless, forgotten, and neglected."

All her mirrors were covered with black stuff of some kind; she did not wish to see the sad relics of her beauty.

At eleven o'clock every evening she took a walk with her maid around the Place Vendôme. She stayed in bed all day, never rising till twilight, and receiving no one but one or two old admirers who were faithful to the end.

Her things (*haillons* they were called in official language) were sold at auction—piles of old ball-shoes, head-gear, gloves stiffened with moisture and age. Apparently, she never gave anything away, but hoarded her treasures, which after her death were swept in corners and smelled of mold and damp.

We are named to Berlin. I am very sorry to leave Paris; I was getting quite accustomed to its little ways. Johan went to the Elysées to present his *lettres de rappel*. It seems only yesterday he went to present his *lettres de créance*. The President gave him the Grand Cordon of the *Légion d'honneur*, and to me the beautiful *service de Sevres* called "*La Chasse*," a *surtout de table* of five pieces. This is only given to royalty or Ambassadors. One cannot buy it, as it belongs to the French government. I heard that they hesitated between giving me that or a piece of Gobelin tapestry. I was glad they chose the *surtout de table*. It will be useful in two ways—as a subject of conversation and as a beautiful souvenir of our stay in Paris.

BERLIN, 1902-1912

BERLIN, *January 22, 1903.*

Dear L.,—J.'s presentation of his *lettres de créance* to the Emperor was a small affair compared with former functions, which were combined with gala coaches, powdered coachmen, and *pourboires*. It was simply taking a train to Potsdam, in which there was a section called *Kaiserlich*. The Minister of Foreign Affairs accompanied him, as was his duty. In a royal carriage from the court they were driven to the Neues Palais. J. was met by the *Introducteur des Ambassadeurs* (Herr von Knesebeck) and conducted into the presence of the Emperor, where J. made his speech. The Emperor was very official and ceremonious when he responded, but in the conversation afterward was affability itself. J.'s audience with the Empress was very hurried, because of the Crown Prince of Denmark, who had arrived the night before in Berlin. He stayed two days at Neues Palais.

I arrived two weeks after this. The custom here is for a Minister's wife to be presented by the *doyenne* (Madame Sjögeny) to the *grande maîtresse* (Countess Brockdorf) on one of her reception-days *before* the *Schleppenkur*. I found her very charming. My audience with the Empress was fixed for a date a week later, and the Swedish and the Peruvian Ministers' wives were to be received at the same time.

We met in the *salon* of Countess Brockdorf on the day appointed, and, preceded by her, went together to the *salon* of the Empress, where we found Her Highness already waiting. We sat about in a circle. The Empress talked French with us and was most gracious. She has a wonderful figure; her white hair and youthful face and her lovely, kind smile make her very beautiful. She said that the Emperor remembered me from Rome and Prince Henry (her brother-in-law) recollected having met me at Monza.

I went in company with these same two ladies at an audience to the Princess Henry, who lives in the pretty pavilion on the left of the palace, overlooking the canal. She only comes to Berlin when there are *fêtes* at court, otherwise she and the Prince live at Kiel.

Our next visit was to Princess Friedric-Leopold, the Empress's sister. She lives in a palace in Wilhelm-strasse when in Berlin. She is very lively, talkative, and extremely natural in conversation. She has a beautiful country place near Potsdam.

The *Schleppenkur* is a great event in Berlin. It takes place before the birthday of the Emperor. I had never seen anything like this ceremony, and it interested me very much. Perhaps it will you. It takes place at a very early hour in the evening—eight o'clock. This makes it necessary for one to begin to dress at six. Naturally, you go without any dinner—a cup of bouillon is considered sufficient to keep you alive.

It is the custom for diplomats to engage for the evening a *Schutzmann*—a heavy mounted policeman. Our particular one was waiting for us before our house and rode by the side of our carriage until we arrived at the entrance of the *Schloss*. He looked very important, but I do not think he was of much use. However, it seems that a *Schutzmann* comes under the chapter of *Noblesse oblige*, and we took him. He did a great deal of horsemanship, but never dared to disobey the chief policeman's orders, and when we arrived at Portal 4 we had to wait for the file like other people. He did not call up our carriage at the end, but had to be called up himself by the police force; then he appeared, bristling with energy, and galloped at our horses' heads to our door, where we laid our offering in his hand and bade him good night. The *Schutzmann* is one of our privileges and nuisances. I felt sorry for people who had been standing in the cold street for hours to watch the procession of carriages and the gala coaches (which the Ambassadors use on this occasion), because they only get a glimpse through the frost-covered windows of glittering uniforms and dazzling diamonds. Your dress (instructions as to which are printed even to the smallest detail on the back of your invitation) must be a ball-dress, with a train four meters long, short sleeves, and a *décolletage* of the Victorian period, and white kid (*glacé*) gloves.

EMPEROR WILHELM IN THE UNIFORM OF THE GUARDS

THE EMPRESS OF GERMANY ON HER FAVORITE MOUNT

We arrived at the Wendel entrance and mounted the long and fatiguing staircase before we reached the second story where the state apartments are. In the hall of the *corps de garde* were several masters of ceremony, who received us with deep bows. I wondered what certain large baskets which looked like clothes-baskets were, and was told that ladies wearing boas or lace wraps around their shoulders were expected to drop them into these baskets. They would then be conveyed to the other staircase, where, after the ceremony, we would find our servants and carriages—and, we hoped, our boas! We passed through different rooms where groups of ladies were assembled. The *Corps Diplomatique* filled two rooms. The ladies were in the first one, which leads to the Throne Room.

The Hungarian and Russian ladies wear their national costumes, which are very striking and make them all look like exotic queens. The English ladies wear the three feathers and the long tulle white veil, which make them look like brides. We others wear what we like, ball-dresses of every hue, and all our jewels. No one can find fault with us if our trains, our *décolletage*, our sleeves and gloves, are not according to regulations.

The chamberlains arranged us, consulting papers which they had in their hands, after the order of our rank. Being the latest member, I was at the very end, only the wives of two *chargés d'affaires* being behind me. The one directly behind me held up my train, just as I held the train of the Peruvian Minister's wife in front of me. I hope that I have made this clear to you. The *doyenne* stood by the door which led into the Throne Room through which she was to enter. Four meters behind her was her daughter holding her train, and behind her were the ladies who had not already been presented at court.

The room not being long enough, we formed a serpentine curve, reminding one of the game called "Follow the leader." It must look funny to any one not knowing why we were so carefully tending the clothes of other people. I never let go the train of the colleague in front until she reached the door of the Throne Room, where I spread it out on the floor. Then, as the lady passed into the room, two lackeys, one on each side of the door, poked the train with long sticks until it lay peacock-like on the parquet.

TWO VIEWS OF ROYALTY From photographs taken at Lyngby, near Copenhagen, in 1894. In the facing photograph the former Czar of Russia is seen, with black hat and light clothes, holding his favorite dog. From left to right the others are: the Princess of Hesse; the Princess Marie; Prince Waldemar with his dog; a *dame d'honneur*; King Christian X. of Denmark; and the present Czar of Russia. The man at the extreme left of the picture is the present King, George of Greece.

This is rather a critical moment. One has a great many things to think of. In the first place, you must keep at the proper distance from your predecessor. Of this you can be pretty sure, because if you walk too fast there is the restraining hand of the chamberlain to prevent you. Still, there is always the fear of dropping your fan or tripping over the front of your gown or of your tiara falling off.

When I came in I saw His Majesty standing on the throne, stately and solemn. For two hours he stands thus. With a mass of officers on my right and a few chamberlains at intervals on my left I advanced very slowly and, I hope, with a certain dignity. I saw the train of my colleague turn the corner around the officers. Two other lackeys darted forth and pronged my train in place. I made my courtesy first to the Emperor and then to the Empress, who stood at his left.

Next to her Majesty stood the *grande maîtresse*. I put myself by her side and presented Frederikke and our secretary's wife, and the *grande maîtresse* said their names to the Empress. Then as we passed out a servant picked up our trains and threw them over our arms, disappearing through the door of the immensely long gallery which is filled with pictures commemorating the numerous battles and events of the last forty years. I wondered, when I looked at the stretch of carpet, how any one carpet could be made so long.

As I am the latest arrived Minister's wife, I and my two acolytes were the last persons to enter the *Weissesaal* where the buffet stood. This buffet extended almost the whole length of the vast room. We refreshed ourselves. My little self was in sad need of being refreshed, and I devoured the sandwiches spread out temptingly under my eyes, and drank some reviving champagne, and waited for my better half, who, with the other better halves, was making his bow to the sovereigns. The ladies of the *Corps Diplomatique* pass before the throne first and are followed by the gentlemen; then come the highest-ranked princesses, and so forth. It is very fatiguing moving about with one's court train dragging on one's arm, and I for one know that I was glad when we went down the marble staircase and found the servant who had sorted our boas from the baskets. There is no antechamber at the foot of the staircase, so one must stay exposed to the wintry blasts when the door is opened to let people out. It is extraordinary how long it takes ladies to disappear after their carriages are announced. They say a few last words, linger over the picking up of their skirts, and go out leisurely; also the servant seems unnecessarily long mounting his box, settling himself before the coachman drives away.

BERLIN, *January, 1903*.

Dear ____,—The 21st was the Emperor's birthday.

The whole city is beflagged, and there are all sorts of illumination preparations. "W's" in every dimension and color, the Emperor's bust surrounded by laurel leaves, and flags in every window. Johan went in gala uniform to the chapel in the *Schloss*, where a religious service is always held, after which every one goes to congratulate his Majesty and see the *défilé cour* afterward.

In the evening was the gala opera. Johan dined at Count Billow's (the *Reichskanzler*) at five o'clock, while I dressed for the theater. We were obliged to be there at eight o'clock sharp. "Sharp" is the word here. There is no loitering where the Emperor is concerned. Everything is on time, and his Majesty is sometimes *before* the hour mentioned, but never *after*.

The Opera-house is rather small, but was beautifully decorated with garlands of artificial flowers hanging from the center of the dome down to the balconies, and from the proscenium boxes to the orchestra. In the center of the house is the royal box, the balustrade of which is covered with real flowers. From all the balconies are hung beautiful carpets covered with festoons. The whole interior was a mass of color.

The Emperor and Empress sat, of course, in the front of the box, while the other chairs were filled by royal guests who had come to Berlin to congratulate the Emperor. The King of Saxony, the King of Würtemberg, and the other German royalties, all sat in the royal box. The Emperor's sons had their seats in the balcony.

The Ambassadors occupied the four proscenium boxes. The highest princesses of the German nobility sat in the next balconies. The *Corps Diplomatique* occupied the boxes and balconies adjoining the royal box. All the officers and secretaries of the Embassies sat in the parquet.

When the audience was seated the *directeur générale des théâtres* entered the royal box, came forward, and rapped with his stick three times, a signal that their Majesties were about to enter. The royal party came in very quietly and took their places. Every one in the house, of course, stood up and bowed. It was a pretty sight from our balcony to see all the men's heads in the parquet bend down while they saluted their Majesties. It looked like the swaying of wheat by the wind.

Gradually all the lights were turned out and the overture commenced. The opera was "Carmen" and Madame Destinn sang.

In the *entr'acte* the diplomats and the ladies and gentlemen in the first balcony were begged to go in the foyer, where they were presented to the different royalties assembled there.

The Empress was covered with magnificent diamonds and pearls, and the jewels displayed by all these royal ladies, and all the glittering uniforms of the princes and officers made a splendid sight.

The Emperor came toward me with a gleam of recognition, and commenced in an entirely unceremonious way, shaking me heartily by the hand:

"How do you do? It's a long time since I saw you."

"Not since Rome, when your Majesty was there in 1889," I answered.

"So long ago? I remember it so well! As if it was yesterday!"

"I, too," I said. "I remember your Majesty being in the Statue Gallery of the Capitol, where you looked like one of the statues itself, in your white uniform."

"I remember," he said. "It was a dreadful glare."

"It was the first time they ever put electricity in the Capitol."

"They put too much in," he said, "and such a lot of people! Dear me! I shall never forget it. Didn't I look bored?"

"No, your Majesty looked very serious and as handsome as a Lohengrin" I answered.

"Lohengrin, really! I did not see any Elsa I wanted to save."

"Oh, I meant only a Lohengrin *de passage*," I replied.

The Emperor laughed. "That is good."

"I recollect what your Majesty wrote on the photograph you gave Monsieur Crispi."

"Really? What was it? I don't remember."

"You wrote: '*Gentilhomme, gentilhomme; corsaire, corsaire et demi*'."

"What a good memory you have!" he said, and added, very kindly, "I am very glad to have you and your husband here, and I hope you will like Berlin. But"—holding a finger warningly—"don't look for many Lohengrins."

In case, my dear, you don't understand this, I will tell you what it means: If you are nice to me I will be equally nice to you, *but* if you are horrid I will (pokerly speaking) see you and go you one better.

BERLIN, *January, 1903.*

Dear ____,—Every diplomatic lady has a reception-day. Mine is Thursday. Last Thursday there were one hundred and sixty people.

My first receptions in January were very perplexing, because so many people came whom I did not know and who did not know me. Our two secretaries, Frederikke and I have a code of signals which help me over many a rough place. Visitors leave their cards in the antechamber. The secretary stands in the first *salon* and waves them into the large *salon* where I am. If I raise my eyebrows the secretary knows that I depend upon him to find out who the person is, and the name, if possible. He, therefore, gets the card and shows it to me by some magical twist. Sometimes he manages to whisper the name. Often I fail to grasp either the whisper or the card; then I am lost, and flounder hopelessly about without bearings of any kind, asking leading-questions, cautiously feeling my way, not knowing whether I am talking to a person of great importance or the contrary. When at last my extreme wariness and diplomacy get hold of a clue, then I swim along beautifully on the top of the wave.

Frederikke helps me by taking odds and ends off my hands and sorting them out behind her teacups. All the young people flock about her, and with their laughter and flutterings add a gay note to the official element around me.

The Emperor desires that all his officers should be accustomed to society, and they receive orders to make afternoon visits, which they do— poor things—I suppose, much to their distaste. As no one knows them and they do not know any one, it must be very awkward for them. They come six at a time, leave a package of cards in the antechamber, present themselves, and each other. They click their heels, kiss the hand of the hostess, give a hopeless glance about them, move in a body toward the tea-table, return, and go through the same ceremony, and leave together, making a great clinking of swords and leaving an odor of perfumed pomade.

BERLIN, *January, 1903.*

Dear L.,—I have been to my first court ball here, I will describe this one to you, and never again.

The invitation we received was very large. It told us that we were invited by order of his Majesty, King and Emperor, to appear at the Königlicheschloss, Thursday, at eight. We were accompanied, as usual, by the policeman on horseback. It amused me, while we were waiting in the carriage, to see standing before one of the entrances to the palace a whole line of soldiers with *serviettes* hung over their shoulders. They were there for the purpose of washing the dishes after the supper.

As I have said before, the *Wendel treppe* is very high and tiresome to mount. We found the hall of the *corps de garde* filled with youthful pages whose ages are anywhere from fifteen to twenty. They were dressed in red coats, with large frills of lace, held in place by their mothers' best diamond brooch, and neat little low shoes with buckles and neat little white silk legs.

I glided along the polished floor through the different rooms, which were empty, save for the numerous chamberlains. All had papers and diagrams in their hands, and they told the gentlemen as they passed who they were to take in to supper, and the name of the supper-room. Each room has a name, like "Marine Room," "Black Eagle Room," and so forth.

The long gallery was filled with officers, whose uniforms were of every imaginable color and description, and gentlemen who looked as if they had just stepped out of a picture-frame. They wear their calling on their sleeves, as it were. The Academician has a different costume from the judge. I noticed a clergyman in his priestly robes, his Elizabethan ruff around his neck, his breast covered with decorations. He was sipping a glass of hot punch and smiling benignly about him. He had a most kind and sympathetic face. I would like to confess my sins to him, but just now I don't happen to have any to confess.

Tea was passed about while we were waiting to enter the ballroom. In the *Weissesaal* the *Corps Diplomatique* has a raised platform reserved for it on the right of the throne where we ladies, beginning with the ambassadress, stand, following precedence. On the other side are all the princesses of the German nobility. I was shown to my place on the platform.

When the two thousand people collected in this room raised their voices a little more than was seemly, the master of ceremonies pounded his stick on the floor—*there was to be no loud talking*—silence reigned a moment, and then the unruly guests burst out again, and were again reduced to silence by another and more ominous thump. The orchestra began the march of "Tannhaüser." This was the signal for the entrance of the sovereigns. No one dared to breathe. People straightened themselves up, the ladies stepped down from their platform. From the middle arcades the young pages—twenty-four in number—entered in pairs. Then came the Oberhof Marshal alone, followed by the four greatest personages in Berlin, the Duke Trachenberg, Prince Fürstenberg, Prince Hohenlohe, and Prince Solms-Baruth. After them came the Emperor with the Empress on his arm. Every one bowed. They were followed by the five sons of the Emperor—the Crown Prince, Prince Adalbert, Prince Eitel Fritz, Prince August Wilhelm, and Prince Joachim; then all the princes and princesses of the house of Prussia.

THE THRONE-ROOM OF THE ROYAL PALACE, BERLIN

It was a very imposing sight as they all marched in. When the Emperor and the Empress reached the throne they made a stately bow to each other and separated, the Empress turning to the *doyenne* (the first ambassadress) and the Emperor crossing to the Ambassadors. Each *chef de mission* stood in front of his secretaries and presented them.

My place was between the wives of the Swedish and the Brazilian Ministers. My neighbor was very unhappy because she was not able to use her eyeglasses. Eye-glasses are one of the things that are not allowed, nor are such things as boas or lace wraps.

The Empress spoke to all the ladies in either German, French, or English. She was accompanied by the *grande maîtresse*, who stood near.

Right behind the Emperor are two gentlemen who are always within speaking distance. The first is the tallest young man to be found. He wears a red uniform, white knee-breeches, very high boots, a breastplate representing a brilliant rising sun, and a high blazing helmet surmounted by a silver eagle. This makes him the most conspicuous person in the room, so that you may always know where the Emperor is by seeing the young officer's towering helmet above the crowd. The other is General Scholl, a dear, kind old gentleman, who is dressed in the costume of Frederick the Great's time, with a white wig, the pigtail of which is tied with black ribbon, a huge jabot of lace with a diamond pin on his breast.

All the other court persons wear dark blue dress-coats, with gold buttons, and carry in one hand the awe-inspiring stick, and in the other the list for the suppers. Some of them are rather vain about their legs, and stand profile-wise so that they can be admired. They do look very well turned out, I must say, with their silk stockings and low buckled shoes.

The ladies of the *Corps Diplomatique* are not always as observant of court rules as they ought to be, and their *décolletage* is not always impeccable. If Worth sends a corsage with the fashionable cut—what do they do? They manage, when they stand on their platform *en vue*, to slip their shoulders out, thereby leaving a tell-tale red mark, only to slip the shoulders in place when royalty has its back turned.

The Empress was followed by a second tall young officer. He wore a red uniform and a hat with a high red feather, easily seen from a distance. Countess Brockdorf, to distinguish her from other ladies, wears a long black mantilla on her head and looks like a *duègne à l'Espagnole*. The other ladies of honor stand near the Empress in the background. I forgot to say that the wives of foreign Ministers have *fauteuils* on their platform, behind which stand their secretaries' wives.

The ball was opened by the Crown Prince, who danced with the youngest *demoiselle d'honneur*, then the other princely couples joined. None but the princes have the privilege of dancing at first. The *valse a deux temps* only is permitted. The court likes better the old-fashioned method of revolving in circles round and round the room, but occasionally it permits the lancers.

The young ladies and gentlemen, who had been practising their dancing for weeks, began their gavotte. The ancient *ballet-danseuse* sat up under an arch in the ceiling, and held up a warning finger if any mistake happened. The dances they learn are gavottes and minuets, which are very ingeniously arranged. Some of the officers looked rather awkward when they had to point their toes or gaze in the eyes of their partners. During one of these dances the Empress went off into the gallery, next to the ballroom, and ladies new to the court were brought up and presented to her.

Princess Henry and Princess Leopold then made the tour of the guests. Each time a royal person came to speak to us we were obliged to descend from our platform, in order to be on the same level. The Emperor talked with all the ladies. To me he spoke in English, which, of course, he speaks perfectly. He was dressed in a Hussar uniform, and held his casque in his left hand, and offered his right. He showed me a new decoration he had just received from the Sultan. He pointed out the splendid diamonds, and seemed very pleased with it.

A *Vortänzer* (the leader of the dance) is chosen in the beginning of the season. His duty is to arrange all balls and lead all cotillions that are given by society during the winter. He gives advice, indicates the officers who dance well—in fact, arranges everything. The young people pass three delightful flirtatious weeks learning these gavottes and minuets. Many a happy couple date their bliss from those dancing-lessons.

As I knew who was to take me in to supper, I waited in my place until my partner, the Minister of Justice, came to fetch me. I was very happy to be portioned off to such a charming gentleman. We were told to go in the Marine Room, where were the Emperor and the Empress. Each Prince had a table for twelve, over which he presided. At ours was Prince Adalbert, the Emperor's naval son. A supper for two thousand guests sounds rather formidable, does it not? With a slight difference in favor of the first three rooms, the same supper is served to all. A supper here is just like a dinner, beginning with soup, two warm dishes, an entrée, dessert, fruit, and coffee.

On our return to the ballroom there was some more dancing. The last dance was the prettiest of them all. Their Majesties took their places on the throne, stood watching with a pleased smile the procession of dancers who came in, four pairs at a time, from the last door of the ballroom. In each group the four officers belonged to the same regiment. First they danced a gavotte, and then twirled off in a waltz. Then the other four couples came in. There were forty or fifty couples altogether. When they had all entered they formed a fan-shaped line and advanced toward their Majesties, making the deepest of courtesies. Then they spread out and made a large circle. The Emperor and the Empress bowed their thanks, and the dancers retired, and the orchestra sounded a fanfare. The ball was over. The Emperor offered his arm to the Empress, and all the Princes followed in the same order in which they had entered. As we went through the long gallery servants handed glasses of hot punch about, which were very acceptable before going out in the cold air. I happened to glance in the open door of a room we passed and saw a Mont Blanc of *serviettes* piled up to the ceiling, and next to that room was a regiment of soldiers wiping plates.

After the *Schleppenkur* and before the Kaiser's birthday comes the *Ordens Fest*. It is a yearly entertainment the Emperor gives to those who have received the Prussian Order of the Red Eagle, the highest in rank of the elder members, and all the newly made. Johan has just received the decoration.

Here every one sees all sorts of people, from cab-drivers to princes. There is a luncheon for two thousand guests. The Emperor and the Empress walk about and talk to as many as they can. The other evening we went to the Winter Garden, and the head waiter said to Johan, "I have not seen you for a long time, your Excellency—not since we lunched together at the *Schloss* at the *Or dens Fest*."

BERLIN, *1903*.

Dear L.,—The dear old King of Denmark came to Berlin to pay a visit to the Emperor. He arrived the night before last. We went to fetch him at the station. Johan was instructed to take rooms at the hotel for the suite, but the Emperor begged the King to stay at the *Schloss*, which he consented to do. The next morning the Emperor came to Berlin and drove the King out to the Neues Palais at Potsdam, where there was a luncheon. Johan said it was quite touching to see how tender and affectionate the Emperor is toward the King. Johan and his secretary were the only persons present outside the family. It was very amusing (Johan said) after luncheon to see the young Princess Victoria Louise and Prince Oscar, who went about with their fingers on their lips. J. wondered why. The Crown Prince told him that his young brother and sister talked so much that he had bribed them to keep silent for ten minutes and had promised them a mark each. They got the two marks! The Kaiser has great affection for the King. His speech of welcome when he drank the King's health at lunch was very touching.

This afternoon the King came to take tea with us. I had not seen him since the death of the Queen. It was a great pleasure to have him in my house. He and I sat in the large *salon*, while Johan, the King's adjutant, and a German gentleman attached to the King during his stay here remained in the next room. The King only talked about the Queen. I, who loved her so much, was all tears. His Majesty once in a while would put his hand on mine and say, "You loved her." We had our tea alone. He told me that the Queen's room in Amalienborg remains just as she had left it. My photograph was on the mantelpiece in her boudoir, and the cushion that I had embroidered for her was still on her *chaise-longue*. Nothing there was to be disturbed.

As the King left I pointed to the portrait of himself he had given me, which was hanging on the wall. I said:

"I prize this, your Majesty, more than anything I own, because you gave it to me yourself."

"I was better-looking then than I am now. Is that not true?"

"Your Majesty is always handsome in *my* eyes," I answered.

"Dear madame, you make me vain." And he took my hand, and the kind King kissed it like a *preux chevalier* of the old school.

As I followed him to the door he said, "Do not come any farther; you will take cold. I will bid you good-by here." He is about eighty-five years old, and as youthful in his movements as a young man.

J. said, "I am sorry we have no lift."

QUEEN LOUISE OF DENMARK
From a photograph taken in 1878. She was the wife of King Christian IX., and the mother of Queen Alexandra of England, Empress Dagmar of Russia, King George of Greece, and various royalties.

"I do not need a lift; I can still run down the stairs." Which he did in a surprising manner.

The King left that evening; and as he begged me not to come to the station, J. went without me.

February, 1903.

As Johan is accredited to the Court of Mecklenburg-Schwerin, we were invited to a great court ball which was to be given. We arrived at Schwerin at twelve o'clock, and found the *maréchal de la cour*, the court servants and carriages at the station awaiting us. We were not installed in the castle, but at the Grand Duchess Marie's palace in the town itself. The *maréchal* who met us informed us that we were expected to luncheon at one o'clock. We just had time to change our dresses and drive to the castle. The lady of honor and the *maréchal de la cour* received us in the hall on the ground floor, and the elevator took us up to the *salon* where the Grand Duke and the Grand Duchess were awaiting us.

The Grand Duchess is very charming and very handsome. She is the daughter of the Duchess of Cumberland, granddaughter of King Christian. We had luncheon in one corner of the vaulted hall—a luncheon of twenty people. I sat on the right of the Grand Duke, who was most amiable. After luncheon the Grand Duchess took me into her boudoir and showed me all her souvenirs—photographs of Bernstorff, a screen painted by the Queen of Denmark, and aquarelles of Gmunden, her home. She has all the charm of her dear mother and her beloved grandmother.

At four o'clock we left and drove about Schwerin, making the obligatory visits. A court carriage with a lackey was put at our service during our stay. I rested, having rushed about since eight o'clock in the morning.

Our apartment in this palace looked as if the mistress had just left it. The drawing-room is filled with knick-knacks, a piano with music on it, and tables with writing-materials. At seven o'clock we dined with the grand master of ceremonies and his wife at their palace. A dinner where you know none of the guests and no one knows you must naturally be uninteresting, and this one did not prove the contrary. At half past nine we went again to the *château* to attend the ball. A chamberlain met us at the antechamber and preceded us into the ballroom. The grand-ducal pair came toward us, and I was led to my place on a raised dais. I danced the *quadrille d'honneur* with the Grand Duke. Very nearly every one in the room was presented to me, and I found among them many people I had known before—therefore we had some subjects of conversation, for which I was thankful.

The *château* is a *bijou*. It has a winding staircase which is worthy of Blois. We mounted this to go to the supper-room. The supper was served at small tables, and was excellent. Frederikke danced the cotillion, and we stayed until the end. It had indeed been a long day for me. The next day we drove to the *château* and bid their Highnesses good-by.

BERLIN, *1904*.

Dear L.,—At one of the Towers's costume balls Mr. X, of American renown, dressed conspicuously as Jupiter (of all ironies!), stalked about, trying to act up to his part by shaking in people's faces his ridiculous tin bolts held in white kid-glove hands, and facetiously knocking them on the head. He happened, while talking to a lady, to be right in front of the young Prince. A friend tapped him discreetly on the shoulder, giving him a significant look. "What is the matter?" said Mr. X, in a loud voice, glaring at his friend. A gentle whisper informed him that he had better turn round and face the Prince. "Heavens!" said the ungracious Jupiter. "I can't help it; I'm always treading on their toes" (meaning the Prince's).

Speaking of indiscretions, I was told (I cannot say whether it is true) that Mrs. Z, one of our compatriots, having met the Emperor in Norway, where their yachts were stationed, and feeling that she was on familiar enough terms, said to him:

"Is it not lovely in Paris? Have you been there lately?"

"No, I have not," answered the surprised Kaiser.

"Oh, how queer! You ought to go there. The French people would just love to see you."

"Do you think so?" said the Emperor with a smile.

Thus encouraged, she enlarged on her theme, and, speaking for the whole French nation, continued, gushingly, "And if you would give them back Alsace and Lorraine they would simply adore you."

The Kaiser, looking at her gravely, as if she had solved a mighty problem, said, "I never thought of that, madame."

The dear lady probably imagines to this day that she is the apostle of diplomacy. She came to Berlin intending (so she said) to "*paint Berlin red.*" She took the list of court people and sent out invitations right and left for her five-o'clock teas, but aristocracy did not respond. Berlin refused to be painted.

BERLIN, *September, 1905.*

Dear ____,—The Kaiser went to Copenhagen on the *Hohenzollern*. Johan and I met Frederick and Nina and stayed with them during the Emperor's visit. There was a very large dinner at Fredensburg, a dinner at Charlottenberg (the Crown Prince's *château*) in honor of the Kaiser. Prince Carl, who is about to be made King of Norway, was there. Princess Maud was in England. The King seemed to be in the best of spirits, and the two sovereigns laughed and joked together. The Emperor has a great affection for the King, and loves to show his respect and devotion. He often puts his arm around the King's shoulder when talking to him. I will just add here that Johan received another decoration, and Frederick, who is now Minister of Foreign Affairs, received a grand cordon, as well as a bust in bronze of the Kaiser. My gift from the Emperor is a beautiful gold cigarette-case with his autograph in diamonds on the front, with the imperial crown, also in diamonds.

The Kaiser went to a dinner given in his honor at the Y's.... Johan, Frederick, Nina, and I were among the guests. At the end of the rather long dinner a little episode happened which shows how quick the Emperor is to understand a situation and perceive its humorous side. According to custom, the Emperor occupies the hostess's place, with her at his right. Herr Y made signs to his wife across the table, and in a stage whisper begged her to find out from the Emperor if he wished coffee served at table or in the adjoining *salon*. The hostess apparently neither heard nor understood; at any rate, she said nothing to the Emperor. The host asked again, in a stagier whisper, and made signs with his head toward the other room. Still no answer. The Emperor, looking over to me (I sat next to the host), said, with a merry twinkle in his eye, "Something wrong in the code of signals." A few moments after he said quite casually to the host, "Would you mind if we had coffee in the other *salon*?"

The Emperor that evening was in excellent spirits. In his short mess-jacket he looked like a young cadet. He told us several amusing anecdotes and experiences in a most witty manner. Nina said to him:

"Your Majesty, I have been looking in all the shop-windows to-day to see if I could find a good photograph of you. I wanted to bring it, and was going to ask you to sign it, but—"

"But you could not find anything handsome enough, *hein?*" inquired the Emperor, laughing.

"That is true," Nina answered. "Your Majesty's photographs do not do you justice."

Beckoning to an adjutant, the Emperor said, "I want you to send to the shops and bring what photographs of me you can find."

The man departed. Although it was nine o'clock and most of the shops must have been shut, he did manage to bring some. Then the Kaiser examined the photographs, with a little amusing remark on each. "I do not think this is handsome enough—I look so cross. And this one looks conceited, which I don't think I am. Do you?"

"Not in the least," Nina answered.

"In this one," he remarked, "I look as if I had just ordered some one to be hanged. And this one [taking up another] looks like a Parsifal *de passage*"—referring to something I had once said.

"I did not say Parsifal, your Majesty. I said Lohengrin."

"All the same thing," said he.

"Not at all," I said. "One was a knight, and the other was a fool."

"Well," he laughed, "I look like both."

He did not like any of the photographs, and sent to the *Hohenzollern* for his own collection. His servant came back almost directly (he must have had wings) and brought a quantity of portraits, which were much finer and larger than those from the shops. He begged us to choose the one we liked best, and he wrote something amusing on it and signed his name.

BERLIN, *January, 1906.*

Dear ____,—The sad news of the death of our adored old King arrived this evening. We were very surprised, as the last account we had heard of him seemed more hopeful. Though he was so very old (eighty-six years), he had a wonderful constitution and always was so active. I am glad that I saw him when he was here last year and had such a pleasant afternoon with him.

Johan was one of the pall-bearers at the King's funeral at Roskilde. I did not go on to Copenhagen. There was a funeral service here at the Scandinavian chapel. We are to have mourning for six months.

BERLIN, *June 6, 1906.*

Dear L.,—If I were going to be married and had to go through all the ceremonies which attend the marriage of a German princess, I think I would remain an old maid.

I will tell you what the wedding of the Princess Cecilia of Mecklenburg was like. As it was the first royal wedding that I had ever attended, my impressions are fresh, if not interesting. I have seen royal silver and golden weddings, but never anything like this.

The day before yesterday, the hottest day of all the tropical days we have been having, the Princess arrived in Berlin. The Emperor and the Empress met her at the station and drove her to Bellevue Castle, where there was a family lunch. She had numerous deputations and visits of all sorts until five o'clock, when she made her public entrance into Berlin, passing through Brandenburger Tor. All the streets where the Princess was to pass were decorated *à l'outrance* with flags and flowers. Carpets were hung from the balconies.

The middle of the Unter den Linden, usually left to pedestrians, was freshly strewn with red earth for the procession of the carriages. All the public buildings were festooned with enormous paper roses as big as cabbages. There were high poles holding gilded baskets filled with flowers.

In order that every one of the populace should have a souvenir these flowers were soaked in a preparation of wax, which made them quite hard, and they were warranted to last for some time. Streamers of paper flowers, graduating from light yellow through the whole gamut of rainbow colors and ending in dark blue, reached to the ground from the tops of the houses. The Opera House outdid itself. It was wise to cover it as much as possible—it is such an ugly building.

The French Ambassador invited us to see the *entrée* from the balcony of the Embassy in Pariser Platz. The little maidens, their heads crowned with wreaths, had been waiting in the sun for hours with their baskets filled with roses, which they were to throw before the Princess as she passed.

It was a splendid procession, headed by the *Hofstalmeister*, followed by a staff of officers spangled with orders and decorations, in the most gorgeous uniforms. Then the blast of trumpets and a mounted military band preceded the gala coach, only used for weddings, drawn by six horses with huge white plumes on their heads. In the coach was the Empress, and on her right the Princess Cecilia in a light-blue dress, white hat, and long blue feathers.

The coach stopped in the Platz, and the Mayor of Berlin approached the window and presented a huge bouquet and delivered an address to the Princess, who bowed graciously and smiled.

The Empress looked very happy.

After this came all the other gala coaches, followed by the *garde du corps*.

There was a family dinner, and after that the gala performance at the Opera. I have already told you about these gala performances, so this will be only a repetition, except that there were more flowers and more carpets. All around on the ledge of the balcony there were fresh and real roses and carnations, so that every lady could take a bouquet away with her. Garlands of paper flowers hung the entire distance from the ceiling to the prompter's box. One wondered how they found hands enough in Berlin to make all these thousands of flowers.

The parquet was a garden of uniforms. The Emperor entered with the bride-elect on his arm, and the Empress with the Crown Prince. The Crown Prince wore the white uniform of the Guards, and a silver helmet. The other princes followed, all entering very quietly. Every one in the theater bowed and courtesied, and save for the rustling of dresses and the rattling of swords there was not a sound to be heard. The Crown Prince and his *fiancée* sat in the middle seats, the Emperor to the right of his daughter.

The overture was a composition made for the occasion, and played while all the lights were blazing, in order that every one could have a good look at the Princess.

Then gradually the theater became dark, and the opera commenced. It was "Orphée," by Glück. Madame Destinn sang the principal part. Her voice is very beautiful, but she is so small, and somewhat dumpy, that she did not look much like an Orphée. To make the opera shorter they combined the first and second acts, and to allow Orphée to go from hell to heaven without letting down the curtain they had invented a sort of treadmill on which Orphée and Eurydice should walk while the landscape behind them moved. It was a very ungraceful way of walking. They looked as if they were struggling up a hill over rough and stony ground.

We went into the foyer after the performance and were presented to the Princess. I had known her as a young girl in Cannes, where her parents lived, therefore we had something to talk about. She is very charming, tall and willowy, and has a pleasant word and smile for every one.

The wedding-day dawned in a relentless haze. We were invited to be at the chapel of the *Schloss* at five o'clock. The regulations about our court dress were the same as for the *Schleppenkur*, only we were begged *not* to wear *white*. My dress was yellow, with a yellow *manteau de cour*. Frederikke wore a light-green *pailletted* dress with a light-green train. We were a little late in starting; our *Schutzmann* had waited patiently in the courtyard for a long time. We drove through the crowded streets, lined with spectators. Each clock we passed pointed in an exasperating way to the fact that we were late. J.'s sword seemed always to be in the way; every time he spoke out of the window to urge on the already goaded coachman the sword would catch on something. The air was more than suffocating, and there was evidently a storm brewing.

We arrived before the portal of the *Schloss* at the last moment. Ours was the last carriage to arrive. The pompous *Suisse* pounded his mace on the ground and said, warningly, "You must hurry; the Kaiser is just behind you." And we *did* hurry.

The staircase makes three turns for each flight, and the chapel is the highest place in the palace, meaning seven turns for us. I grasped the tail of my ball dress in one hand and my heavy court train in the other and prepared to mount. On each turn I looked behind and could just see the eagle on the top of the Emperor's silver helmet. We hurried as I never hurried in my life, for if his Majesty had got ahead of us on any of these turns where the two flights meet and part, we would have been shut out from the chapel. As it was, one door was already closed. They opened it for us, and we were the last to enter before the princes. We crossed the chapel to reach the *estrade* on which stood the *Corps Diplomatique*. In my hurry I forgot to let down my dress, and I don't dare to think how much stocking I must have exhibited. When finally I did reach my place I was so out of breath it took me a long time before I was in it again.

THE ROYAL PALACE AND LUSTGARTEN, BERLIN

There was a general who stood before me with his plumed hat in his hand, and the plumes waved about like palm-trees, so near were they to my panting!

Then the Emperor appeared with his suite, and stood at the right of the altar. He was a little ahead of time. There were about seventy-two princes and princesses. Each of the princesses had a page or a young lady to hold up her train.

The Empress then entered, followed by her suite. The youngest *demoiselle d'honneur* held her train, which was of red velvet covered with heavy embossed gold embroidery.

After the Empress came the Crown Prince in his white *garde de corps* uniform. He looked very young and slender and quite pale.

A moment after the bride came in. Six young ladies held her train, which was light-blue velvet embroidered in silver, over a white-satin gown covered with beautiful point lace. The train was carefully spread on the floor.

The choir of boys high up in the dome sang psalms with many verses. Then the clergyman commenced his exhortation, which was very long. The heat was intense. Some ladies about me thought they were going to faint, but happily they could not make up their minds.

Although the music was delicious, I longed to hear the organ. Especially when the ceremony was finished I hoped that we should hear Mendelssohn's March. But there was no organ in the chapel.

It took the royal persons a long time to leave the chapel, each princess taking up a great deal of space with her train and her train-bearer. The last princely couple were strangely contrasted. The young Duchesse d'Aosta, who is unusually tall, walked with a tiny Siamese prince. We followed down the steps to the *Weissesaal*, where the members of the Diplomatic Corps defiled before the throne and made our courtesy—*one only*—before the Emperor. All the suites and court gentlemen stood massed together opposite the throne. It was quite an ordeal to walk under the fire of so many eyes, as the parquet was without any carpet and very slippery, and the length of the room immense.

After waiting what seemed an hour, the royalties, headed by the Emperor and the Empress, walked past us.

The spectacle of these fifty princesses with their magnificent dresses, blazing with jewels, made one gasp.

Besides all the royal people of Germany, representatives from other countries were present. Prince Christian and his wife, who is the sister to the bride, represented Denmark.

They all disappeared in the banqueting-hall at the end of the gallery. We others sat down at tables each containing twelve people, and were served a regular dinner.

Each table in our room had a superb *surtout de table* in silver, and silver drinking-cups worthy of a museum. The *ménus* and bonbons were trimmed with white-satin frills and had the photographs of the Crown Prince and Princess, and were laid by each plate. A dinner for three thousand people! The young ladies and officers had their dinner at a standing buffet.

We went back to the ballroom after the royalties had passed us again. The clouds outside were very oppressive.

Then the traditional *Fackeltanz* commenced. The *Corps Diplomatique* had a platform to itself, fenced in with cords. We were so crowded that had it not been for the cord which held us in our places we would have tumbled out.

The ladies of the nobility also had a platform. The herald, dressed in a short medieval, red-velvet costume, with the embroidered coat of arms of Germany on his breast, advanced, trumpet in hand, and announced that the *Fackeltanz* was about to begin. The orchestra played a gavotte; and the Crown Prince, giving his hand to the Empress, and the Crown Princess giving hers to the Emperor, preceded by eight pages with torches and by Prince Fürstenberg, walked around the room. When they arrived before the throne they made the most reverential of bows before parting with their Majesties, who took their places on the throne. The Princess's train was carried by four young ladies, and by her side walked Countess Harrach, one of the *dames de palais*. After this the Princess walked with every prince according to his rank, sometimes with two, one on each side, and the Prince walked with two ladies. Each tour of the *salon* they made they stopped in front of the Emperor and bowed and received their next partner. Fancy what fatigue!

The storm which we had expected now really burst upon us. Peals of thunder mingled with the strains of the orchestra, and almost shook the ground.

At eleven o'clock the Princess had danced with every one and had made hundreds of courtesies, and on the signal given by their Majesties retired with her suite. We went down the *Hölletreppe* (in English, *hell-stairs*), a rather diabolical name, but I hope it was paved with better intentions than the *Wendeltreppe*, where we went up. My intention was, *bed*.

We found our carriages and drenched coachman and dragged our trains home to their resting-places.

We had been eight hours under arms.

Every one received a white ribbon with a little gold fringe on the end, bearing the monogram of the married couple. It was a *honi soit qui mal y pense* remembrance of the royal wedding.

Prince Wilhelm Hohenzollern,[2] cousin of the Emperor, is a great philatelist, and brought his magnificent collection of albums (eight or ten large ones) to show me, and a pile of duplicates. His victoria was quite filled when he drove up to our door, and his *chasseur* had to make two trips to bring them all up. Collectors of postage-stamps make a brotherhood in themselves. He knew each stamp in his books, and explained all to us.

He has twelve thousand! I brought out my little collection very shyly—it was so insignificant beside his. We passed two hours going through the two collections. He left six thousand duplicates with me to look over and chose from, so my collection was enriched by one thousand new specimens. He told me he had inherited a whole collection from his uncle, the King of Rumania. He came to drink with us, and was always most amiable. He does not play cards, nor is he musical in any way, therefore conversation was our only resource. I brought in all my animals and put them through their tricks; the parrot played up wonderfully. He followed me about the room, sat on my shoulder, sang, and whistled. What amused people most was, when I sang "Medje," a very sentimental song, he imitated a *rire-fou* which seemed so inappropriate that every one was convulsed with laughter. Then I showed my doves, which were pronounced "perfect darlings." My seven dogs did their best to amuse us. The parrot ran after them and bit their tails, which the dogs did not resent in the least.

Prince Friedrich Wilhelm of Prussia also dined with us—a very formal dinner. He is rather serious for such a young man. He is tall and thin, and in his high, buttoned-to-the-chin uniform he looks even taller than he really is. He is very musical, and brought his violin and several books of music. He only approves of Bach, Beethoven, and Mozart in his severer moods. He likes Bach best of all. He plays very correctly, one might say without a fault, but I have heard violinists who play with more *brio*. He listened with kindness to a young Danish girl who executed a dashing solo by Brahms divinely, and nodded his head in approval when she had finished. The Prince was begged to play several times, and he went through the entire *répertoire* of sonatas he had brought with him. The guests were immensely pleased, and the *soirée* was very successful.

His brother, Prince Joachim Albrecht, is also a very good musician, but differs radically from Prince Wilhelm. He plays the violoncello very well, and favors modern music. He composes ballads, and leads his own regimental orchestra. He is as jolly and unconventional as his brother is reserved and grave. When he dines with us he brings his violoncello, and I accompany him on my piano. He composed two very pretty and successful ballets, both given for charity. The first one was danced by Frederikke and two other girls and three young officers. It was called "*La Leçon de Danse*." On the top of the program, instead of the English device, "*Honi soit qui mal y pense*," I put "*Honi soit qui mal y danse*" in the same shield. Hardly any one in the German audience saw the joke—nothing more than that it was a *druckfehler* (printer's error). The rehearsals were in my *salon*, and we had great amusement over them. The second ballet was more pretentious, and was danced in one of the largest theaters in Berlin. It was called the "Enchanted Castle." A parvenu buys an ancestral castle, and on his arrival there falls asleep in the great hall, filled with the portraits of ancestors and knights in armor. The ladies, in their old-fashioned dresses, step out from their frames, and with the knights in armor move in a stately quadrille. After they return to their frames, thirty young couples dance a ballet, and when they finish, the parvenu wakes up. It was very pretty and brought in a lot of money, and there was a question of its being repeated for the Emperor, but this was not done.

February, 1908.

Dear L.,—The Crown Prince and the Crown Princess gave a small *bal-costume*. It was their first entertainment of any importance, though there were very few people invited. As Frederikke is a dancing young person, we were invited, enabling me to take many girls under my protecting wing. The Emperor was dressed as the Grand Elector of Brandenburg. The Empress had copied an old family portrait at San Souci. She had a voluminous blond peruke and a flowing blue dress. She looked very handsome. The Princes were generally dressed as their ancestors and looked very familiar, as almost all of them stand in the *Sièges Allée*. I learned much of German history that evening. The Emperor was very kind and gave me a spirited and concise history of those whom his six sons represented. No one except the Kaiser would ever have had the persistency to stay booted and spurred during the whole evening without a murmur, though he must have suffered from the heat and been uncomfortable to a great degree. He had thick, brown curls which hung close about his ears; thick, high, and hot leather boots; and heavy leather gloves which he conscientiously kept on till the very end.

The Kaiser is a wonderful personality. The more I see him the more I admire him. He impresses you as having a great sense of power and true and sound judgment. And then he is kind and good. I do not think him capable of doing a mean or small action.

Mrs. Vanderbilt drove me out to Potsdam in her motor, and, going through the forest, we passed in our hurried flight an automobile which we did not have time to remark upon. That evening there was a ball at court. When the Emperor spoke to me he said: "You flew by the Empress and me like lightning this afternoon when we were walking in the forest."

"Was that your Majesty's motor?" I asked. "We went so fast that I did little else than hold on to my seat. It must have seemed ill-mannered to have flown by like that."

There is to-night a *Gesinde Ball* to which we are going. I know that you have no idea as to what a *Gesinde Ball* is, so I will tell you that it is a ball given at some kind house by a kind lady. People dress themselves up as servants. It is our wildest dream, and we are never so happy as when we are gotten up to look like ladies' maids. I can tell you how some of them will look—self-made and to the manner born. I am going, since commands from superior quarters make it imperative, as a giddy old housekeeper or a care (worn) taker who has taken a smart gown from her mistress's wardrobe on the sly.

Several evenings later I heard your *prima donna* with patience (because you sent her), but not with enthusiasm. She is like a hundred other would-be *prima donnas* who cannot sing now and never can. These flock to Berlin, study with all their might for two or three years, and sing worse each year. Then they give a concert, for which they give away the tickets. They say they must have the Berlin criticism. In the mean time their families are eating dry bread and their friends are squeezed like lemons. They get their criticism in some paper, cut it out, stick it on a nice piece of paper, and send it to their countrymen, who are out of pocket for a thousand marks or so. Then they go back to their homesteads, discouraged and unhappy, and sing for nothing in the village choir for the rest of their lives.

Our winters are very much alike—always the same routine. The season commences with the reception of the *grande maîtresse*, then comes the *Schleppenkur*, the *Ordensfest*, and after that the Emperor's birthday, with a gala opera in the evening; then the first, second, and third balls at court, and the gala performances at the Opera when any sovereign comes to Berlin on a visit. In Lent there is always one entertainment at court. After Easter every one disappears and all the blinds are pulled down. Those who remain in Berlin pretend they are away.

The Emperor speaks French and English with equal ease, but he likes best to speak English. He can be very lively at times, and then the next moment just as serious again. While talking to you he never takes his eyes off your face. He is seemingly all attention. Sometimes when the diplomatic ladies stand side by side he glances to the next lady, evidently making up his mind about what he will talk with her. His voice is singularly clear, and what he says is straight to the point. He has the rare gift of making the person to whom he is talking appear at his very best. The life in Potsdam is, I have been told, very home-like and cozy. The Emperor often spends the evening reading aloud, while the Empress sits near with her knitting. They love to be in the Neues Palais and stay there until after Christmas. Their Christmas festivities must be worth seeing. Each prince has a Christmas tree and a table of his own, makes his own choice of presents, and ties up his own packages—as it were—and lights the Christmas candles. These festivals are held in the mussel-room, on the ground floor, original if not pretty—a combination of shells, mother-of-pearl, and glass stone, which must be very effective in the brilliantly lighted room.

The Empress is very fond of riding, but often drives a little pony-carriage with two English "high-steppers." Once when the Shah of Persia was spending the day at Potsdam the Empress offered to take him out for a drive in the park. Half-way to their destination the lively pace of the horses alarmed the Shah. He put his hand over hers, which held the reins, and said in his pigeon-French, "*Vous-mourir seule*" and got out and walked back.

The Emperor said to me, "Do you know Mr. Carnegie?"

I said that I did not.

"He is a clever gentleman," continued the Emperor. "Can you guess what he said to me?"

I shook my head.

The Emperor then quoted Mr. Carnegie: "You and Mr. Roosevelt would make a nice tandem."

"That shows tact and discrimination," I remarked.

The Emperor laughed. "I asked him which he thought would be the wheel-horse?"

"What did he answer to that?" said I.

"I am afraid Mr. Carnegie did not find anything to answer just then. He has not your talent for repartee."

"In this case," I assured his Majesty, "I should not have answered at all, for I have no idea what a wheel-horse is. If it is the horse which makes all the wheels turn, then it must be your Majesty."

"You see!" said the Emperor, shaking his finger and laughing.

We had the great pleasure of welcoming Prince Hans (King Christian's brother). Johan was with him in Greece many years ago and has never ceased to love him. He is the most polite gentleman I ever saw; he almost begs your pardon for being kind to you. He dined with us yesterday. We invited to meet him Prince Albert Schleswig-Holstein (his nephew) and Prince and Princess Wied[3]. This young couple are delightfully charming. The Prince has the most catching smile. It is impossible not to be in good spirits when you are with him. We sat out on the balcony after dinner and took our coffee and looked out into the brilliantly lighted square of Brandenburger Tor with its network of trams. I think our apartment is the most beautifully situated in all Berlin.

March, 1908.

Dear L.,—The King of Spain is in Berlin now on a visit of a few days to the Emperor. We only saw him at the gala performance at the Opera. The Kaiser had chosen "The Huguenots." It was beautifully put on. Madame Hempel sang the part of Marguerite de Valois, and Madame Destinn sang Valentine. The house was decorated in the usual manner, with carpets hanging from the balconies and flowers in great profusion everywhere. The King of Spain sat between the Kaiser and the Kaiserin. He looks very young and very manly. After the first act, when we all met in the foyer, the

Emperor stood by him, and sometimes would take him by the arm and walk about in order to present people to him. I was presented to him, but I did not get more than a smile and a shake of the hand—I could not expect more. Johan was more favored, for the King asked him how long he had been in Berlin. You must confess that even that was not much.

I was compensated by having quite a long talk with the Kaiser—long for him, as he has so many people to talk to, and he feels, I am sure, every eye of the hoping-to-speak-to-him person in the room. He said:

"I have just been reading the memoirs of General von Moltke. Did you ever know him?"

"No," I said, "I never saw him, but I have a letter from him, written in 1856 to my father-in-law, dated from the Tuileries."

"He often speaks in his letters of your husband's grandparents' home in Copenhagen—how he always felt at home and happy there, and was always sure to find a charming circle of interesting and literary people. You must read it; it would interest your husband, too."

"Did your Majesty ever hear about Moltke's visit to some grand-ducal court? Moltke thought, of course, that as he had all the grand cordons and decorations in creation, he had also that of this court. When he was going to visit the Grand Duke he said to his servant, 'Don't forget my decoration,' The servant looked high and low, but could not find it, and, thinking that he had mislaid it, went and bought one. Moltke put on his uniform, the decoration being in place on his breast. When the Grand Duke entered he had in his hand an *étui* containing the decoration, intending to hang it around Moltke's neck himself. Imagine his surprise at seeing it there already!"

BERLIN, *November, 1908.*

Dear L.,—Our King and Queen visit Berlin.

When the Emperor learned of the date for the visit, and that their Majesties were to be accompanied by the Minister of Foreign Affairs (Frederick) he proposed that Nina should also come, and he invited them to be his guests at the *Schloss*. This was joyful news for me. Though Nina had just had a dreadful fall while riding and had broken her arm and wrist, she had the courage to undertake the journey. They traveled with their Majesties.

The *Lehrter Bahnhof* is particularly well adapted to receive royalties. It has a fine *façade*, and the open square in front is large enough to contain the military bands and the hundreds of carriages of all sorts. Today it was overflowing.

Inside the station a broad flight of steps lead down to the platform, where was spread the traditional red carpet; the plants, bushes, and flowers all made it look very gay and festive. The train was expected at eleven o'clock. We hoped to get there very early, but found the Emperor and his staff already on the platform, waiting. As our little party arrived (we and the Secretaries) the Emperor came forward, took my hand, and kissed it very graciously. We stood talking until the Empress came, accompanied by all her ladies and suite. The train was announced by many signals and many whistlings, but no train came in. The locomotive had given out and the train had stopped a good way out of the station. The carpet not reaching so far, their Majesties were obliged to walk quite a distance on the wet platform. By means of shunting and jerking the royal train was brought in under the station roof, but nowhere near the carpet. The small steps were put up to the carriage door, and the King and Queen descended. The Emperor kissed the King on both cheeks. The Empress received the Queen affectionately and gave her a bouquet, which she carried in her hand. I saw Nina's pale face, pinched with pain, in the distance, and longed to fly to her, but etiquette compelled me to stay to make my obeisance to their Majesties. The band which was in the station struck up the Royal Danish March, and we could hardly hear ourselves speak on account of the tremendous resonance. The procession of resplendent uniforms and the bright colors of the ladies' dresses made a brilliant sight as they walked through the station. The Empress led the way, and we all followed to the waiting-room, where presentations to the Queen took place. The Empress presented every one of the ladies to the Queen, *even me*. All the royal carriages seemed to be out—two open barouches with four horses were for the four royalties. I drove to the castle to see Nina, who was already installed in her regal apartment. I went up the *Wendeltreppe*, through two antechambers and a small *salon*, before reaching her magnificent drawing-room. It had superb tapestries on the walls and was filled with fine old Dutch inlaid furniture. It is called the Braunschweig suite, nine rooms in all. Frederick had a separate staircase and entrance. Nina and I went to the window to look out onto the *Platz* in front of the castle, and saw the parade pass before the Emperor and the King, who stood in the rain while the troops marched by.

Nina had a court carriage and lackey at her disposal all the time she was in Berlin. In the evening there was a state dinner in the superb *Weissesaal*. Johan and I and the members of the Legation were the only diplomats present. We all met in the Grand Gallery; the Emperor took in the Queen of Denmark, placing her on his right, and the King gave his arm to the Empress and sat facing the Emperor. The table was in the shape of a horseshoe, and there were about eighty people present. Prince Schleswig-Holstein (familiarly called Prince Abby) took me in, and the Emperor's son, Prince Adalbert, sat on my left. The *ménu* was in German. Some of the French dishes seemed to have puzzled the translator. The Empress wore a dress of blue brocade and many beautiful jewels. Our Queen wore a light-gray satin trimmed with lace, and her famous diamond-and-pearl necklace. The Emperor wore the Danish uniform, and the King was in the uniform of his Prussian regiment. A military band played throughout dinner.

I was amused when the fruit and bonbons were passed. Both the princes next to me piled their plates high with them and passed them over their shoulders to the young gentlemen pages who stood behind each royal person, thus depriving many ladies of the longed-for bonbons, which were adorned with the portraits of their Majesties.

The Emperor made a very charming and touching speech in German, when we all stood up and emptied our glasses. The King replied in German, and we again got up and drank. After dinner every one went into the long gallery, and their four Majesties talked very informally with us while taking their coffee. At eleven o'clock their Majesties retired. I was glad, for Nina's sake, that she could rest after her fatiguing day. I knew that she was suffering agonies from her tightly bandaged wrist. Her arm was in a plaster cast, and she carried it in a sling cleverly hidden under her laces. The next day the Empress took the Queen with her to visit some charitable institutions. The King and the Queen had graciously promised to lunch at our house, which was surrounded by a cordon of police, on foot and on horseback, in front and in the courtyard belonging to the Legation.

At two o'clock quite a procession of court carriages entered our *porte-cochère*, where I met the Queen, presenting her with a bouquet tied with ribbons of the Danish colors—red and white. Our lunch was for forty people, and was served in two rooms. The King gave me his arm. The Emperor had sent in the morning a life-sized crayon portrait of himself by Lenbach as a present. The whole staircase was lined with palms and bushes, and of course there were plenty of flowers in the rooms.

After luncheon a deputation of the Danish colony met in the large *salons* and were presented to their Majesties. It was after five o'clock before every one had departed. The policemen had filed off, and the crowds which had collected in the street disappeared.

The gala opera in the evening was like all the other gala operas I have described. At eight o'clock every one had assembled and was in his place. The opera was called "*Der Lange Kerl*," written at the Emperor's command by some German composer. It was a beautiful production, and represented Frederick the Great at Sans-Souci. In the first act the interior of Sans-Souci was copied after the famous picture of Mezzler where Frederick the Great is playing on the flute. The "Long Fellow" was a giant, who, it seems, was a common soldier in the King's regiment. Madame Destinn took the part of a peasant woman, and washed up the pavement and prepared her vegetables for sale in the most realistic manner. The second scene, when Potsdam wakes up in the morning, reminded me of the opening of the second act of "Lohengrin." The last act was very sad, and rather lugubrious, representing Frederick the Great seated in the garden in front of Sans-Souci. There was no singing in this act at all, only pantomime. The respectful manner and the sad faces of the lackeys as they helped the poor old King to his chair and covered his knees with rugs, leaving him alone, was very pathetic.

We went into the foyer after the performance. The Empress presented all the notable people to the Queen, and I stood near her in order to present others if necessary.

BERLIN, *May, 1910*.

Dear L.,—Do not be surprised that you have not heard from me. We have been motoring. A most delightful tour. One does not know the bliss of traveling until one motors through Germany as we have just done. I would send you my diary, but it reads too much like a ship's log. We started from Berlin on the 1st of May and went as far as Eisenach. In trying to climb the steep hill which leads to the halls where Tannhauser sang his naughty description of Venusberg our motor broke down, as if to commemorate the spot. We had to spend the night at Eisenach for repairs. The next day we passed Gotha, where we lunched, and passed the night at Fulda. The next day we went on to Weimar, where Liszt's memory is as green as the trees in the grand-ducal park.

Everything is beautiful in this time of the year, and the days are long. What could be more enchanting I leave to your imagination.

In Munich we galleried from morning to night, and were utterly exhausted and hardly had the courage to dress for the opera; but, having tickets, economy got the better of prudence, and we sat through the long performance of "Don Giovanni" with *Geduld*.

Andrada, the Portuguese barytone, was very good and looked the part to perfection. In real life I am told he is a Don Juan himself. If the list of his victims has not yet reached *mille et un* the fault cannot be laid at his door. His stage victims were all fat German *Frauen*. Zerlina wore a blond wig, showed very black eyebrows and red lips. Her golden molars showed from afar. Our visit to the artist Lenbach and his wife was followed by an invitation to tea the next day. Lenbach is divorced from his first wife, married to a Countess Arnim (also divorced). They have a dear little girl whom Lenbach has painted several times. The studio is in a charming garden, arranged in the most artistic manner, full of broken columns and antique relics resembling the gardens on the Venice canals. Lenbach seen in the bosom of his family is a different Lenbach from the one we knew in Rome and Paris—half society man, half artist. Here he is simply *all papa*.

We motored over the mountain to Oberammergau. I do not dare to say that I was disappointed in the performance. I suppose years ago, when people began to go to Oberammergau, it was more interesting, but now it is simply an enterprise, speculation kept alive by travelers and sight-seers. As a representation it is impressive in a way, but your illusions are dimmed by the prosaic manner in which everything is done. I felt a little queer when I met Jesus Christ smoking and wiping his muddy sandals with a dirty handkerchief, and saw Mary Magdalene flirting with the chauffeurs. When we sat at a *café*, enjoying a mug of beer and a sausage, we were surrounded by St. Joseph and a brood of angels, all drinking beer. People may rave about the *Stimmung*, the poetry, and the romance of it, but I saw beauty neither in the acting nor in the play. I do not speak of the music, there was so little of it. Physical comfort goes a long way with yours lovingly. To sleep in a narrow bed having a piece of flannel buttoned between two coarse pieces of linen, to eat bad food, to sit on hard benches for hours under an open heaven which lets down occasionally a mild shower—this is what the Germans call *Stimmung* and others call "local color" and what I call discomfort. Still, it is one of the things one must do once in ten years. For a European to say, "I have not been to Oberammergau," is like an American saying, "I have never been to Niagara."

Whoever has been to see the crazy King Ludwig's *châteaux* knows more about them than I do, for I hated to go inside them. I gazed at the magnificent view and wondered how any but a crazy person could have furnished the interiors.

What a life the King led his faithful subjects! They are still taxing all they can tax in order to pay his debts. Poor things! They won't finish for a long time yet!

BERLIN.

Dear L.,—The visit to the Berlin court by King Edward and Queen Alexandra is already a thing of the past, but I must tell you about it while it is still fresh in my mind. We, as *légation de famille*, went to the Lehrter station to meet them on their arrival. When the train steamed in the Emperor and the Empress went forward to the door of the carriage, and as the King and the Queen descended they all embraced affectionately.

The Empress led the Queen to the waiting-room, where she presented all the ladies who were there. There was music inside and outside of the station. In fact, everything was so exactly like the reception of our King and Queen, which I have described before, that I will not repeat myself.

King Edward looked tired and coughed constantly. The Queen, whom I had not seen for a long time, seemed quite unchanged and charming as ever. There is not much time on such occasions to say more than a few words to each. We saw them drive off amid the most enthusiastic greetings from the populace massed together in the square.

That evening there was a state banquet, served in the *Weissesaal*, at which the Kaiser read his speech in English to the King, and the King read his reply.

I sat between Lord Granville and Sir Charles Hardinge, between a cross-fire of wit and fun. The court orchestra, up in the gallery, played subdued music during the dinner, so that conversation was possible. Their four Majesties sat next to one another on one side of the table, and the *Chancelier de l'Empire* sat opposite the Empress. The English Embassy and ourselves were the only diplomats among the hundred guests. The bonbons which were served with the fruit had photographs of King Edward, the Queen, and the German Imperial family, and were, as is the custom, handed to the pages. These offerings are meant, I suppose, as a polite attention, and little souvenirs of the occasion, but the guests for whom the bonbons are intended go away empty-handed. These pages belong to the highest families in Germany, and are present at all court functions, such as balls and dinners, and stand behind the chairs of the royal personages at the table.

COUNT HATZFELDT

From a recent photograph. He was Prime Minister of Germany and German Ambassador to London, brother-in-law of Madame de Hegermann-Lindencrone. The picture shows over sixty decorations, all the important ones of Europe, which have been given him. It is custom that the decorations of orders in diamonds are kept by the family after the death of the recipient. All other orders go back to the governments bestowing them.

After dinner we went into the long gallery, which in one part was arranged as a *salon*, with *fauteuils* and chairs in circle.

To show what a wonderful memory King Edward has, he said to me:

"Do you remember a song you used to sing [I thought he was going to say 'Beware'] with something about, 'I mean the daughter'?"

"Yes, your Majesty, I remember very well. It was, 'I know a lady, a Mrs. Brady.'"

"Yes, that was it...'and has a daughter,' wasn't it?"

I said, "What a memory your Majesty has! Fancy remembering that all these years. It was when your Majesty came to Sommerberg to play tennis with Paul Hatzfeldt."

"That was a long time ago," continued King Edward. "I was stopping then with the King and the Queen of Denmark at Wiesbaden. I remember it all so well. Poor Hatzfeldt. You know what Bismarck said about him?"

"Was it not something about his being the best horse in his stable?"

"That is it," the King answered. "You have a good memory, too. How is Countess Raben?"

"You mean 'the daughter'?"

The King laughed. "Yes, I mean 'the daughter.'"

We did not stay long after the dinner, as evidently their Majesties were fatigued after their journey. The King coughed incessantly, and the Queen looked very tired. I think that she is beginning to look very like her mother, the dear old Queen.

The next day hundreds of court carriages were flying about Berlin; I wish you could see the packages of cards that were sent to us. In the evening was the gala opera. The Opera House is always decorated in the same way, and there is always the same audience.

"Sardanapal" was the play chosen by the Emperor for this performance. I thought it very interesting to look at, but impossible to understand. It was a combination of orchestral music, choruses, and pantomime. A dreadful-looking Nubian came out before the curtain between acts and told us in German poetry what was going to happen. The Emperor had taken a great interest in the play, and had indicated all the costumes himself. Every dress was a study and entirely correct, you may be sure, if the Kaiser had anything to do with it. The ornaments which the actors wore were copied from specimens in the museums. The scenery was very fine, and when Sardanapal was burned up, with his wives and collection of gold and silver things, the whole stage seemed to be on fire. This almost created a panic, and would have done so if the audience had not seen that their Majesties sat calmly in their seats. It was very realistic. The Emperor told me afterward in the foyer that the flames were nothing but chiffon, lighted with electric lights, and blown up with a fan from beneath. When the fire had done its work there was nothing left upon the stage but red-hot coals and smoldering *débris*. It was all very well, if we only had been spared the lugubrious man with the beard made of tight black curls, who did the talking.

The next day the luncheon in honor of their English Majesties at the English Ambassador's, Sir Edward Goschen, was full of emotion. King Edward wore the uniform belonging to his German regiment, which, besides being buttoned tightly and apparently much padded, has a high and tight collar. He had received a deputation of most of the English colony and already looked wearied before we went in to luncheon. This was served in the ballroom, and was a long and elaborate affair. The King sat opposite the Queen, and Sir Edward and Lady Goschen sat at either end of the table. All the princes, the German nobility, and ministers of state were present.

The King apparently had a good appetite, and talked with his neighbors right and left and opposite, and seemed to enjoy himself. When we re-entered the drawing-room the King lit an enormous cigar and, seating himself on a low sofa, talked and smoked, when suddenly he threw his head back against the sofa, as if gasping for breath. The Queen, who was on the other side of the room, rushed instantly to the King and quickly unbuttoned his collar and opened his coat. The two English physicians who had come with the King were finishing luncheon in another room. They were instantly called in, and they begged the guests to leave the *salon* in order that the King might have more air. The King had not fainted, but on account of the tight collar, the heat of the room, the big cigar, and the violent fit of coughing, it was almost impossible for him to get his breath. The physicians helped him up from the low sofa into a high chair, and took away the cigar; but the King, as soon as he could speak, said, "Give me another cigar." The physicians protested, but the King insisted upon the cigar, which they were obliged to give him. The guests returned, and the conversation rallied for a while, but the emotion of the few moments before could not be easily calmed.

The King left the room quietly, hardly any one seeing him, reached the automobile, and drove to the castle. The Queen followed him a few moments later.

We were prepared to receive notice at any moment that the ball fixed for that evening would be countermanded. But it was not, and at eight o'clock—the hour one goes to court balls here—found every one assembled. As usual, we took our places on the platform reserved for the ladies of the *Corps Diplomatique*, and then, with the ceremonial which I have so often described, their Majesties, preceded by the pages and court notables, entered. The Emperor gave his arm to Queen Alexandra, and the Empress entered with King Edward. It is customary for the Emperor and the Empress to make a tour of the invited guests, but this evening the royal persons stayed on the throne and did not move during the dances.

King Edward and the Queen supped at the table of the Emperor, and immediately afterward retired to their rooms and were seen no more. During the whole evening they had not spoken to a single person.

The next morning their Majesties took their departure from the Lehrter station. We went to bid them good-by. The Emperor, in speaking to me, said, "You know, my uncle had such a fright the other night when he saw the fire, he wanted to leave the theater; it was only when I told him that the flames were chiffon that I could quiet him."

When King Edward bade me good-by he said, "Please remember me to Countess Raben," and added, laughingly, "I mean the daughter."

Saint-Saëns and Massenet came to Berlin to assist at a sort of *Congrès de musique*. Massenet was invited to lead the orchestra in "Manon," and Saint-Saëns that of "Samson and Delilah." They accepted an invitation to lunch at our house, and I was delighted to see them again. They had come, they said, with prejudices on fire. They were sure that they would dislike everything German; but, having been begged to visit the Kaiser in his *loge* after the performance, they came away from the interview burning with enthusiasm. How charming the Emperor was! How full of interest! So natural! etc., etc. They could not find words for their admiration. That is the way with the Emperor. He charms every one.

The first of my articles about Compiègne appeared in *Harper's Magazine* in the summer. At the ball at court in the following January the Kaiser came to speak to me, his face beaming with the kindest of smiles.

"I can't tell you how I have enjoyed your articles, I read them to myself and read them out loud to the Empress."

"How," said I "did your Majesty discover them?"

"I have always taken *Harper's Magazine*, ever since I was a little boy. You may imagine how astonished I was when I saw something from your pen. Your description of Napoleon the Third is quite historical. You gave me a new idea of him. In many ways I always regret that I never saw him. I could have once, when I was quite small. I was with my parents at Nice, and the Emperor came there, but I did not see him."

BERLIN, *May 1912*.

Dear L.,—On the 14th we had just returned from a long motor trip, arriving late in the evening. How fortunate that we did not arrive a day later! The next morning Johan was called on the telephone. The message was from Hamburg, to say that our King (Frederick VIII) had died there, suddenly in the night. Johan, of course, took the first train for Hamburg.

This was dreadful news.

The King was traveling with the Queen, Princess Thyra, Prince Gustave, and the usual suite. His Majesty had bade them good-night and retired— alas! not to his room, for he wished to take a stroll through the streets of the town. It was only at two o'clock that the valet noticed that the King had not been in his room. Then he alarmed the *Hof-Marshale*, who, with the other gentlemen, commenced a search. At five o'clock they found his Majesty in the *Krankenhaus*. He had fainted in the street and had been put into a cab, in which he died. Johan stayed all the next day in Hamburg, accompanying the Queen on board the *Daneborg* (the royal yacht), which had been sent to take the King's body back to Denmark.

THE EMPEROR IN 1905
From an autographed photograph given to Madame de Hegermann-Lindencrone.

The Queen was overwhelmed with grief, but showed the greatest self-control.

It has been a distressing time indeed for the Duchess of Cumberland. She has lost her eldest son (killed in an automobile accident on the way to Schwerin to see his sister, the Grand Duchess) and now it is her brother who is taken so tragically. The young duke was very unwise to take that particular road. We had passed over the same route, or tried to, on our way to pay a visit to the grand-ducal pair not more than two weeks before. Our chauffeur was appalled at the dreadful condition of the road and advised turning back. We made a great *détour* and avoided an accident. The Duke was driving himself, and the ruts in the road made the car jump so that the wheel struck him under the chin, he lost control, and the machine struck a tree, killing the Duke instantly. The chauffeur was saved.

BERLIN.

Mr. Roosevelt and family arrived in Berlin three days ago. Society was on tiptoe with expectation. They talked of giving Arthur Nevin's Indian opera, "Poia," in order that the ex-President should have the thrill of seeing his compatriots in a German setting. This idea was abandoned, though Count Hülsen had accepted the opera and at an enormous expense had had it mounted at the Grand Opera.

The Kaiser received Mr. Roosevelt and was charmed with him, just as Mr. Roosevelt was charmed with the Kaiser. Of course, who could resist the magnetic forces of these two *dii ex machinâ*.

Ambassador and Mrs. Hill gave a large and all-comprising reception at the Embassy in honor of their distinguished guest, which is much too small to contain the entire society of Berlin and *embrace* (I like that word) all the American colony.

To gain a little more space they very practically turned the *porte-cochère* into a *vestiaire*, where we took off our mantles before crossing the carpet-covered carriage-drive.

Mr. Roosevelt was most amiable. He greeted people with a cordiality which bordered on *épanchement*—giving their hands a shaking the like of which they had never had before. Mr. Roosevelt remained by Mrs. Hill's side and smiled kindly at the guests as they poured in and out of the *salon*. That was about all the guests did—pour in and pour out. One could not expect even the most favored to exchange more than a few words with the great man.

Our conversations were in the style of the reception, short and quickly done with.

MRS. HILL: "This is Madame de Hegermann. She is American, from Cambridge, Massachusetts."

MR. ROOSEVELT: "Ah!... I am a Harvard man."

ME: "So am I! I mean I am a Harvard woman! I was born and brought up in Radcliffe College."

MR. R.: "Ah!" (*Puzzled, trying to match the possible date of my birth with the birth of Radcliffe College.*)

ME: "Radcliffe College was my grandparents' home."

MR. R.: "Oh, I see! Well, madame, I am delighted to shake hands with any one from Cambridge."

Johan's was like this:

MRS. HILL: "Monsieur de Hegermann was Danish Minister in Washington some years ago."

MR. R.: "I am sorry I was not President then. Ha! ha! Pleased to have met you, sir!"

We were told that there would be speeches under the flag, but we poured out without anything of the kind occurring.

BERLIN, *1912.*

Dear L.,—It is not only the unexpected that arrives: the expected arrives also.

The news we have been expecting these last years arrived yesterday.

Diplomacy has decided to divorce us.

We are to leave Berlin.

Johan ought to have left the service four years ago. According to the *protocole* in Denmark, a Minister must retire when he reaches the *d'age limite*—the Ambassador retiring at the age of seventy.

The Prime Minister asked him to remain, and he did. But now it seems that the powers that be have decided.

It is very sad, but true.

Countess Brockdorf came to make me a visit of condolence. She said that her Majesty had begged her to express her regrets. In the course of the visit she asked me when my book[4] would come out, and when I told her that I thought in October she said, "I know that the Emperor is counting on your giving him a copy." I promised that I would not forget it.

On the day fixed for Johan's audience to present his letters of recall we were invited to luncheon at Neues Palais with their Majesties. At Wildpark, the Emperor's private station, a few miles from Potsdam, we were met by his carriage and drove through the beautiful park to the palace. The carriage stopped at the principal entrance, where a broad red carpet was stretched from the carriage-drive to the door. Johan got out there. Then I was driven to the other side of the palace, where I found another red carpet. This was the entrance which leads to the Empress's suite of apartments.

Countess Keller (the lady of honor) was waiting for me and led me to the Empress.

Her Majesty was most gracious; no one could have been more so. We remained talking until a lackey announced that Johan's audience was finished and that the Emperor was waiting in the dining-room for us. The Kaiserin kindly took me by the arm, and we went together into the adjoining *salon*, where we found the Emperor, the Princess Victoria Augusta, Johan, William von Kidderling (Minister of Foreign Affairs), who is always present at these official audiences, a chamberlain, an adjutant—not more than ten people in all.

The Kaiser, on seeing me, kissed my hand, and was, as usual, most kind and altogether delightful. I sat at his left, the young Princess being at his right. I tried to say how grieved we were at the idea of leaving Berlin, where we had spent ten happy years. He was gracious enough to say that both he and the Empress were very sorry to lose us. He said many appreciative things about what I had written in *Harper's*, and asked many questions showing that he had really read them. He seemed interested to hear about the Emperor Napoleon and the life at Compiègne. He said that he met Empress Eugénie for the first time when in Norway, three years ago. He had made a visit to her on her yacht, and she had "honored" him by taking tea with him on the *Hohenzollern*. He said, "How beautiful she must have been when she was young!"

"I saw her," I replied, "last spring at her villa at Cape Martin. She is *still* beautiful, though she is eighty years old."

"Eighty years!" cried the Kaiser, "and still a *charmeuse*! That is unique."

All through luncheon I was thinking that this was the last time I should be talking to the interesting and wonderful *charmeur* who was sitting next to me. The Kaiser has a way of fixing those discerning gray eyes of his on you when he talks, and you have the feeling that he is sifting and weighing you in his mind—and when he smiles his face lights up with humor and interest. You feel as if a life-buoy were keeping you afloat. He has that wonderful gift of making people appear at their best. I gave him my book after luncheon. It looks very fitting in its red morocco binding. He appeared greatly delighted with it and begged me to write my name on the first page, which, of course, I was happy to do.

The Empress exclaimed: "'Do give me one, too! Once the Emperor has it, I shall never get it."

The Kaiser's last words to us were, "Promise not to forget Berlin!"

Forget Berlin—never!

THE END

Footnotes:

[1]

King George of Greece who was assassinated in 1913.

[2]

Father of the princess who married the young ex-King of Portugal, Manuel, in 1913.

[3]

Now King and Queen of Albania.

[4]

In the Courts of Memory, published in the autumn of 1912.